# STUDY GUIDE

**David Mitchell**
*University of South Alabama*

# STUDY GUIDE

to accompany

Modern Principles:
## MACROECONOMICS
Cowen ■ Tabarrok

**WORTH PUBLISHERS**

**Study Guide**
by David Mitchell
to accompany
Cowen ■ Tabarrok: *Modern Principles: Macroeconomics*

© 2010 by Worth Publishers
All rights reserved.

The contents, or parts thereof, may be reproduced for use with *Modern Principles: Macroeconomics* by Tyler Cowen and Alex Tabarrok but may not be reproduced in any form for any other purpose without prior written permission of the publisher.

ISBN 13: 978-1-4292-3180-0
ISBN 10: 1-4292-3180-7

First Printing 2009

Printed in the United States of America

**Worth Publishers**
41 Madison Avenue
New York, NY 10010
www.worthpublishers.com

# Contents

|  |  |  |
|---|---|---|
| | *Key to Corresponding Chapter Numbers* | vii |
| | *Preface* | ix |
| CHAPTER 1 | **The Big Ideas** | 1 |
| CHAPTER 2 | **Supply and Demand** | 13 |
| CHAPTER 3 | **Equilibrium: How Supply and Demand Determine Prices** | 35 |
| CHAPTER 4 | **Price Ceilings and Price Floors** | 53 |
| CHAPTER 5 | **GDP and The Measurement of Progress** | 73 |
| CHAPTER 6 | **The Wealth of Nations and Economic Growth** | 91 |
| CHAPTER 7 | **Growth, Capital Accumulation and the Economics of Ideas: Catching Up vs. The Cutting Edge** | 105 |
| CHAPTER 8 | **Saving, Investment, and the Financial System** | 127 |
| CHAPTER 9 | **Stock Markets and Personal Finance** | 145 |
| CHAPTER 10 | **Unemployment and Labor Force Participation** | 157 |
| CHAPTER 11 | **Inflation and the Quantity Theory of Money** | 171 |
| CHAPTER 12 | **Business Fluctuations and the Dynamic Aggregate Demand–Aggregate Supply Model** | 187 |
| CHAPTER 13 | **The Real Business Cycle Model: Shocks and Transmission Mechanisms** | 207 |
| CHAPTER 14 | **The Federal Reserve System and Open Market Operations** | 223 |
| CHAPTER 15 | **Monetary Policy** | 239 |
| CHAPTER 16 | **The Federal Budget: Taxes and Spending** | 257 |
| CHAPTER 17 | **Fiscal Policy** | 271 |
| CHAPTER 18 | **International Trade** | 285 |
| CHAPTER 19 | **International Finance** | 303 |

# Key to Corresponding Chapter Numbers

|  | Microeconomics | Economics | Macroeconomics |
|---|---|---|---|
| The Big Ideas | Chapter 1 | Chapter 1 | Chapter 1 |
| Supply and Demand | Chapter 2 | Chapter 2 | Chapter 2 |
| Equilibrium: How Supply and Demand Determine Prices | Chapter 3 | Chapter 3 | Chapter 3 |
| Elasticity and Its Applications | Chapter 4 | Chapter 4 | |
| The Price System: Signs, Speculation and Prediction | Chapter 5 | Chapter 5 | |
| Price Ceilings | Chapter 6 | Chapter 6 | |
| Price Floors, Taxes and Subsidies | Chapter 7 | Chapter 7 | |
| International Trade and Globalization | Chapter 8 | Chapter 8 | Chapter 18 |
| Externalities: When Prices Send the Wrong Signals | Chapter 9 | Chapter 9 | |
| Profits, Prices and Costs under Competition | Chapter 10 | Chapter 10 | |
| Monopoly | Chapter 11 | Chapter 11 | |
| Price Discrimination | Chapter 12 | Chapter 12 | |
| Cartels, Games, and Network Goods | Chapter 13 | Chapter 13 | |
| Labor Markets | Chapter 14 | Chapter 14 | |
| Getting Incentives Right: Lessons for Business, Sports, Politics, and Life | Chapter 15 | Chapter 15 | |
| Stock Markets and Personal Finance | Chapter 16 | Chapter 16 | Chapter 9 |
| Public Goods and the Tragedy of the Commons | Chapter 17 | Chapter 17 | |
| Economics, Ethics, and Public Policy | Chapter 18 | Chapter 18 | |
| Political Economy | Chapter 19 | Chapter 19 | |
| GDP and the Measurement of Progress | | Chapter 20 | Chapter 5 |
| The Wealth of Nations and Economic Growth | | Chapter 21 | Chapter 6 |

|  | **Microeconomics** | **Economics** | **Macroeconomics** |
|---|---|---|---|
| Growth, Capital Accumulation and the Economics of Ideas: Catching Up vs. The Cutting Edge | | Chapter 22 | Chapter 7 |
| Savings, Investment, and the Financial System | | Chapter 23 | Chapter 8 |
| Unemployment and Labor Force Participation | | Chapter 24 | Chapter 10 |
| Inflation and the Quantity Theory of Money | | Chapter 25 | Chapter 11 |
| Business Fluctuations and the Dynamic Aggregate Demand-Aggregate Supply Model | | Chapter 26 | Chapter 12 |
| The Real Business Cycle Model: Shocks and Transmission Mechanisms | | Chapter 27 | Chapter 13 |
| The Federal Reserve System and Open Market Operations | | Chapter 28 | Chapter 14 |
| Monetary Policy | | Chapter 29 | Chapter 15 |
| The Federal Budget: Taxes and Spending | | Chapter 30 | Chapter 16 |
| Fiscal Policy | | Chapter 31 | Chapter 17 |
| International Finance | | Chapter 32 | Chapter 19 |
| Price Ceilings and Price Floors | | | Chapter 4 |

# Preface

This **Study Guide** is designed for use with *Modern Principles: Macroeconomics* by Tyler Cowen and Alex Tabarrok. Economics is not just an interesting subject for study; it is an integral part of life—from shopping at the local grocery store to buying a house to understanding national and local legislation. To help you reach your goal of understanding economics, this study guide includes a number of exercises that involve active learning and repetition. Together, these activities will enhance your learning of text material and will help you to evaluate your understanding of important concepts.

Have you ever taken a test thinking you were well prepared only to discover that you really didn't understand a particular concept? Ideally, working through a study guide chapter will enable you to actively learn the text chapter's contents while also discovering and focusing on material you thought you had mastered but had not.

## Why Learn About. . .?

Each chapter begins with a brief motivational introduction. Some chapters have a hypothetical dialog between an instructor and his or her students. Other chapters explain why the material is important and lists categories of people who are most likely to be interested in the chapter topics—for example, consumers, businesspeople—making it clear that most of economics will be useful to you even in the years following graduation.

These motivational introductions are intended to pique your interest in the chapter contents and so to motivate you to read on.

## Summary and Key Terms

Each summary contains only the essential points of the chapter, including useful tables and graphs from the text. To make the material easier for you to digest, the summary is deliberately brief and straightforward. Reading the summary does not replace reading the text. However, it will help solidify your understanding of the text material. For your convenience, the key terms in the text chapter are listed separately and defined.

## Traps, Hints, and Reminders

This short section first identifies concepts that from experience we have found can be difficult for undergraduate students new to economics. Helpful hints for understanding that material are then provided. The section also includes information about concepts that we think are among the most important.

## Practice Exercises: Learn by Doing

When you feel comfortable that you understand the chapter contents, try to complete these practice exercises, using your own words. These exercises include some questions (marked with an asterisk [★]) that duplicate the text end-of-chapter questions. Answers to these exercises are provided at the end of the chapter. In addition, the topic or topics covered by the question are given, so that you can check the text when you don't understand a topic. Remember: learning is best when it is active.

## Multiple-Choice and Short-Answer Questions

Each chapter contains a self-test review, which includes about 20 multiple-choice questions and about 10 short-answer questions. Answers are provided at the end of the chapter. The short-answer questions are very similar to the practice exercises. We feel that repetition can help you continue to learn right though this section. The self-test review is yet another opportunity for active learning.

## Acknowledgements

A number of people and institutions have greatly contributed to the writing of this study guide. In particular I would like to thank my wife Jen who put the eyes of a non-economist on each chapter and found many places to help make this study guide more readable for undergraduate students. Eva Long found typos and was very helpful.

Jim Swofford was always willing to share ideas and encouragement with me while we wrote the study guides for **Modern Principles**. I would also thank Tom Acox and Matt Driskill who worked the closest with us on writing and formatting the chapters. Finally, I also wish to thank Laura McGinn and Stacey Alexander for their assistance in producing this study guide.

*David Mitchell*
*November 2009*

# STUDY GUIDE

# 1
# The Big Ideas

## Why Learn about Economics?

Economics is a difficult subject, not just because it involves learning lots of material, but because it is way of thinking. So, why would anyone want to learn about economics? Economics is a requirement for many business majors because it helps them think about trade-offs, prices, costs, and labor markets.

Who else would want to learn about economics? Political science majors will want to learn about economics because so much policy is based on it. Nursing majors will be interested in economics because they will want to understand the incentives of policy makers, doctors, patients, health maintenance organizations (HMOs), and other nurses. A sociology or anthropology major might want to understand why some countries are so rich and others are so poor. Environmental science majors need to know economics because there is often a trade-off between industry and the environment.

## Summary

This chapter discusses the reasons for studying economics and the ten key (big) ideas in economics.

*Institutions* are overall rules for making rules. These include the rule of law, democracy, the Constitution, and property rights. Good institutions provide good **incentives**. Incentives are things that encourage people to act a certain way. Good institutions encourage people to save, work, and innovate.

*Trade-offs* are the idea that in order to get one thing, you must give up something else. The benefits that you give up are called the **opportunity cost**. Economists think about trade-offs at the *margin*. "Margin" means small change.

Sometimes governments implement *price controls*. Price controls are government intervention with prices. Price controls can limit how high a price can go, or they can limit how low a price can go.

*Booms and busts* are periods of economic expansion and contraction. During a boom, the economy is thriving. During a bust the economy is not doing well. During a boom, output is high and unemployment is low. Though the economy may go up and down in the short term, hopefully it is experiencing economic growth in the long term. *Economic growth* is a long-run increase in a country's ability to produce more goods and services.

The *central bank* is a nation's banking authority. It is usually responsible for controlling the money supply, as well as for conducting monetary policy. That might include taking actions to promote economic stability, low **inflation**, and full employment. When the central bank prints too much money, inflation occurs. Inflation is a general increase in prices.

## Key Terms

**incentives** are rewards and penalties that motivate behavior

**opportunity cost** of a choice is the value of the opportunities lost

**inflation** is a general increase in prices

## Traps, Hints, and Reminders

Opportunity cost is a trap for students because it has the word "cost" in it, but it is really the "benefit" foregone. This is a common test question.

*Marginal analysis* is changing by small units. Many of the later chapters also discuss marginal analysis. The opposite of marginal analysis is all or nothing. Think of it this way—rarely do people drive at the exact speed limit or go as fast as their car will go. Many people choose how fast they want to drive (within limits).

For example, you might decide to drive 9 miles per hour (mph) over the speed limit, but you choose not to drive as fast as your car can go. So, why not drive 10 mph over the speed limit instead of 9 mph? Because at 10 mph over the speed limit you are more likely to get pulled over by a traffic patrol officer. The cost of going 9 mph over the speed limit (instead of 10 mph over) is low. In addition, speeding tickets are considerably more expensive for driving 10 mph over the speed limit than 9 mph for driving over.[1] The benefit of going 9 mph over the speed limit is high (since it will get you to your destination faster). Make sure that you read all of the above closely, as understanding the fine details of benefits and costs can be confusing.

*Marginal thinking* is thinking about making a small change. You will sometimes hear the expression "thinking at the margin." Being "at the margin" is a similar term that means that you are only a small change away from being in a new category. If your professor says that you are at the margin between a "C" and a "D," this means that you are right between the two grades. A bit more work would mean a "C," while a bit less work would mean a "D."

---

[1] The authors of this study guide and Worth Publishers do not endorse speeding of any kind. Driving over the speed limit is dangerous, and besides, getting a speeding ticket is not good for your driving record or your insurance payment!

# Practice Exercises: Learning by Doing

1. Why are test questions about opportunity cost difficult for students?

2. What evidence is there that "direct incentives" matter more than "appeals to sensitivity"? Use an example from the text.

3. How could a drug be "too safe"?

4. Why are lost wages counted in the opportunity cost of college, but your college food bill is not?

## Multiple-Choice Questions

1. Opportunity cost is
   a. the cost of your next-best alternative.
   b. the cost of your second-next-best alternative.
   c. the benefit of taking your best alternative.
   d. the benefit from all your other alternatives.

2. A baseball star has been drafted to play major league baseball and is offered a $100,000 signing bonus; a young mathematician in need of advanced training could make $30,000 working now; and an aspiring accountant could make $15,000 working now. They all attend Big State U for their freshman year. Which one has the highest opportunity cost?
   a. the baseball player
   b. the future mathematician
   c. the future accountant
   d. They all have equal opportunity costs.

3. Which of the following is a marginal choice?
   a. the decision to build a new factory or not
   b. the decision to hire one more worker
   c. the decision to explore the oceans
   d. the decision to learn how to speak Spanish

4. Which of the following is not listed in your text as a benefit of economic growth?
   a. longer life expectancy
   b. more rights for women
   c. better vacations
   d. more fairness

5. If governments decide to ban high prices during catastrophes, then economists would predict that during catastrophes
   a. people would be happy because they are getting all their goods for low prices.
   b. fewer goods will be available and people will have to wait.
   c. suppliers will bring in even more goods at low prices.
   d. suppliers will not be affected in any way by the rule.

6. Economic growth is measured by
   a. how happy the populace is getting.
   b. the increase in how much a country can produce.
   c. the increase in the number of people employed in a country.
   d. the increase in the amount of taxes in a country.

7. Why is North Korea poorer than South Korea?
   a. Countries farther from the equator are poorer.
   b. All of the capitalist countries are conspiring against North Korea.
   c. South Korea has institutions that provide incentives for innovations and investment.
   d. North Korea is too mountainous for companies to build factories.

8. According to your text, the Great Depression was
   a. prolonged by bad policy.
   b. a natural occurrence in a capitalist society.
   c. caused by a famine in India.
   d. caused by the beginning of World War II.

9. The central bank of the United States is called
   a. Bank of America.
   b. the National Bank of the United States.
   c. the Federal Reserve.
   d. Washington Mutual.

10. When the central bank prints too much money,
    a. people cannot get paper anymore.
    b. inflation occurs.
    c. prices fall too fast.
    d. All of the answers are correct.

11. Which of the following is not a reason that central banking is hard?
    a. There is often a time lag between when the central bank changes policy and when the effects of the changes are known.
    b. It is difficult to foresee the future.
    c. A central bank often has conflicting goals.
    d. There are not enough hard challenges to make central banking interesting.

12. A student attends the local college instead of working as a customer service representative making $20,000. Tuition is $15,000. Books and fees are $2,000. He lives at home. What is the out-of-pocket cost of going to college for this student?

    a. $15,000

    b. $17,000

    c. $20,000

    d. $37,000

13. A student attends the local college instead of working as a customer service representative making $20,000. Tuition is $15,000. Books and fees are $2,000. He lives at home. What is the opportunity cost of going to college for this student?

    a. $15,000

    b. $17,000

    c. $20,000

    d. $37,000

14. Good institutions

    a. eliminate trade-offs.

    b. align self-interest with the social interest.

    c. eliminate incentives.

    d. eliminate self-interest.

15. The Boudreaux family and the Williams family are both making decisions about pets. The Boudreaux family is deciding whether or not to keep all 20 pets that currently live on their farm or to move to the city and get rid of all their pets. The Williams family has one cat and one dog. The Williams are thinking of getting one more dog. Which family is thinking "at the margin"?

    a. Neither family is thinking at the margin.

    b. the Williams family

    c. the Boudreaux family

    d. Both families are thinking at the margin.

16. Your professor has a strict grading rule. An average grade from 90 to 100% is an "A." An average grade from 80 to 89.99% is a "B." An average grade from 70 to 79.99% is a "C." There are no pluses or minuses. Patty has an average grade of 89.95 before the final exam. Selma has an average grade of 85 before the final exam. Which student is "on the margin"?

    a. Patty

    b. Selma

    c. both Patty and Selma

    d. neither Patty nor Selma

**17.** Jerome's favorite flavor of ice cream is chocolate. His second-favorite flavor is black cherry, and his third-favorite is coffee. If he cannot get one of those flavors, he would rather not eat ice cream. If Jerome goes to a well-stocked ice cream store and gets chocolate, what is his opportunity cost?

   a. There is never an opportunity cost when you eat ice cream.

   b. chocolate

   c. black cherry

   d. coffee

**18.** Bubba's average tax rate is 20%, but his marginal tax rate is 30%. If Bubba works an extra hour, what is his tax rate on that extra hour?

   a. 20%

   b. 25%

   c. 25.87%

   d. 30%

**19.** Tyra's favorite TV shows, in order of preference, are *America's Next Top Model*, *America's Funniest Home Videos*, and *CSI*. If each show is an hour and she wants to study for one hour this week, what is the opportunity cost of studying?

   a. Giving up *America's Next Top Model*, *America's Funniest Home Videos*, and *CSI*.

   b. Giving up *America's Next Top Model*.

   c. Nothing: it is free to watch TV.

   d. Giving up *CSI*.

**20.** If prices are rising in general, that is known as

   a. deflation.

   b. inflation.

   c. rationing.

   d. appreciation.

# Short-Answer Questions

21. Sarah moves to a new city. She gets an apartment that costs $6,000 a year. Her food costs are $6,000 a year. Her job pays $28,000 a year. She is thinking of giving up her job and going to the local college full-time, including summers. Tuition, fees, and books will cost $20,000 a year. What is the opportunity cost of going to college?

22. Elizabeth is dating Jeremy, but she is also thinking of going back to her high school boyfriend, David. Since Jeremy does not charge her to date him, is there any cost to Elizabeth?

23. Could a car be too safe? Explain.

24. If you do not have lunch with your friends at the school cafeteria and instead eat a "free lunch" given by an on-campus recruiter, what was the cost of the lunch?

25. What is a trade-off? How are trade-offs related to opportunity cost?

26. What are institutions, and how are they related to incentives?

**27.** From 1949 to 1990 Germany was separated into two countries. The German Democratic Republic (East Germany) was a communist country. The Federal Republic of Germany (West Germany) was a capitalist country. Despite similar history and culture, West Germany had more innovations and inventions than East Germany did. Why might this be?

**28.** What are price controls?

**29.** How is the production of innovative ideas different from the production of other goods?

**30.** What are booms and busts?

**31.** What is a central bank and how does it cause inflation?

# Answer Key

## Answers to Practice Exercises: Learning by Doing

1. During the stress of an exam, students sometimes forget that opportunity cost is the benefit foregone. It is easy for students to get definition questions and application-type questions wrong.
   **Topic: Big Idea Three: Trade-offs Are Everywhere**

2. Paying ship captains for prisoners delivered to Australia alive instead of for prisoners loaded on to ships provided an incentive to bring prisoners to Australia alive. This incentive worked much better than simply asking ship captains to bring prisoners alive.
   **Topic: Big Idea One: Incentives Matter**

3. When we make drug companies prove that their products are super safe, we miss out on the opportunity to have some risky drugs available on the market that can save some lives.
   **Topic: Big Idea Three: Trade-offs Are Everywhere**

4. When you go to college full-time, you miss out on the benefit of earning money by working full-time. Regardless of whether you go to college or work, you would still eat.
   **Topic: Big Idea Three: Trade-offs Are Everywhere**

## Answers to Multiple-Choice Questions

1. c, Topic: Opportunity Cost
2. a, Topic: Opportunity Cost
3. b, Topic: Big Idea Four: Thinking on the Margin
4. d, Topic: Big Idea Six: The Importance of Wealth and Economic Growth
5. b, Topic: Big Idea Five: Tampering with the Laws of Supply and Demand Has Consequences
6. b, Topic: Big Idea Six: The Importance of Wealth and Economic Growth
7. c, Topic: Big Idea Seven: Institutions Matter
8. a, Topic: Big Idea Eight: Economic Booms and Busts Cannot Be Avoided but Can Be Moderated
9. c, Topic: Big Idea Ten: Central Banking Is a Hard Job
10. b, Topic: Big Idea Nine: Prices Rise When the Government Prints Too Much Money
11. d, Topic: Big Idea Ten: Central Banking Is a Hard Job
12. b, Topic: Opportunity Cost

13. **d,** Topic: Opportunity Cost
14. **b,** Topic: Big Idea Two: Good Institutions Align Self-Interest with the Social Interest
15. **b,** Topic: Big Idea Four: Thinking on the Margin
16. **a,** Topic: Big Idea Four: Thinking on the Margin
17. **c,** Topic: Opportunity Cost
18. **d,** Topic: Big Idea Four: Thinking on the Margin
19. **d,** Topic: Opportunity Cost
20. **b,** Topic: Big Idea Nine: Prices Rise When the Government Prints Too Much Money

## Answers to Short-Answer Questions

21. If Sarah goes to college, she gives up $28,000 a year in salary and the use of $20,000 (for tuition, fees, and books). She has to pay for her apartment and food whether or not she is in college. Sometimes students are confused about opportunity cost, including only the tuition, but could not Sarah have spent the $20,000 on something else? Thus, her opportunity cost is $48,000.
    **Topic: Big Idea Three: Trade-offs Are Everywhere**

22. Yes, Elizabeth has opportunity cost. When she dates Jeremy, she gives up dating David.
    **Topic: Big Idea Three: Trade-offs Are Everywhere**

23. Yes, if a car is made so safe that no one can afford to drive it. This could lead to people missing the financial benefits that owning a car brings or being in unsafe situations. For example, having a car enables people to drive to work. If people could not afford to buy cars to commute to work, this could put a restriction on job opportunities. Also, if people living in areas prone to natural catastrophes (such as forest fires or floods) cannot afford to buy cars, they may not be able to escape during an emergency situation.
    **Topic: Big Idea Three: Trade-offs Are Everywhere**

24. You endure the presentation from the on-campus recruiter and give up lunch with your friends. The benefit of enjoying lunch with your friends is the opportunity cost.
    **Topic: Big Idea Three: Trade-offs Are Everywhere**

25. A trade-off is the idea that when you do one thing, you cannot do something else. You cannot study economics and watch TV. You do one or the other. The benefit you forego is the opportunity cost.
    **Topic: Big Idea Three: Trade-offs Are Everywhere**

26. Institutions are overarching rules that govern the way that rules are made. They can be thought of as rules for making rules. Some institutions, such as communism, are set up so that everyone benefits from your hard work. That type of institution would provide you with less of an incentive to work hard. Other institutions, such as those found in capitalist countries, have laws that give you the right to the benefits of your hard work. Those types of institutions provide an incentive to work hard.

    **Topic: Big Idea Seven: Institutions Matter**

27. West Germany's capitalism provided the right incentives for people to invent and innovate. In West Germany, if people worked hard, then they were able to save more money and benefit. In East Germany's communist system, whether or not people worked hard, invented, or innovated, their financial status did not change. As a result, this type of system did not provide incentives.

    **Topic: Big Idea Seven: Institutions Matter**

28. Price controls are government rules that limit how high or low a price can go.

    **Topic: Big Idea Five: Tampering with the Laws of Supply and Demand Has Consequences**

29. Innovative ideas are easily replicable. Regular goods are not. If you invent a new way to harness solar energy, everyone who sees that invention can use it (and pay you for patent usage). If you bake a pizza and more people eat that pizza, then less pizza will be available for you to eat. More people seeing pizza does not mean that there is more pizza.

    **Topic: Big Idea Seven: Institutions Matter**

30. Booms and busts are the economic cycles. The most famous bust was the Great Depression.

    **Topic: Big Idea Eight: Economic Booms and Busts Cannot Be Avoided but Can Be Moderated**

31. The central bank is a nation's banking authority. It is usually responsible for controlling the money supply, as well as for conducting monetary policy. Responsibilities might involve taking actions, such as keeping inflation low, to maintain economic stability. Inflation is a general increase in prices. When the central bank prints too much money, inflation occurs. The Federal Reserve is the central bank of the United States.

    **Topic: Big Idea Ten: Central Banking Is a Hard Job**

# 2

# Supply and Demand

## Why Learn about Supply and Demand?

As the authors say in the text, if you understand little else, you may rightly claim to be literate in economics if you understand supply and demand. If you fail to understand supply and demand, you will understand little else in economics. Thus, supply and demand are the fundamental building blocks of economics.

Supply and demand can be used to understand many human interactions, ranging from the supply and demand of oil (gasoline) for automobiles to the supply and demand of human organs for transplanting.

Who will be interested in supply and demand?

> Elected public officials and candidates for political office that implement programs (affecting taxes and taxpayers), set prices for city services (such as buses), or need to understand the economic effects of government policies
> Businesspeople who want to decide how much to produce and at what price to sell their product
> Students of economics, who, as the authors say in the text, will be lost if they fail to understand this chapter

## Summary

This chapter covers supply and demand. A **demand curve** is a function that shows the quantity demanded at different prices. As shown in Figure 2.1, **quantity demanded** is the quantity buyers are willing and able to buy at a particular price.

**Figure 2.1**

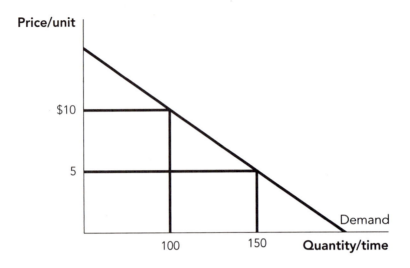

Demand curves are typically downward sloping, implying that if the price falls, the quantity demanded increases. In Figure 2.1, if the price falls from $10 to $5, the quantity demanded increases from 100 units to 150 units. Similarly, if the price rises from $5 to $10, then the quantity demanded decreases from 150 units to 100 units.

**Consumer surplus** is the consumer's gain from exchange, or the difference between the maximum price a consumer is willing to pay for a certain good and the market price. For example, if you are willing to pay $1,000 for a Super Bowl ticket, and the market price is $480, then your consumer surplus is $520 = $1,000 − $480.

In Figure 2.2, the **total consumer surplus** is measured by the area beneath the demand curve and above the price.

**Figure 2.2**

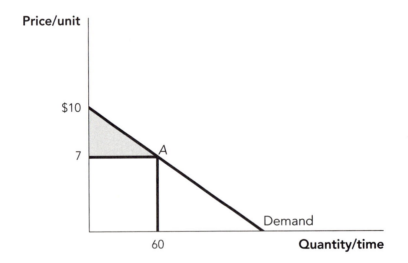

With a market price of $7, the total consumer surplus is the triangle determined by points $7, A, and $10, and it is shaded. The amount of this area can be calculated using the formula for the area of a triangle, which is (height × base)/2. In this example, the height is $3 = $10 − $7 and the base is 60. The height × base is $180 = $3 × 60. The total consumer surplus is $90 = $180/2.

It is important to understand what things cause demand to shift when they change. If, in Figure 2.3, the demand curve shifts from $D_1$ to $D_3$, then it is said that demand has increased. This means at every price the quantity of the good that people want to buy is larger. If, in Figure 2.3, the demand curve shifts from $D_1$ to $D_2$, it is said that demand has decreased. This means at every price the quantity of the good that people want to buy is smaller.

Figure 2.3

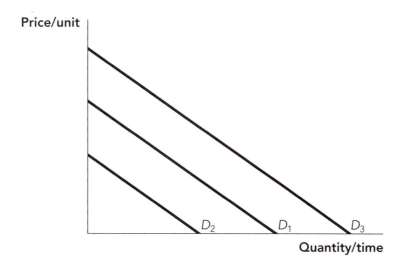

Among the important things that shift demand are changes in consumer income, population, the price of substitutes and complements, expectations, and tastes (how desirable a good is at a specific point in time).

For some goods, when consumer incomes rise, demand increases. These goods are called **normal goods**. For other goods, when consumer incomes rise, demand decreases. Such goods are called **inferior goods**.

If, when the price of another good goes up and the demand for the original good rises, then the two goods are called **substitutes**. Consumers use one good instead of the other and buy more of the now relatively cheaper of the two goods. If, when the price of another good goes up and the demand for the original good falls, then the two goods are called **complements**. Consumers use the two goods together and buy less of both goods when the price of one of them rises.

If population, tastes (desire) for a good, and the expected future price of the good all increase at the same time, then the demand for the goods will also increase. Again that would be a shift like $D_1$ to $D_3$, as shown in Figure 2.3.

A **supply curve** is a function that shows the quantity supplied at different prices. In Figure 2.4, **quantity supplied** is the quantity that sellers are willing to sell at a particular price.

Supply curves are typically upward sloping, implying that if the price rises, then the quantity supplied also increases. In Figure 2.4, if the price rises from $5 to $15, then the quantity supplied increases from 50 units to 200 units. Similarly in Figure 2.4, if the price were to fall from $15 to $5, then the quantity supplied would decrease from 200 units to 50 units.

**Figure 2.4**

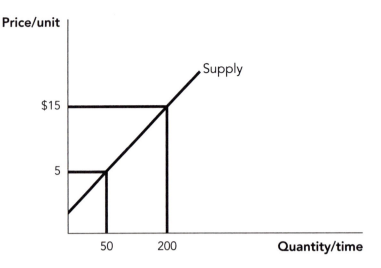

**Producer surplus** is the producer's gain from exchange, or the difference between the market price and the minimum price at which a producer would be willing to sell a certain quantity. For example, if you are willing to sell your car for $10,000 and the market price is $15,000, then your producer surplus would be $5,000 = $15,000 − $10,000 on that transaction.

**Total producer surplus** is measured by the area above the supply curve and below the price, as shown in Figure 2.5.

**Figure 2.5**

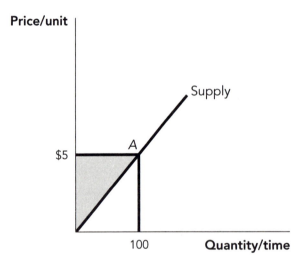

With a market price of $5, the total producer surplus is the triangle determined by points $5, $A$, and the origin 0,0. Again, the amount of this area can be calculated using the formula for the area of a triangle, which is (height × base)/2. In this example, the height is $5 and the base is 100. The height × base is $500 = $5 × 100. The total consumer surplus is $250 = $500/2.

As with demand, it is important to understand what things will cause supply to shift when they change. If, in Figure 2.6, the supply curve shifts from $S_1$ to $S_3$, it is said that supply has increased. This means at every price the quantity of the good that sellers want to sell is larger. If, in Figure 2.6, the supply curve shifts from $S_1$ to $S_2$, it is said that supply has decreased. This means at every price the amount of the good that sellers want to sell is smaller.

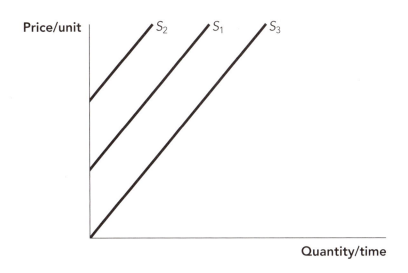

Figure 2.6

Among the important things that shift supply are technological change, changes in the price of inputs in production, taxes and subsidies, changes in expectations, entry and exit of producers, and changes in opportunity costs.

If a technology involved in producing calculators improves, then the supply of calculators increases. Similarly, if the price of any input involved in producing calculators falls, then the supply of calculators increases.

If the government taxes the production of calculators, then the supply of calculators decreases. With the tax added, it costs the producer more money to supply calculators. A subsidy is the negative of a tax. If the government subsidizes the production of calculators, then the supply of calculators increases. With the subsidy factored in, it costs the producer less money to produce calculators.

When producers expect a higher price for the product tomorrow (future markets), they have less incentive to sell today (current markets). To the extent that producers can store their product, they will reduce supply today so that they can sell more in the future (when prices are expected to be higher).

An increase in the number of producers also increases supply. For any given amount of supply, if a new producer comes into the market, the supply is increased. Similarly, when any producer leaves the market, this causes a decrease in the amount supplied. In a similar manner, opportunity costs can affect supply. For example, if a self-employed glazier accepts a job installing air-conditioning units that pays more than a job installing glass and mirrors, then the opportunity cost of installing glass and mirrors has increased. The glazier left the business of glass and mirror installation, thereby reducing supply in that market.

## Key Terms

**demand curve** a function that shows the quantity demanded at different prices

**quantity demanded** the quantity that buyers are willing and able to buy at a particular price

**consumer surplus** the consumer's gain from exchange, or the difference between the maximum price a consumer is willing to pay for a certain good and the market price

**total consumer surplus** the area beneath the demand curve and above the price

**normal good** a good for which demand increases when income increases

**inferior good** a good for which demand decreases when income increases

**substitutes** two goods are substitutes if a decrease in the price of one good leads to a decrease in the demand for the other good

**complements** two goods are complements if a decrease in the price of one good leads to an increase in the demand for the other good

**supply curve** a function that shows the quantity supplied at different prices

**quantity supplied** the quantity that sellers are willing and able to sell at a particular price

**producer surplus** the producer's gain from exchange, or the difference between the market price and the minimum price at which a producer would be willing to sell a particular quantity

**total producer surplus** the area above the supply curve and below the price

## Traps, Hints, and Reminders

Consumer surplus and producer surplus should not be confused with a surplus on a market. Though these terms have the word "surplus" in them, they are not related to surplus on a market or quantity supplied greater than quantity demanded (these concepts will be discussed in Chapter 3).

Inferior goods are not necessarily substandard goods. They are simply goods that are negatively related to consumer income. If a person became rich enough, he or she might buy fewer small jets and more custom-fitted commercial jets. This implies that the small jet might be an inferior good to some people at a certain income level, but says nothing about the quality.

Whether goods are complements or substitutes is up to the consumer. To you, butter and margarine may be substitutes, but for the heart patient only margarine is acceptable, and for the pastry chef only butter will be used. You may think of peanut butter and grape jelly as complements, that is, you may only use them together on bread. However, someone else may think of them as substitutes, that is, he may put only peanut butter on his toast and not jelly.

On a supply curve, any increase in supply is a shift to the right and down. This can be confusing. With supply or demand, "increase" or "decrease" describes the change along the quantity axis. Thus, an increase in supply is a shift to the right and down, because that moves supply to the right (that is, increasing quantities) along the quantity axis. Similarly, a decrease in supply is a shift up and to the left, because that moves supply to the left (that is, decreasing quantities) along the quantity axis.

A *subsidy* is a negative tax, that is, the government is giving someone money rather than taking it away. You could also think of a tax as a negative subsidy. So quite naturally, taxes and subsidies have opposite effects on supply. That is, a tax on a product decreases supply, while a subsidy for a product increases supply.

The *area of a triangle* is one-half the height times the base. The area of a triangle can be calculated as (1/2) × height × base (or .5 × height × base).

# Practice Exercises: Learning by Doing

1. What is a demand curve? What is quantity demanded? Draw a demand curve on the graph below and use it to explain what a demand curve shows.

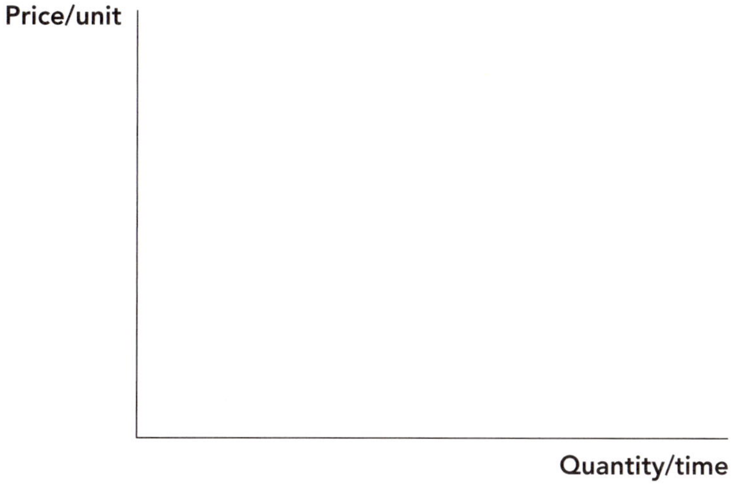

**Price/unit**

**Quantity/time**

2. What is a supply curve? What is quantity supplied? Draw a supply curve on the graph below and use it to explain what a supply curve shows.

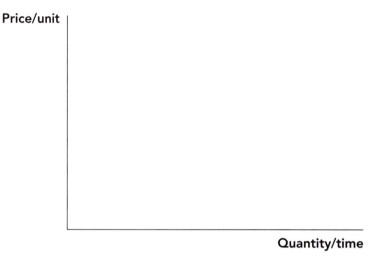

3. What is consumer surplus? If the market price for a calculator was $10, the most that Bob was willing to pay was $20, the most that Kaitlin was willing to pay was $15, and the most that Cindy was willing to pay was $8, how much consumer surplus did each get?

4. How is total consumer surplus measured? On the graph below, mark the total consumer surplus at a market price of $10. Then calculate the amount of total consumer surplus.

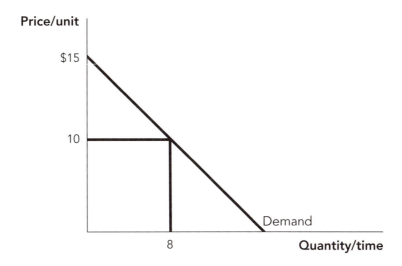

5. What is producer surplus? If the market price of a used textbook is $80, the least that Bob was willing to sell for was $90, the least that Kaitlin was willing to sell for was $40, and the least that Cindy was willing to sell for was $25, how much producer surplus did each get?

6. How is total producer surplus measured? On the graph below, mark the total producer surplus at a market price of $10. Then calculate the amount of total producer surplus.

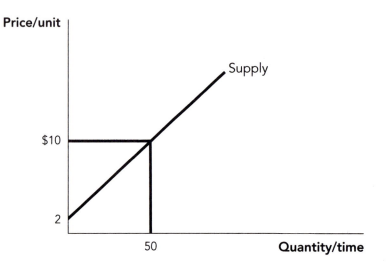

7. On the first graph below, draw an increase in demand.

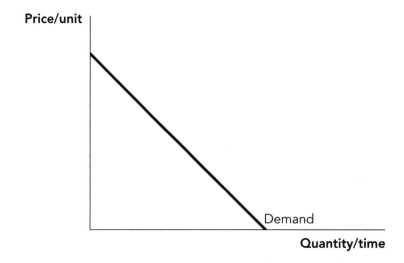

On the next graph below, draw a decrease in demand.

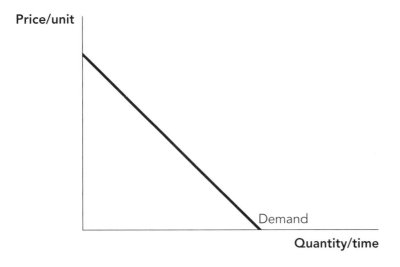

8. What are some of the important things that cause demand to change when they change? Why do they cause demand to change? And what is the direction of the change in demand caused by each?

9. On the first graph below, draw an increase in supply.

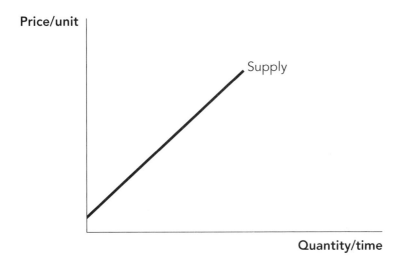

On the next graph below, draw a decrease in supply.

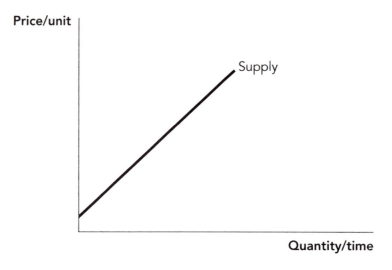

10. What are some of the important things that cause supply to change when they change? Why do they cause supply to change? And what is the direction of the change in supply caused by each?

*11. When the price of Apple computers goes down, what probably happens to the demand for Windows-based computers?[1]

## Multiple-Choice Questions

1. If the price of oil rises, then
   a. the quantity of oil demanded falls.
   b. the demand for oil rises.
   c. the supply of oil rises.
   d. All of the answers are correct.

---

[1] Questions marked with a ★ are also end-of-chapter questions.

2. A demand curve shows
   a. the maximum willingness to pay for particular quantities.
   b. quantity demanded at different prices.
   c. different combinations of prices and quantities that consumers are able and willing to buy.
   d. All of the answers are correct.

3. If the most Tom is willing to pay for an ice cream cone is $5 and the market price is $2, then by purchasing an ice cream cone, Tom will get a consumer surplus of
   a. $2.
   b. $3.
   c. $5.
   d. $10.

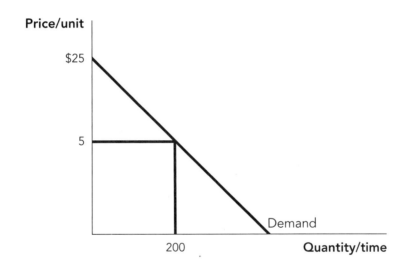

4. In Figure 2.7, if the market price is $5, then the consumer surplus is
   a. $25.
   b. $500.
   c. $1,000.
   d. $2,000.

5. If consumer incomes rise, then the demand for
   a. inferior goods increases.
   b. normal goods decreases.
   c. inferior goods decreases.
   d. complements decreases.

**26 • CHAPTER 2 • Supply and Demand**

6. If peanut butter and jelly are complements, then an increase in the price of peanut butter will cause
   a. an increase in the price of jelly.
   b. a decrease in the demand for jelly.
   c. an increase in the demand for peanut butter.
   d. a decrease in the demand for peanut butter.

7. If the price of a substitute for butter rises, then
   a. the demand for butter increases.
   b. the demand for butter decreases.
   c. the price of butter falls.
   d. the supply of the substitute decreases.

8. Inferior goods are
   a. substandard.
   b. those with expected future price decreases.
   c. those that are negatively related to consumer income.
   d. those that few people buy.

9. If the price of oil is expected to fall in the future, then
   a. the demand for oil today decreases.
   b. the demand for oil in the future decreases.
   c. the supply of oil today decreases.
   d. the supply of oil in the future increases.

10. If tastes for a good goes up due to a fad, then
    a. the current price falls.
    b. the good is a normal good.
    c. the supply of the good decreases.
    d. the demand for the good increases.

11. If the price of oil falls, then
    a. the supply of oil decreases.
    b. the quantity of oil demanded decreases.
    c. the demand for oil increases.
    d. the quantity of oil supplied decreases.

12. Quantity supplied is
    a. negatively related to price.
    b. the amount of a good that sellers are willing and able to sell at a particular price.
    c. price without the willingness to sell.
    d. All of the answers are correct.

13. Producer surplus is
    a. the difference between the market price and the minimum price at which a producer would be willing to sell a particular quantity.
    b. the difference between the maximum price that a consumer would be willing to pay for a particular quantity and the market price.
    c. when the quantity supplied is greater than the quantity demanded.
    d. when the quantity demanded is greater than the quantity supplied.

Figure 2.8

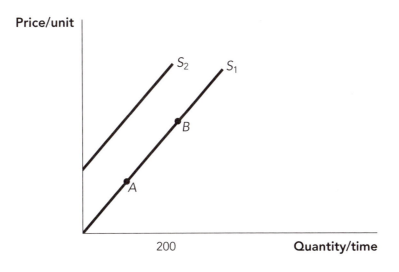

14. In Figure 2.8, an increase in supply is
    a. a move from point $A$ to point $B$ on $S_1$.
    b. a move from point $B$ to point $A$ on $S_1$.
    c. a shift from $S_2$ to $S_1$.
    d. a shift from $S_1$ to $S_2$.

15. If technology increases, then the
    a. supply curve decreases.
    b. demand curve decreases.
    c. supply curve increases.
    d. demand curve increases.

16. If the price of an input, such as the number of autoworkers, increases, then
    a. the supply of cars will decrease.
    b. the supply of cars will increase.
    c. the price of cars will decrease.
    d. the supply of autoworkers will decrease.

17. If firms expect the price of their product to increase in the future, then
    a. the demand today will decrease.
    b. the price today will decrease.
    c. the price in the future will decrease.
    d. the supply today will decrease.

18. If a firm's opportunity cost of producing a product increases, then the supply of that product will
    a. increase as the number of firms in the industry grows.
    b. decrease as the number of firms in the industry grows.
    c. increase as the number of firms in the industry falls.
    d. decrease as the number of firms in the industry falls.

19. If Al's Used Cars sells a car for a market price of $10,000 and the minimum that they would have sold it for was $4,000, then the producer surplus of Al's Used Cars is
    a. $4,000.
    b. $6,000.
    c. $10,000.
    d. $40,000,000.

Figure 2.9

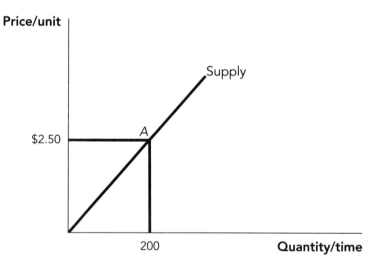

20. In Figure 2.9, total producer surplus is
    a. $2.50.
    b. $197.50.
    c. $250.
    d. $500.

## Short-Answer Questions

21. What is a demand curve? What is quantity demanded?

22. What is a supply curve? What is quantity supplied?

23. What is consumer surplus? How is total consumer surplus measured?

24. What is producer surplus? How is total producer surplus measured?

25. If the market price for a good is $6 and the maximum that Tom is willing to pay is $8, what is his consumer surplus? Assume that the market price is $6 and 50 units are sold. The demand curve hits the vertical axis at $9. What is the total consumer surplus?

26. If the market price for burgers is $7 and the minimum that Big Bun Burgers would have sold a burger for is $4, then what is the producer surplus of Big Bun Burgers on a burger? If the market price is $7, all local burger restaurants sell 400 burgers, and the supply curve passes through the origin, then what is the total producer surplus?

**27.** Describe and graph an increase in demand. What might cause an increase in demand for a good?

**28.** Describe and graph a decrease in supply. What might cause a decrease in supply of a good?

**29.** When does the demand for an inferior good rise? What does it mean for a good to be normal or inferior? What does it *not* mean when it is said that a good is normal or inferior?

**30.** What determines if two goods are complements or substitutes? Are two goods always substitutes or complements?

# Answer Key

## Answers to Practice Exercises: Learning by Doing

1. A demand curve is a function that shows the quantity demanded at different prices. Quantity demanded is the quantity that demanders are willing and able to buy at a particular price. The demand curve should be drawn with a negative slope. The demand curve should demonstrate that price decreases lead to increases in quantity demanded.

   **Topic: The Demand Curve for Oil**

2. A supply curve is a function that shows the quantity supplied at different prices. Quantity supplied is the amount of a good that sellers are willing and able to sell at a particular price. The supply curve should be drawn with a positive slope. The supply curve should demonstrate that price increases lead to increases in quantity supplied.

   **Topic: The Supply Curve for Oil**

3. Consumer surplus is the consumer's gain from exchange, or the difference between the maximum price the consumer is willing to pay for a certain quantity and the market price. Bob received a consumer surplus of $10 = $20 − $10 from buying a calculator. Kaitlin received a consumer surplus of $5 = $15 − 10 from buying a calculator. Cindy received zero consumer surplus from buying a calculator, because the exchange would not take place. Cindy's potential consumer surplus was negative, that is, −$2 = $8 − $10.

   **Topic: Consumer Surplus**

4. Total consumer surplus is measured by the area beneath the demand curve and above market price. The area between demand and market price should be marked on the graph. The calculation for total consumer surplus is $20 = ($15 − $10) × 8 × (½).

   **Topic: Consumer Surplus**

5. Producer surplus is the producer's gain from exchange, or the difference between the market price and the minimum price at which a producer would be willing to sell a particular quantity. Bob received zero producer surplus from selling the textbook, because the exchange would not take place: his potential consumer surplus was negative, that is, -$10 = $80 − $90. Kaitlin received a producer surplus of $40 = $80 − $40 from selling the textbook. Cindy received a producer surplus of $55 = $80 − $25 from selling the textbook.

   **Topic: Producer Surplus**

6. Total producer surplus is measured by the area above the supply curve and below market price. The area between supply and market price should be marked on the graph. The calculation for total producer surplus is $200 = ($10 − $2) × 50 × (½).

   **Topic: Producer Surplus**

7. In the first graph, the new demand curve should be above and to the right of the old demand curve. In the second graph, the new demand curve should be below and to the left of the old demand curve.

   **Topic: What Shifts the Demand Curve?**

8. For normal goods, demand increases as income rises because the consumer buys more of the good. For inferior goods, demand decreases as income rises because the consumer shifts to other goods. For substitutes, demand rises when the price of the other good increases, because the consumer substitutes one good for the other. For complements, demand falls when the price of the other good increases, because the consumer uses the two goods together. If population, taste (desire) for a good, and expected future prices each increase, then the demand for the good will also increase. More buyers mean more demand. Increased taste means that each person wants more of the good. Consumers will try to buy today because the good is expected to be more costly in the future.

   **Topic: What Shifts the Demand Curve?**

9. In the first graph, the new supply curve should be to the right of and below the old supply curve. In the second graph, the new supply curve should be above and to the left of the old supply curve.

   **Topic: What Shifts the Supply Curve?**

10. If technology improves, or if the prices of inputs decline, supply increases because production is cheaper. A tax increase makes production more costly and decreases supply, while a subsidy makes production cheaper and increases supply. If a firm expects a higher price in the future, then to the extent its product is not perishable, the firm will reduce supply today to sell later when the price is expected to be higher. The more firms in the market, the greater the supply, since each supplier adds to the supply. Finally, if the opportunity cost for suppliers rises, some suppliers will leave the business for the higher-valued opportunity, thereby reducing supply in the first industry.

    **Topic: What Shifts the Supply Curve?**

11. Apple computers and Windows-based computers are likely substitutes. Thus, when the price of Apple computers falls, the demand for Windows-based computers likely falls. In this scenario, some consumers will purchase Apple computers rather than Windows-based computers. These consumers would most likely have purchased Windows-based computers when the Apple computers were more expensive.

    **Topic: What Shifts the Demand Curve?**

## Answers to Multiple-Choice Questions

1. a, **Topic: The Demand Curve for Oil**
2. d, **Topic: The Demand Curve for Oil**
3. b, **Topic: Consumer Surplus**
4. d, **Topic: Consumer Surplus**

5. c, Topic: What Shifts the Demand Curve?
6. b, Topic: What Shifts the Demand Curve?
7. a, Topic: What Shifts the Demand Curve?
8. c, Topic: What Shifts the Demand Curve?
9. a, Topic: What Shifts the Demand Curve?
10. d, Topic: The Demand Curve for Oil
11. d, Topic: The Supply Curve for Oil
12. b, Topic: Producer Surplus
13. a, Topic: Producer Surplus
14. c, Topic: What Shifts the Supply Curve?
15. c, Topic: What Shifts the Supply Curve?
16. a, Topic: What Shifts the Supply Curve?
17. d, Topic: What Shifts the Supply Curve?
18. d, Topic: What Shifts the Supply Curve?
19. b, Topic: Producer Surplus
20. c, Topic: Producer Surplus

## Answers to Short-Answer Questions

21. A demand curve is a function that shows the quantity demanded at different prices. Quantity demanded is the quantity that buyers are willing and able to buy at a particular price.

    **Topic: The Demand Curve for Oil**

22. A supply curve is a function that shows the quantity supplied at different prices. Quantity supplied is the quantity that sellers are willing and able to sell at a particular price.

    **Topic: The Supply Curve for Oil**

23. Consumer surplus is the consumer's gain from exchange, or the difference between the maximum price a consumer is willing to pay for a certain quantity of goods and the market price. Total consumer surplus is measured by the area beneath the demand curve and above the price.

    **Topic: Consumer Surplus**

24. Producer surplus is the producer's gain from exchange, or the difference between the market price and the minimum price at which a producer would be willing to sell a certain quantity. Total producer surplus is measured by the area above the supply curve and below the price.

    **Topic: Producer Surplus**

25. Tom's consumer surplus is $2 on that unit. Total consumer surplus is $75.

   **Topic: Consumer Surplus**

26. The producer surplus of Big Bun Burgers is $3 on that burger. Total producer surplus is $1,400.

   **Topic: Producer Surplus**

27. An increase in demand is a shift up and to the right. A graph would be similar to Figure 2.3, with the increase in demand shown as the movement from $D_2$ to $D_1$. An increase in demand might be caused by an increase in consumer income for normal goods, a decrease in consumer income for inferior goods, an increase in the price of a substitute good, a decrease in the price of a complementary good, an increase in population, an increase in tastes (desire) for the good, or an expectation of higher future prices for the good.

   **Topic: What Shifts the Demand Curve?**

28. A decrease in supply is a shift up and to the left. A graph would be similar to Figure 2.6, with the decrease in supply shown as the movement from $S_1$ to $S_2$. A decrease in supply might be caused by a negative change in technology, an increase in input prices, an increased tax or a decreased subsidy, an expectation of higher future prices for the good, the exit of some producers of the good from the industry, and a higher opportunity cost of producing the good.

   **Topic: What Shifts the Supply Curve?**

29. The demand for an inferior good rises when consumer income falls. The terms "normal" and "inferior" just describe the relationship between consumer income and the demand for a good. Normal goods are positively related to consumer income. Inferior goods are negatively related to consumer income. These terms do not necessarily tell us anything about the quality of different goods.

   **Topic: What Shifts the Demand Curve?**

30. Whether two goods are complements or substitutes depends on how consumers use them. Different consumers do not necessarily use two goods in the same manner. For some people and in some uses, two goods may be complements, and for other people and in other uses, two goods may be substitutes. For example, for some people, sausage and pepperoni are substitutes on pizza. They prefer having only one of the substitutes (sausage or pepperoni) on the pizza. For other people, the more toppings, the better, and they would allow both sausage and pepperoni (complements) to be added to the pizza.

   **Topic: What Shifts the Demand Curve?**

# 3
# Equilibrium

## Why Learn about Equilibrium?

**Interested student:** It is nice that there is an equilibrium price and quantity in each market, but does it really matter?
**Old professor:** Sure it matters. It tells us how the price of anything from beer to human tissue is determined.
**Interested student:** Ok, but how does it matter in real life?
**Old professor:** Well, someday you might work for a business that depends on the price of its products. And certainly you will care about the wages you receive, because that is the price of your labor. Also, you may vote in an election in which one political candidate thinks that a new policy can reduce the price of some important good. Understanding equilibrium will make you a better-informed voter in such an election.
**Interested student:** Sure that makes sense.
**Old professor:** Plus, Chapters 2 and 3 are fundamental to understanding economics, and you are a student taking an economics class.

## Summary

The interaction of supply and demand leads to a market equilibrium. As shown in Figure 3.1, market equilibrium occurs where supply and demand intersect.

Figure 3.1

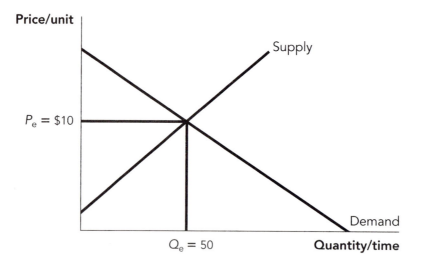

This intersection yields the **equilibrium price**, $P_e = \$10$, and **equilibrium quantity**, $Q_e = 50$ units of the good.

The market equilibrium is stable, as shown in Figure 3.2, where the equilibrium is still at a price of $10 and a quantity of 50 units.

Figure 3.2

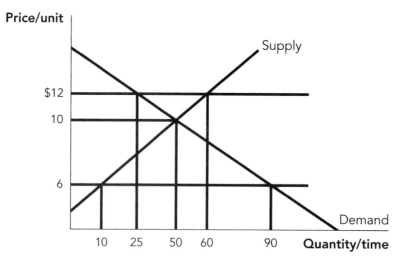

A price of $12 is above equilibrium. At $12, more of the product (60 units) is offered for sale than people want to purchase (25 units). Quantity supplied is greater than quantity demanded by 35 units, implying an excess quantity supplied, or **surplus**.

What will consumers and producers do about the excess quantity supplied? Producers who have rising inventories will start lowering prices below $12. Consumers who see that producers have extra product on hand will start offering prices below $12. Lower prices decrease quantity supplied and increase quantity demanded, moving the market toward equilibrium.

Similarly a price of $6 is below the equilibrium price. At $6, consumers want to buy more of the product (90 units) than producers want to sell (10 units). This time, quantity demanded is greater than quantity supplied by 80 units, implying an excess quantity demanded, or **shortage**.

What will consumers and producers do about the excess quantity demanded? Consumers, many of whom cannot get the item, will start offering prices above $6. Producers, who see their product flying off the shelf, will start asking prices above $6. Higher prices increase quantity supplied and decrease quantity demanded, again moving the market toward equilibrium.

So whether the price is above or below equilibrium, competitive pressures move price and quantity toward the market equilibrium. Only at the equilibrium does quantity supplied equal quantity demanded, implying no pressure from either consumers or producers to change price.

Gains from trade are maximized at the market equilibrium. This can be seen in Figure 3.3, where the 26th unit is worth slightly less than $12, say $11.99, to the consumer and costs the producer only slightly more than $8, say $8.01.

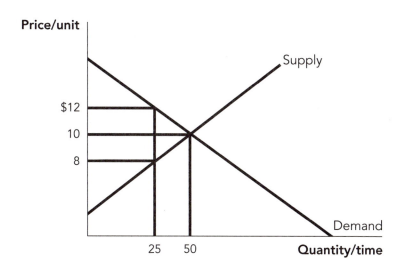

Any price between $11.99 and $8.01 makes both the buyer and seller better off. This is called an unexploited gain from trade. As long as the quantity is below the equilibrium quantity, there will be these unexploited gains from trade.

What if the quantity is above the market equilibrium of 50 units in Figure 3.3? In that case, the cost to producers of producing the unit is greater than what any consumer is willing to pay. So, while consumers are willing to consume the product at some specified price, that price is below the cost of producing the good. Producing such units would waste resources that would be better spent producing something consumers value more.

**38** • CHAPTER 3 • Equilibrium

The free market's, maximizing gains from trade means three closely related things. First, the supply of goods is bought by buyers with the highest willingness to pay. Second, the supply of goods is sold by sellers with the lowest costs. Third, between buyers and sellers there are no unexploited gains from trade, nor any wasteful trades.

As shown in Figure 3.4, a change in demand causes a movement along the supply curve and a change in quantity supplied.

Figure 3.4

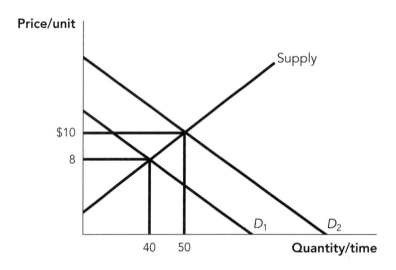

Originally with demand $D_1$, quantity supplied was 40 units. As demand increased to $D_2$, quantity moves along the supply curve and quantity supplied becomes 50 units.

For markets with upward-sloping supply curves and downward-sloping demand curves, an increase in demand increases equilibrium price and quantity. As shown in Figure 3.4, the movement of demand from $D_1$ to $D_2$ causes the equilibrium price to rise from $8 to $10 and the equilibrium quantity to rise from 40 to 50 units. If demand had decreased from $D_2$ to $D_1$ the reverse would have happened. The equilibrium price would have fallen from $10 to $8, and the equilibrium quantity would have fallen from 50 to 40 units.

Similarly, as shown in Figure 3.5, a decrease in supply causes a movement along the demand curve and a change in quantity demanded.

Originally with demand $S_1$, quantity demanded was 60 units. As supply decreased to $D_2$, quantity moves along the demand curve and quantity demanded becomes 35 units.

For markets with upward-sloping supply curves and downward-sloping demand curves, a decrease in supply increases equilibrium price and decreases equilibrium quantity. As shown in Figure 3.5, the movement of supply from $S_1$ to $S_2$ causes the equilibrium price to rise from $11 to $13 and the equilibrium quantity to fall from 60 to 35 units. If supply had increased from $S_2$ to $S_1$ the reverse would have happened. The equilibrium price would have fallen from $13 to $11, and the equilibrium quantity would have risen from 35 to 60 units.

Figure 3.5

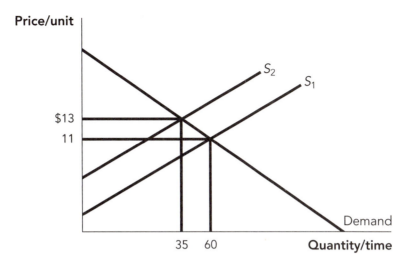

## Key Terms

**surplus** a situation in which the quantity supplied is greater than the quantity demanded

**shortage** a situation in which the quantity demanded is greater than the quantity supplied

**equilibrium price** the price at which the quantity demanded is equal to the quantity supplied

**equilibrium quantity** the quantity at which the quantity demanded is equal to the quantity supplied

## Traps, Hints, and Reminders

A surplus should not be confused with consumer or producer surplus, both of which were defined in Chapter 2. A surplus on a market is when quantity supplied is greater than quantity demanded. Consumer surplus is the maximum the consumer is willing to pay less market price. Producer surplus is market price less the minimum price at which the producer would sell.

A free market maximizes the gains from trade, or maximizes producer surplus plus consumer surplus.

A change in demand causes a movement along the supply curve and a change in quantity supplied. Similarly, a change in supply leads to a movement along the demand curve and a change in quantity demanded. The things that can cause changes in quantity demanded or supplied are different from the things that can cause demand and supply to change, as discussed in Chapter 2.

Also recall from Chapter 2 that changes in supply can be somewhat counterintuitive. An increase in supply is a shift to the right and down, while a decrease in supply is a shift up and to the left.

# Practice Exercises: Learning by Doing

1. What is the market equilibrium? Draw supply and demand on the graph below. Note the equilibrium price and quantity.

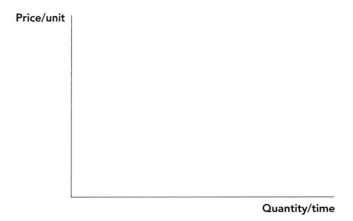

2. On the graphs below, draw a surplus and a shortage in a market.

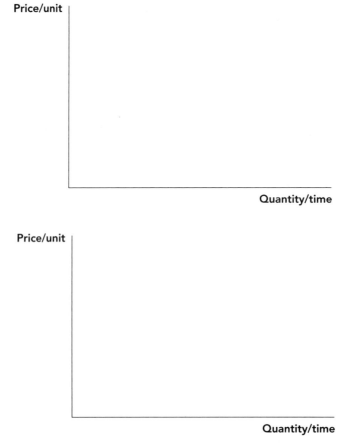

3. Explain why the market equilibrium is a position the market will tend to. Why is it stable?

4. Explain how the market maximizes the gains from trade, or the sum of consumer and producer surplus.

5. Explain why the market will not produce beyond the equilibrium quantity.

6. In the graph below, draw an increase in supply. Explain what happens.

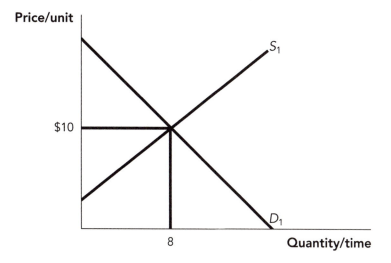

7. In the graph below, draw a decrease in demand. Explain what happens.

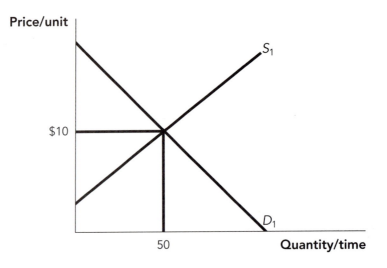

8. What are the three things implied by the free market's maximizing the gains from trade?

*9. In the last 10 years India and China became wealthier and oil prices increased. What is the best way to think about the rise in oil prices during that time? Was the rise in oil prices due to a rise in demand, a fall in demand, a rise in supply, or a fall in supply?[1]

[1]Questions marked with a ★ are also end-of-chapter questions.

# Multiple-Choice Questions

1. In an equilibrium market
   a. quantity demanded equals quantity supplied.
   b. total surplus is minimized.
   c. the market price is unstable.
   d. All of the answers are correct.

2. If price is above the equilibrium price, some
   a. consumers will offer to pay a higher price to get the product.
   b. producers will ask a higher price of consumers to sell the product.
   c. producers will have excess supplies and thus start reducing price to get customers.
   d. All of the answers are correct.

3. If price is below the equilibrium price, some
   a. consumers will offer to pay a higher price to be sure to get the product.
   b. consumers will offer to pay a lower price because the product is so available.
   c. producers will have excess supplies and thus start reducing price to get customers.
   d. All of the answers are correct.

4. If price is below the equilibrium price, then
   a. every consumer who wants the product can get it.
   b. quantity supplied is greater than quantity demanded for the product.
   c. there is a shortage of the product.
   d. All of the answers are correct.

5. If price is above the equilibrium price, then
   a. every producer who wants to sell the product can do so.
   b. quantity supplied is greater than quantity demanded.
   c. there is a shortage of the product.
   d. All of the answers are correct.

Figure 3.6

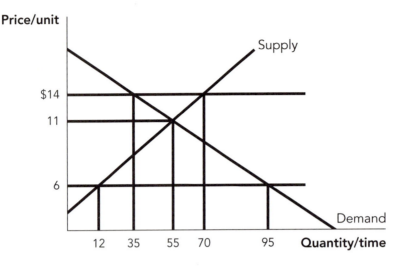

6. In Figure 3.6, the equilibrium price and quantity are
   a. $14 and 70 units.
   b. $11 and 55 units.
   c. $11 and 70 units.
   d. $6 and 12 units.

7. In Figure 3.6, at a price of $14, producers will want to sell
   a. 70 units.
   b. 55 units.
   c. 35 units.
   d. 12 units.

8. In Figure 3.6, at a price of $6, consumers will want to buy
   a. 12 units.
   b. 55 units.
   c. 70 units.
   d. 95 units.

9. In Figure 3.6, at a price of $14, there is an excess quantity
   a. demanded of 83 units.
   b. supplied of 83 units.
   c. demanded of 35 units.
   d. supplied of 35 units.

10. In Figure 3.6, at a price of $6, there is a
    a. shortage of 83 units.
    b. surplus of 83 units.
    c. shortage of 35 units.
    d. surplus of 35 units.

11. In a free market equilibrium,
    a. consumer plus producer surplus is maximized.
    b. gains from trade are maximized.
    c. no potential gains from trade are left unexploited.
    d. All of the answers are correct.

12. The market will not produce a quantity greater than equilibrium because
    a. there are unexploited gains from trade left.
    b. it is illegal.
    c. resources are wasted on production to the right of the equilibrium quantity.
    d. consumer plus producer surplus grows in that region.

13. The free market's maximizing gains from trade implies that
    a. the supply of goods is bought by buyers with the highest willingness to pay.
    b. the supply of goods is sold by sellers with the highest costs.
    c. between buyers and sellers there are unexploited gains from trade.
    d. All of the answers are correct.

14. The free market's maximizing gains from trade implies that
    a. the supply of goods is bought by buyers with the lowest willingness to pay.
    b. the supply of goods is sold by sellers with the lowest costs.
    c. between buyers and sellers there are wasteful trades.
    d. All of the answers are correct.

15. The free market's maximizing gains from trade implies that
    a. the supply of goods is bought by buyers with the lowest willingness to pay.
    b. the supply of goods is sold by sellers with the highest costs.
    c. between buyers and sellers there are no unexploited gains from trade, nor any wasteful trades.
    d. All of the answers are correct.

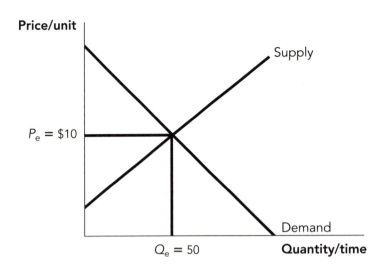

**Figure 3.7**

16. In Figure 3.7, if demand increases, then the equilibrium
    a. price and quantity fall.
    b. price and quantity rise.
    c. price falls and quantity rises.
    d. price rises and quantity falls.

17. In Figure 3.7, if supply decreases, then the equilibrium
    a. price and quantity fall.
    b. price and quantity rise.
    c. price falls and quantity rises.
    d. price rises and quantity falls.

18. In Figure 3.7, if the good is normal, and consumer income falls, then the equilibrium
    a. price and quantity fall.
    b. price and quantity rise.
    c. price falls and quantity rises.
    d. price rises and quantity falls.

19. In Figure 3.7, if there is a technological improvement in producing this good, then the equilibrium
    a. price and quantity fall.
    b. price and quantity rise.
    c. price falls and quantity rises.
    d. price rises and quantity falls.

20. In a free market equilibrium,

    a. quantity demanded is greater than quantity supplied.

    b. the sum of consumer and producer surplus is maximized.

    c. resources are wasted.

    d. there are unexploited gains from trade.

## Short-Answer Questions

21. Describe market equilibrium.

22. What are the three things implied by the free market's maximizing gains from trade?

23. If the price in a market happens to be below equilibrium, what is the situation in the market? Describe what happens in the market in response to this situation.

24. What is the difference between a change in demand and a change in quantity demanded? What causes each to occur?

25. Graph an increase in demand in a market. Explain what happens to the market when this occurs.

26. Graph an increase in supply in a market. Explain what happens to the market when this occurs.

27. What is meant by trades that waste resources?

28. What is a shortage? What is a surplus?

29. If quantity is less than equilibrium quantity, why are there unexploited gains from trade?

30. What does the free market equilibrium maximize?

# Answer Key

## Answers to Practice Exercises: Learning by Doing

1. Market equilibrium is where supply and demand intersect. At the equilibrium price, quantity supplied equals quantity demanded. Draw a graph like Figure 3.1.

   **Topic: Equilibrium and the Adjustment Process**

2. Draw two graphs. Draw one graph like 3.2 with a price above equilibrium. Show how this leads to excess quantity supplied, that is, a surplus. Draw another graph with a price below equilibrium. Show how this leads to an excess quantity demanded, that is, a shortage.

   **Topic: Equilibrium and the Adjustment Process**

3. If price is above equilibrium, there is an excess quantity supplied. Producers have too much product on hand, and some will start selling at a lower price, moving the market toward equilibrium. If price is below equilibrium, there will be an excess quantity demanded. Not all consumers can get the good, and some will start offering a higher price to be sure to get the good. This also moves the market toward equilibrium. At the equilibrium price and quantity each producer sells all it wants and each consumer is able to buy all he or she wants. This makes the market equilibrium stable.

   **Topic: Equilibrium and the Adjustment Process**

4. The market maximizes gains from trade by allowing all producers (who want to sell) to sell at the going price and all consumers (who want to buy) to buy at the going price. This maximizes consumer surplus and producer surplus.

   **Topic: Gains from Trade Are Maximized at the Equilibrium Price and Quantity**

5. The market will not produce beyond the equilibrium, quantity because doing so would waste resources. Consumers will not value the product enough to make up for the costs to the producers of producing the product.

   **Topic: Gains from Trade Are Maximized at the Equilibrium Price and Quantity**

6. The new supply curve should be below and to the right of the old supply curve. The increase in supply leads to a movement along the demand curve. Quantity demanded increases, the new equilibrium price is lower, and quantity is larger.

   **Topic: Shifting Demand and Supply Curves**

7. The new demand curve should be below and to the left of the old demand curve. The decrease in demand leads to a movement along the supply curve. Quantity supplied falls, and the new equilibrium price and quantity are lower.

   **Topic: Shifting Demand and Supply Curves**

8. The supply of goods is bought by the buyers with the highest willingness to pay. The supply of goods is sold by sellers with the lowest costs. Between buyers and sellers there are no unexploited gains from trade, nor any wasteful trades.

   **Topic: Gains from Trade Are Maximized at the Equilibrium Price and Quantity**

9. India and China becoming richer in the last 10 years is best thought of as leading to an increase in the demand for oil that has led to some upward movements in the price of oil.

   **Topic: Shifting Demand and Supply Curves**

## Answers to Multiple-Choice Questions

1. a, Topic: Equilibrium and the Adjustment Process
2. c, Topic: Equilibrium and the Adjustment Process
3. a, Topic: Equilibrium and the Adjustment Process
4. c, Topic: Equilibrium and the Adjustment Process
5. b, Topic: Equilibrium and the Adjustment Process
6. b, Topic: Equilibrium and the Adjustment Process
7. a, Topic: Equilibrium and the Adjustment Process
8. d, Topic: Equilibrium and the Adjustment Process
9. d, Topic: Equilibrium and the Adjustment Process
10. a, Topic: Equilibrium and the Adjustment Process
11. d, Topic: Gains from Trade Are Maximized at the Equilibrium Price and Quantity
12. c, Topic: Gains from Trade Are Maximized at the Equilibrium Price and Quantity
13. a, Topic: Gains from Trade Are Maximized at the Equilibrium Price and Quantity
14. b, Topic: Gains from Trade Are Maximized at the Equilibrium Price and Quantity
15. c, Topic: Gains from Trade Are Maximized at the Equilibrium Price and Quantity
16. b, Topic: Shifting Demand and Supply Curves
17. d, Topic: Shifting Demand and Supply Curves
18. a, Topic: Shifting Demand and Supply Curves
19. c, Topic: Shifting Demand and Supply Curves
20. b, Topic: Equilibrium and the Adjustment Process

## Answers to Short-Answer Questions

21. The market equilibrium is where supply and demand intersect. This is also where, at one price, quantity demanded equals quantity supplied. At this point, the market has captured all gains from trade and maximized the sum of consumer and producer surplus. The equilibrium is stable because every consumer can buy all they want at the market price and every seller can sell all they want at the market price.

    **Topic: Equilibrium and the Adjustment Process**

22. The supply of goods is bought by the buyers with the highest willingness to pay. The supply of goods is sold by sellers with the lowest costs. Between buyers and sellers there are no unexploited gains from trade, nor any wasteful trades.

    **Topic: Equilibrium and the Adjustment Process**

23. When price is below the equilibrium price, quantity demanded is greater than quantity supplied, that is, there is a shortage. Not all consumers who want to consume at that price will be able to purchase the good. Some consumers will start offering higher prices to ensure that they can get the good. The higher price will cause quantity supplied to increase and quantity demanded to decrease, thus moving the market toward equilibrium.

    **Topic: Equilibrium and the Adjustment Process**

24. A change in demand is a shift of the entire curve. Shifts in the entire curve are caused by the items discussed in Chapter 2, such as tastes and consumer income. A change in quantity demanded is a movement along the demand curve. A movement along the demand curve is caused by a shift in the supply curve or a change in price in the market.

    **Topic: Shifting Demand and Supply Curves**

25. The new demand curve should be above and to the right of the initial demand curve. The equilibrium price and quantity increase.

    **Topic: Shifting Demand and Supply Curves**

26. The new supply curve should be below and to the right of the initial supply curve. The equilibrium price falls and the equilibrium quantity rises.

    **Topic: Shifting Demand and Supply Curves**

27. Exchanges beyond the equilibrium quantity are not made, because the cost to the producers of producing the product is greater than the value that consumers place on the product. Thus, if such trades were made, scarce resources would be wasted. A better use of these resources would be to produce something that consumers would value more. Thus if those units were produced and sold, the difference between the cost of producing them from the supply curve, and the value consumers place on them from the demand curve, would be wasted.

    **Topic: Gains from Trade Are Maximized at the Equilibrium Price and Quantity**

28. A shortage is when quantity demanded is greater than quantity supplied, that is, there is excess quantity demanded. A surplus is when there is excess quantity supplied; that is, quantity supplied is greater than quantity demanded.

   **Topic: Gains from Trade Are Maximized at the Equilibrium Price and Quantity**

29. For each unit less than the market equilibrium quantity, some consumer values that unit more than it costs some producer to produce it. This is another way of saying that demand is above supply. Thus there is some price between the value the consumer places on the good and the producer's cost of producing the good that would make both consumer and producer better off. Those are the unexploited gains from trade when quantity is less than equilibrium quantity.

   **Topic: Gains from Trade Are Maximized at the Equilibrium Price and Quantity**

30. A free market equilibrium maximizes both the sum of producer and consumer surplus and gains from trade.

   **Topic: Gains from Trade Are Maximized at the Equilibrium Price and Quantity**

# 4

# Price Ceilings and Price Floors

## Why Learn about Price Controls?

Consumers often want laws that make prices lower (price ceilings), but they don't always benefit from these laws. Students as consumers will be interested in the way that these laws lead to shortages and other problems. Producers want laws that make prices higher, but producers don't always benefit from them either. In this chapter we get to see how price controls lead to unintended consequences.

## Summary

*Price controls* are laws about what can happen to prices. A price control can limit how high a price can go—a **price ceiling.** Price controls can also limit how low a price can go—a **price floor.** Minimum wages, agricultural price controls, and rent control are examples of price controls. Price controls are more interesting when they are binding. A binding price control just means that it has an effect. Accountants aren't really affected by the minimum wage (a price floor) because accountants already make more than the minimum wage. Unskilled workers are affected by the minimum wage. It is binding for unskilled workers.

A price ceiling creates a *misallocation of resources*. With the price system, those that are willing to pay the market price get the item and those who are not willing to pay the market price forego the good. With a price ceiling, the buyer that is willing to pay the most may or may not get to consume the good. A price ceiling therefore encourages bribery, selling to friends first, or if the good is not allocated in other ways, waiting in line.

Price ceilings cause

> shortages,

> reductions in product quality,

> wasteful waiting in line and other search costs,

> loss of gains from trade,

> and misallocation of resources.

**Figure 4.1 Price Ceilings Create Shortages**

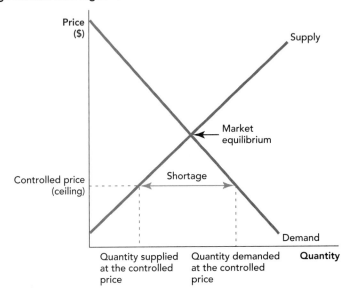

Price floors cause

> surpluses,

> loss of gains from trade,

> wasteful increases in quality,

> and misallocation of resources. (See Figure 4.2.)

**Deadweight loss** is when there is less consumer surplus and less producer surplus because of some interference in the market by the government. It is surplus that people could get but that they don't. The surplus is not available to anyone.

In Figure 4.3, area $A$ is consumer surplus. Area $E$ *would* be consumer surplus but that quantity is unavailable. Area $B$ *would* also be consumer surplus but it is the value of wasted time. Area $D$ is producer surplus. Area $F$ *would* be producer surplus but that quantity is unavailable. Area $C$ *would* also be producer surplus but instead it is wasted time spent by consumers looking for unavailable surplus.

*Rent control* is a regulation that prevents rents from rising to equilibrium levels. As with any other price ceiling, rent control creates a shortage of the good. It has several other problems. It encourages landlords to quit maintaining their properties. Rent control leads to people wasting resources searching for available properties. There are deadweight losses or lost gains from trade with rent control because people are willing to pay more than landlords are able to charge for rent. Finally, resources are misallocated, as fewer apartments are constructed and people often end up living in apartments smaller or bigger than those of their optimal choice.

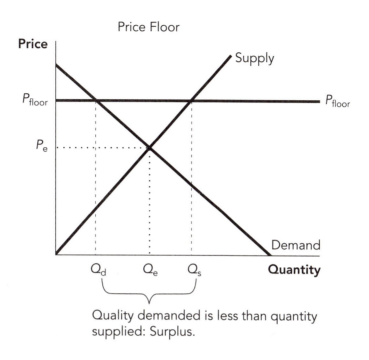

Figure 4.2

Quality demanded is less than quantity supplied: Surplus.

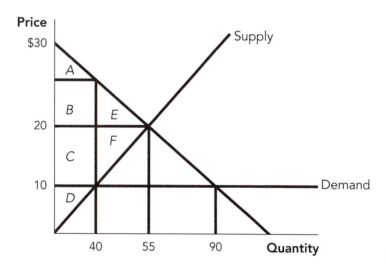

Figure 4.3

Rent controls and other price ceilings often start with a "freezing" of prices or rents due to public pressure about prices or rents rising too quickly. Since, as we learned in Chapter 3, supply in a shorter time frame is relatively inelastic, at first there is not a huge impact on quantity supplied and the shortage is therefore not huge. But over time the shortage grows, as supply is more elastic over a longer time frame. Politicians who pass rent control or other price ceiling laws operate over 2- or 4- or at most 6-year election cycles. So, if they see "freezing" rents as a way to get reelected, then a price ceiling may be worth it to politicians, even if in the long term, the public does not care for price ceilings or rent controls.

## Key Terms

**price ceiling** is a maximum price allowed by law

**deadweight loss** is the total of lost consumer and producer surplus when not all mutually profitable gains from trade are exploited. Price ceilings (and price floors) create a deadweight loss

**price floor** is a minimum price allowed by law

## Traps, Hints, and Reminders

Price floors go above the equilibrium price and price ceilings go below. It is very easy to mix them up on an exam. Some students draw silly pictures when they are studying because drawing silly pictures is actually quite helpful. Draw balloons going up to the equilibrium price in the case of a price ceiling (the balloon can't go above the ceiling) or draw a person standing on the price floor trying to push the price down toward the equilibrium. See the next section. Those are visual mnemonics.

Keep in mind that exam questions often ask students to "show" the effect of a price control. That normally means to draw a supply and demand graph with the price control. It is not uncommon for professors to take points off for not drawing a correctly labeled supply and demand graph.

This is a drawing-intensive chapter. Being able to draw the graph correctly is very important for getting test questions correct; also, make sure to label everything.

Figure 4.4

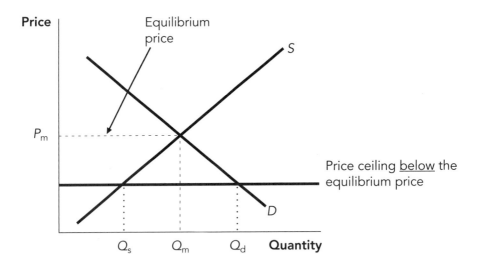

It is important to make sure that you understand the difference between *demand* and *quantity demanded* as well as *supply* and *quantity supplied*. Those terms come up again and again in this chapter.

Don't forget that $Q_m$ is the quantity bought and sold in a free market. $P_m$ is the price in a free market.

Some professors use other nomenclature for equilibrium price and quantity. You might also see $P_e$ for Price in equilibrium and $Q_e$ for Quantity in equilibrium. Don't be confused by that. You may even see your professor use $Q^\star$ and $P^\star$. Don't be one of the students who gets confused just because a symbol has changed. These are all the same thing. You know that the market equilibrium comes from where Supply and Demand cross.

## Practice Exercises: Learning by Doing

1. Draw a graph that shows a price ceiling. The price ceiling should be *below* the equilibrium price. Now draw a silly little cartoon helium balloon with the word "market" on it below the price ceiling. Imagine that the market is pushing up like a helium balloon to the equilibrium price. [Yes, this is silly but being silly helps you remember it on the exam.]

2. Draw a graph that shows a price floor. The price floor should be *above* the equilibrium price. Now draw a silly little stick figure with the word *market* on it above the price floor. Imagine that the market is pushing down or even stomping down on the price floor to get to the equilibrium [Yes, this is silly, but it is a useful mnemonic or way of remembering something.]

3. Draw two supply and demand curves side by side. One should have a price floor and the other, a price ceiling. Make sure that you correctly label the *quantity supplied* and quantity *demanded* for each. You don't need the silly pictures. Point out how much surplus or shortage there is.

4. Draw the price ceiling one more time.

   a. This time shade in where both consumer and producer surplus would be with no price ceiling.
   b. Show the deadweight loss **and** the area that can be the value from wasted time. (If you are a visual learner, this is the time to bring out colored pencils, crayons, or at least two different colored pens.)
5. If you were looking at a price control graph on an exam, how would you know if you were looking at a price floor or price ceiling?

6. If the federal government put a price ceiling on college education, would that help all students?

7. Would a price floor that is only a few cents above the equilibrium price of milk have the same effect as a price floor that is $1.00 above the equilibrium price?

8. Imagine that the government imposes a price ceiling on lumber after a hurricane. What sort of misallocation problems could occur?

9. Imagine that you work at the local beach giving surf lessons. You are not allowed to charge below $60 for surf lessons even though the market price would probably be about $30. How else could you compete for customers?

10. If a price ceiling is imposed on beer such that the price falls from $1 per beer to $.50 per beer, you would expect there to be a shortage. Who will spend the most time looking for places that have beer and what happens to the time that they spend looking?

## Multiple-Choice Questions

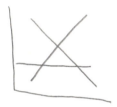

b 1. A price ceiling is
   a. the maximum a consumer is willing to pay for a good.
   b. a maximum price allowed by law.
   c. the maximum value of all the inputs used to produce the good.
   d. All of the answers are correct.

a 2. A price ceiling causes
   a. a shortage.
   b. a surplus.
   c. pressure on the producer to lower the price.
   d. pressure on consumers to offer lower prices.

c 3. An example of a price ceiling is
   a. farm price supports.
   b. the minimum wage.
   c. rent control.
   d. All of the answers are correct.

d 4. Price ceilings lead to
   a. wasted resources.
   b. consumers searching for product availability.
   c. consumers waiting in line to buy the product.
   d. All of the answers are correct.

C 5. With a price ceiling if nothing else is set up, the good will be allocated by
   a. income.
   b. price.
   c. first come first serve and waiting in line.
   d. All of the answers are correct.

Figure 4.5

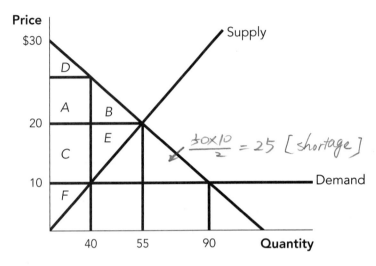

a 6. In Figure 4.5, the price ceiling is
   a. $10.
   b. $20.
   c. $30.
   d. None of the answers is correct.

7. In Figure 4.5, the price ceiling quantity demanded is
   a. 40 units.
   b. 55 units.
   c. 90 units.
   d. None of the answers is correct.

8. In Figure 4.5, the price ceiling quantity supplied is
   a. 40 units.
   b. 55 units.
   c. 90 units.
   d. All of the answers are correct.

9. In Figure 4.5, the price ceiling causes a shortage of
   a. 15 units.
   b. 35 units.
   c. 50 units.
   d. None of the answers is correct.

CHAPTER 4 • Price Ceilings and Price Floors • **61**

10. In Figure 4.5, the deadweight loss associated with the price ceiling is the area
    a. *A* + *B*.
    b. *B* + *E*.
    c. *F*.
    d. *A* + *C*.

11. In Figure 4.5, with the price ceiling, producer surplus is the area
    a. *A* + *B*.
    b. *B* + *E*.
    c. *F*.
    d. *A* + *C*.

12. In Figure 4.5, the consumer surplus is the area
    a. *A* + *B*.
    b. *C*.
    c. *F*.
    d. *D*.

13. In Figure 4.5, which area represents the total value of wasted time?
    a. *A* + *B*
    b. *C*
    c. *F*
    d. *A* + *C*

14. In Figure 4.5, what is the dead weight loss?
    a. *A*
    b. *B* + *E*
    c. *C*
    d. *F*

15. In Figure 4.5, if a magical computer allocated all of the goods so there was no wasteful search cost, what areas would be the consumer surplus?
    a. *A* + *C* + *D*
    b. *B* + *E*
    c. *C*
    d. *D* + *F*

16. Rent controls
    a. cause shortages.
    b. create lost gains from trade.
    c. misallocate resources.
    d. All of the answers are correct.

17. With a price ceiling
    a. gains from trade are maximized.
    b. there are unexploited gains from trade.
    c. there are wasteful trades.
    d. the supply of goods is bought by the buyer with the highest willingness to pay.

18. With a price ceiling
    a. quality of the good improves.
    b. there is a surplus on the market.
    c. resources are misallocated.
    d. All of the answers are correct.

19. With a price ceiling, goods may be allocated by all *except*
    a. bribery.
    b. publically announced price.
    c. personal connections.
    d. first come, first serve and waiting in line.

20. A price floor is
    a. the maximum a consumer is willing to pay for a good.
    b. a maximum price required by law.
    c. the minimum a consumer is willing to pay for a good.
    c. a minimum price required by law.

21. A price floor causes
    a. surpluses.
    b. deadweight loss gains from trade.
    c. misallocation of resources.
    d. All of the answers are correct.

22. An example of a price floor is
    a. gasoline price controls.
    b. the minimum wage.
    c. rent control.
    d. All of the answers are correct.

23. In Figure 4.6, with the price floor the amount of the shortage is
   a. 20 units.
   b. 50 units.
   c. 90 units.
   d. None of the answers is correct.

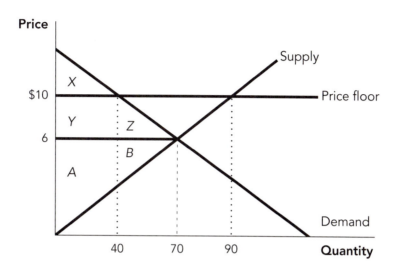

Figure 4.6

24. In Figure 4.6, with the price floor the dead weight loss gains from trade is/are the area
   a. X.
   b. Z + B.
   c. A + B.
   d. Y.

25. A minimum wage
   a. increases unemployment of low wage workers.
   b. creates extra gains from trade.
   c. creates a shortage of workers.
   d. All of the answers are correct.

26. A price floor
   a. causes wasteful increases in quality.
   b. creates a shortage.
   c. increases gains from trade.
   d. leads to a better allocation of resources.

## Short-Answer Questions

27. In the following graph find the **mistakes**.

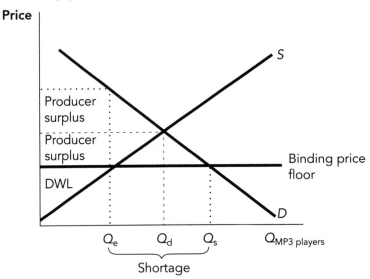

28. What is a price floor and what effects does one have?

29. How do people react to a shortage caused by a price ceiling, and what is the limit on consumer's reaction?

30. In a graph showing the deadweight losses caused by a price ceiling, why do these lost gains from trade occur?

**31.** How is a good with a price ceiling allocated and what problems can this cause?

**32.** Why do price ceilings cause declines in the quality of goods?

**33.** If the federal government put a price ceiling on college text books, would that help all students?

**34.** Would a price ceiling that is only a few cents below the equilibrium price of milk have the same effect as a price ceiling that is $1.00 below the equilibrium price?

**★35.** If the government forced all sellers of loaves of bread to sell at a price equal to half the current price, what would happen to the quantity supplied of bread? To keep it simple, assume that people wait in line to get the bread they need. Would consumer surplus rise, fall, or are you unable to tell with the information given?

**★36.** With price controls as given in the question, would you expect bread quality to rise or fall?

# Answer Key

## Answers to Practice Exercises: Learning by Doing

1.

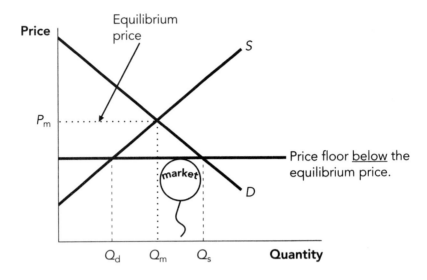

Topic: Price Ceilings

2.

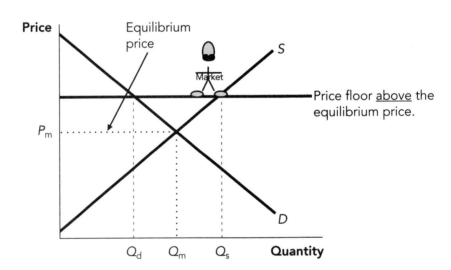

Topic: Price Floors

3.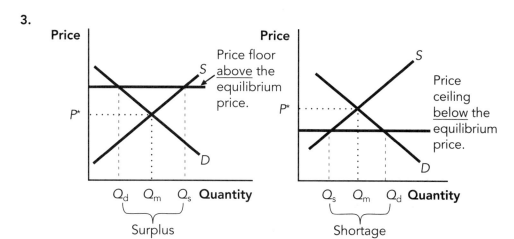

**Topic: Price Floors and Price Ceilings**

4.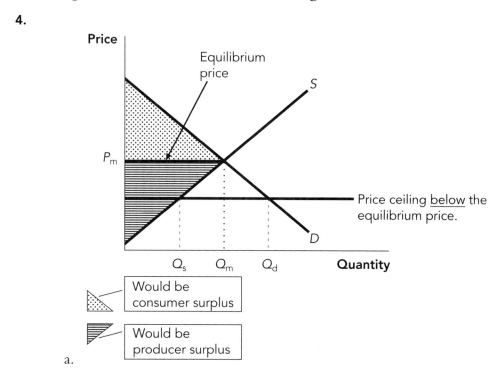

a.

**Topic: Price Ceilings**

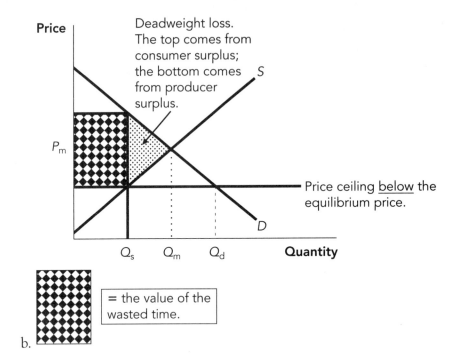

b.

**Topic: Price Ceilings Create Wasteful Lines**

5. If the picture is of a price ceiling, the price control will be below the equilibrium price because the point of a ceiling is to keep prices from going up to the market price. Also, $Q_d$ will be greater than $Q_s$ with a price ceiling. If the picture is of a price floor, the price control will be above the equilibrium price because the point of a price floor is to keep prices from falling. Also, the $Q_d$ will be less than the $Q_s$ with a price floor. Keep in mind that these are *binding* price controls.

**Topic: Price Floors and Price Ceilings**

6. A price ceiling on college education would reduce the amount of resources that would go to colleges, and would increase the number of people who would like to attend college. This would lead to a shortage. Some students would benefit from lower tuition, but others would be shut out of college.

**Topic: Price Ceilings**

7. A price floor that is only a few cents above the equilibrium price of milk would not have the same effect as a price floor that is $1.00 above the equilibrium price even though the graph is quite similar. A price floor that is only a bit away from the equilibrium will cause less misallocation and a smaller surplus than a price floor that is far from the equilibrium.

**Topic: Price Floors**

8. Misallocation of lumber would occur because some people who really needed lumber to rebuild their homes after a hurricane can not buy it, while other people build extra skate board ramps with the cheap lumber.

**Topic: Misallocation of Resources**

9. Since the surf lessons would be priced above the market equilibrium, you would have to compete in other ways. You might combine surf lessons with a free drink and sandwich afterwards. You might only hire very attractive people to get customers. But customers would probably rather save the money and buy their own drink and sandwich.

   **Topic: Wasteful Increases in Quality**

10. People who have the highest willingness-to-pay will spend the most time looking for available beer. They will wait in line and search the most. That time is wasted because they give it up, but no one benefits from the loss.

    **Topic: Wasteful Lines and Other Search Costs**

## Answers to Multiple-Choice Questions

1. b Topic: Price Ceilings
2. a, Topic: Price Ceilings
3. c, Topic: Price Ceilings
4. d, Topic: Misallocation of Production Chaos
5. c, Topic: Misallocation and Production Chaos
6. a, Topic: Misallocation and Production Chaos
7. c, Topic: Price Ceilings
8. a, Topic: Price Ceilings
9. c, Topic: Price Ceilings
10. b, Topic: Price Ceilings
11. c, Topic: Lost Gains from Trade
12. d, Topic: Price Ceilings
13. d, Topic: Lost Gains from Trade
14. b, Topic: Lost Gains from Trade
15. a, Topic: Lost Gains from Trade
16. d, Topic: Lost Gains from Trade
17. b, Topic: Price Ceilings
18. c, Topic: Price Ceilings
19. b, Topic: Price Ceilings
20. d, Topic: Price Floors
21. d, Topic: Price Floors
22. b, Topic: Price Floors

23. d, Topic: Price Floors
24. b, Topic: Surpluses
25. a, Topic: Lost Gains from Trade
26. a, Topic: Surpluses

## Answers to Short-Answer Questions

27.

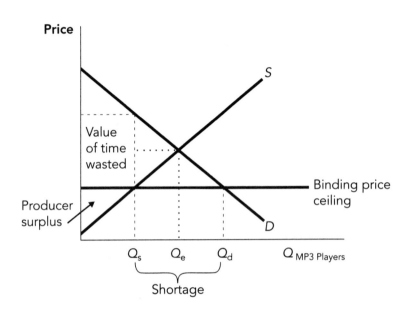

**Topic: Wasteful Lines and Other Search Costs**

28. A price floor is a legal minimum that a good or service can be sold for. The minimum wage is an example of a price floor. You can not sell your labor below the minimum wage. Price floors cause surpluses and wasteful quality competition.

**Topic: Price Floors**

29. People react to the shortages caused by price ceilings by searching for product availability and forming lines to be sure to get to consume the product. The time spent waiting in line and searching for the good is not received by the seller of the good and thus is wasted. The limit on this behavior is willingness-to-pay. Consumers will not spend more on the good, including the ceiling price plus time waiting in line and on search costs than their willingness to pay, as seen from the demand curve.

**Topic: Wasteful Lines and Other Search Costs**

1)

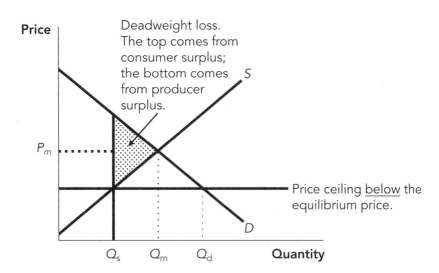

30. These deadweight losses happen because there are unexploited gains from trade. That is there are units consumers would be happy to pay more than it would take to get producers to sell them, but these trades are prohibited because they are at prices above the price ceiling.

   **Topic: Lost Gains from Trade**

31. If there is a price ceiling, it is not clear how the good will be allocated. It is possible that bribes or other under-the-table payments will develop to get the good to those who want it the most. Or the good may be allocated on a first come first serve basis and that leads to wasted resources due to searching for product availability and waiting in line to buy the product.

   **Topic: Wasteful Lines and Other Search Costs**

32. A price ceiling reduces quality, as since firms can not raise price, they try to reduce costs. Thus, a landlord may not maintain a property, a retail outlet may reduce service, or a soup company may put more broth and fewer noodles in the can. A restaurant might even reduce the number of matzo balls in its soup.

   **Topic: Reductions in Quality**

33. A price ceiling on college text books would lead to fewer books being written and produced. More students would be chasing the same books, which would lead to shortages.

   **Topic: Price Ceilings**

34. The basic effect is the same regardless of whether the price control is big or small, but the *effect* will be different. A price ceiling that is $1.00 below the equilibrium price will have a much bigger effect than a price ceiling a few cents below the equilibrium price.

   **Topic: Price Ceilings**

**72** • CHAPTER 4 • Price Ceilings and Price Floors

*35. If the government forced all sellers of loaves of bread to sell at a price equal to half, the current price the quantity supplied of bread would go down as the market moved along the supply curve to the new price ceiling. Assuming that people wait in line to get the bread they need, we would expect consumer surplus to fall since some consumer surplus would be wasted with waiting and other consumer surplus would turn to dead weight loss.

**Topic: Wasteful Lines and Other Search Costs *and* Price Ceilings**

*36. With price controls as given in the previous answer, bread quality would fall because bread companies wouldn't have to compete for customers. There would be more $Q_d$ than $Q_s$, so companies could cut the size of the loaves and the quality of the loaves.

**Topic: Reductions in Quality *and* Price Ceilings**

# 5 (20)
# GDP and the Measurement of Progress

## Why Learn about GDP?

**Business major:** Hey why do I have to learn about GDP? I don't care about poor people. Shouldn't the sociology majors deal with this?

**Professor:** Well, when you understand how wealthy a country is you can begin to think about trends. Is a country getting richer? From there you can think about where you want to invest and where you want to market your products.

**Political science major:** Well, what about me? I'm not some greedy business major. I want to help people.

**Professor:** Well, understanding GDP lets you analyze policy across countries and across time. One way to know if your policies have been successful is to see how much your country has grown compared to earlier growth and growth in other countries. You can't measure growth rates without knowing GDP first.

**Student in back:** Is this going to be on the test?

**Exasperated professor:** Yes, GDP will be on the test. You can't think about business cycles or economic growth without understanding GDP. Those are the two fundamental questions in macroeconomics.

## Summary

This chapter is an introduction to the two main questions or topics in macroeconomics: growth and business cycles. The growth question is about why some countries are rich and others desperately poor. And of course it asks what we can do to get richer. The business cycle question is why the economy is booming sometimes and hurting other times. **Business fluctuations** or **business cycles** are the short-run movements in real GDP around its long-term trend. Once again the obvious additional question is what we can do to reduce the pain of recessions.

The chapter begins with a focus on measuring a country's economic production and growth. It gives a full definition of GDP. **Gross domestic product (GDP)** is the market value of all final goods and services produced within a country in a year. The chapter explains how to avoid double counting. Students also learn how to measure the *growth* of GDP.

GDP does have some problems. It doesn't account for leisure or damage to the environment. It doesn't count the black market economy. Some goods don't have market prices. GDP doesn't count non-market production. It does *not* measure the distribution of income.

There is much vocabulary in this chapter related to measuring the economy. **GDP per capita** is GDP divided by population. **Gross national product (GNP)** is the market value of all final goods and services produced by a country's permanent residents, wherever located, in a year. **Nominal variables**, such as nominal GDP, have not been adjusted for changes in prices. **Real variables**, such as real GDP, have been adjusted for changes in prices by using the same set of prices in all. A **recession** is a significant, widespread decline in real income and employment.

There is quite a bit of numerical material in this chapter. GDP, GNP, nominal GDP, and real GDP are all calculated.

The chapter introduces students to business cycles and the way in which economists break up GDP into the national income identity. Students also learn that GDP can be measured by adding up all the income that is received or all the money spent on expenditures. Either method should work just the same. Both methods have the same outcome.

There are many problems in adjusting nominal to real GDP. One is that some goods did not exist earlier. What was the price of Guitar Hero in the year 2000? What about changes in quality? An iPod today has more memory and more features than when the iPod first came out.

In the National Income Identity, ($Y = C + I + G + NX$), $Y$ stands for national income. Sometimes students panic and forget that $Y$ is just national income. And of course the *national income identity* just means "national income defined algebraically." Economists break down $Y$ into several areas: $C$—consumption, $I$—investment, $G$—government, and $NX$—net exports. This breakdown allows economists to analyze the different parts of the economy. **Consumption** spending is private spending on final goods and services. **Investment** spending is private spending on tools, factories, and equipment used to produce future output. **Government purchases** are spending by all levels of government on final goods and services. Transfers are not included in government purchases. **Net exports** are the value of exports minus the value of imports.

# Key Terms

**gross domestic product (GDP)** is the market value of all final goods and services produced within a country in a year

**GDP per capita** is GDP divided by population

**gross national product (GNP)** is the market value of all final goods and services produced by a country's permanent residents, wherever located, in a year

**nominal variables**, such as nominal GDP, have not been adjusted for changes in prices

**real variables**, such as real GDP, have been adjusted for changes in prices by using the same set of prices in all time periods

**recession** is a significant, widespread decline in real income and employment

**business fluctuations** or **business cycles** are the short-run movements in real GDP around its long-term trend

**consumption spending** is private spending on final goods and services

**investment spending** is private spending on tools, plant, and equipment used to produce future output

**government purchases** are spending by all levels of government on final goods and services, transfers are not included in government purchases

**net exports** are the value of exports minus the value of imports

## Traps, Hints, and Reminders

Make sure that you don't count sales of used houses, stocks, and bonds. Make sure that you do count real estate commissions and consulting fees.

Make sure you know the difference between GNP and GDP, which is an easy question to miss on an exam because the definitions are similar. Overall this is a vocabulary intensive chapter.

There are *two* tricky parts of National Income Identity to break down. Purchases of stocks are not included in investment. They are a transfer of corporate ownership. Government transfers aren't counted either. When the government buys missiles or builds bridges, those purchases are added to GDP. When the government sends out social security checks, these aren't counted.

Investment is not money, stock, or bonds. Investment is purchases of things that will make the country more productive in the future. Investment can be more computers, factories, and machines. Investment can even be more education.

It is important to make sure that you understand that GDP can be calculated by either adding up all the income or adding up all the expenditures on *finished goods*.

Make sure that you know how to find real GDP growth by using the first year's prices. Sometimes students get confused because they don't know what to divide by.

The concept between real and nominal is important. *Real* variables have been adjusted for changing prices. If your dad says that he only earned $1 an hour, remind him that prices were lower and you care more about his *real* wage than his *nominal* wage. Real GDP and real wages are the two most common variables that you will see in the news.

# Practice Exercises: Learning by Doing

1. Calculate GDP in this simple economy:
   Consumer purchases: $6000
   Investment Purchases: $1,000
   Government purchases (not counting transfers): $2,500
   Total exports: $1,000
   Total imports: $500

2. What is counted in GDP? What isn't counted in GDP?

3. Smithsonia is a small country named after Adam Smith. In 2005, it had a GDP of 4 billion Smiths (its currency). In 2006, it had a GDP of 4.3 billion Smiths. What was Smithsonia's GDP growth?

4. Calculate the annual growth rate of *nominal* GDP between the following years.
   1969 GDP in Billions: 948.6
   1970 GDP in Billions: 1012.2

5. What is the difference between *real* and *nominal*?

6. What are the reasons why it is difficult to convert nominal variables (GDP or wages, for example) into real variables?

7. Would a significant decline in the economic activity of construction workers qualify as a recession?

8. Anuradha is a recent immigrant from India. She currently works as a software programmer in Silicon Valley. Are her earnings counted in India's GDP or America's GDP? What about GNP?

9. When Anuradha set up her programming shop in Silicon Valley she had to purchase new office furniture, cables, and surge protectors. Are these purchases counted in GDP?

## Multiple-Choice Questions

1. Orrin mines iron ore, which he sells to Thorin, who turns iron ore into steel. The steel is sold to Gorin, who turns the steel into battle axes. The battle axes are sold by a merchant in the city to adventurers. Which of the following would be considered final goods?

    a. the iron ore

    b. the battle axes sold to the merchant

    c. the battle axes sold to the adventurer

    d. All of these are final goods.

2. Imagine that Jack and Jill Day Care buy $500 worth of milk and cookies and $200 worth of crayons and coloring books. Then Jack and Jill Day Care hire a day care attendant at $14,000 per year. If Jack and Jill sell $101,000 worth of day care to parents, what has GDP risen by?
   a. $101,000
   b. $500
   c. $101,700
   d. $115,700

3. Imagine that Worth Publishers buys $100,000 worth of paper from Hammermill paper company, which buys $40,000 worth of wood from various suppliers all over the U.S., and that pulping the wood and turning it into paper uses $30,000 worth of energy. Worth is able to sell text books for $1,000,000 in the U.S. alone. What is the increase in GDP due to Worth's textbooks?
   a. $100,000
   b. $140,000
   c. $1,000,000
   d. $1,170,000

4. What percent of social security payments is counted in GDP?
   a. 14
   b. 7
   c. 100
   d. 0

5. The market value of final goods and services produced by a country's citizens in one year is called
   a. GDP.
   b. GNP.
   c. CGP.
   d. NNI.

6. Which of the following is *not* considered investment when we look at the national income identity?
   a. when the government builds roads and bridges
   b. when people buy and sell stocks
   c. when companies buy and sell bonds
   d. None of these is considered investment.

7. When economists look at the national income identity, which of the following is counted in investment?
   a. The government prints more money.
   b. People buy stock for their retirement.
   c. Farmers buy better tractors.
   d. All of these are considered investment.

8. What does "factor income" mean?
   a. the income that comes from the various factors in production; these factors being land, capital, and labor
   b. the factors relating to income such as education and experience
   c. the income that is earned by factories
   d. Whenever vocabulary like *factor income is used*, its best to just close your eyes or ears and hope it disappears from the language.

9. Veronique is French Canadian working in the U.S. as a welder for a Korean company. Her earnings are counted
   a. in U.S. GDP and Korean GNP.
   b. in U.S. GNP and Canadian GDP.
   c. in U.S. GNP and French GDP.
   d. in U.S. GDP and Canadian GNP.

10. The Golden Gate Bridge connects San Francisco with Marin County and was built in 1937. The Golden Gate Bridge
    a. is counted in GDP but not national wealth.
    b. is counted in national wealth but not GDP.
    c. is not counted in national wealth or GDP.
    d. is counted in national wealth and GDP.

11. If South Korea produces final goods and services worth $835 billion, and that number has been increasing by an average of 6% per year, what will next year's GDP be?
    a. South Korea's GDP is $835 billion and its GDP growth is 835/6 or $139.16.
    b. South Korea's GDP is 6% but its growth rate is 835%.
    c. South Korea's GDP is 835 ★ 1.06 or 885.1.
    d. South Korea's GDP is $835 billion and its GDP growth rate is 6%.

12. Which of the following *is not* considered a government purchase?
    a. new rifles for the military
    b. unemployment checks
    c. salaries for public school teachers
    d. levees built by the Army Corps of Engineers

13. In the national income identity, what has the largest share of GDP?
    a. consumption
    b. government spending
    c. investment
    d. net exports

14. Two imaginary countries, Ricardia and Smithsonia, had the same GDP per capita in 1960, $500. In 2008, Ricardia had a GDP per capita of $20,000 and Smithsonia had a GDP per capita of $200. Which country is more likely to have lower life expectancy and higher infant mortality?
    a. Ricardia
    b. Smithsonia
    c. GDP per capita, life expectancy, and infant mortality are unrelated.
    d. Ricardia should have higher life expectancy and Smithsonia should have higher infant mortality.

15. If a country is experiencing inflation, it would mean that
    a. nominal and real GDP are the same.
    b. nominal GDP is going up faster than real GDP.
    c. real GDP is going up faster than nominal GDP.
    d. neither nominal nor real GDP is related to inflation.

16. If nominal GDP is $12 trillion this year and real GDP is $10 trillion this year, then inflation must be
    a. 2%.
    b. 12%.
    c. 10%.
    d. 20%.

17. What has happened to the frequency of recessions since World War II?
    a. They are less common.
    b. They are more common.
    c. There were no recessions before World War II.
    d. There have been no recessions since World War II.

18. What do economists mean when they say that the economy is in an expansion?
    a. The economy is producing the same as before and people are working.
    b. The economy is producing but people aren't working.
    c. People are working but the economy isn't producing much.
    d. People are working and the economy is producing more than before.

19. Imagine that your country has averaged 7% GDP growth over the last twenty years but this year GDP growth is negative. What would that tell you about your country's business cycle?

    a. It tells you nothing because business cycles and GDP growth are two separate problems.

    b. Your country is in the recession part of the business cycle.

    c. Your country is in the boom part of the business cycle.

    d. Your country is neither in the boom part nor the recession part; output is lower but you are still richer than you were 20 years ago.

20. Don Julio's Precision Robotics makes robots that help disabled people function better. The company sold $200 million worth of robots last year. The company also caused $50 million worth of pollution. Don Julio's contribution to GDP in the official statistics is

    a. $200 million because that is what it produced as final good and services.

    b. $150 million because you have to subtract the cost of pollution.

    c. $250 million because you have to add that someone will get the job of cleaning up the pollution.

    d. more than $250 million because the cost of cleaning up the pollution is more than the cost of the pollution alone.

21. Billy Bob and Bubba are two economists. Billy Bob is interested in whether workers are getting a bigger or smaller share of GDP over time. Bubba is interested in looking at how investment changes over the business cycle. How would these two economists look at breaking up GDP?

    a. Billy Bob would look at the factor income approach, and Bubba would look at GDP through the national income approach.

    b. Bubba would look at national expenditure components, and Billy Bob would look at GDP through the income approach.

    c. Either method is equally good for looking at all questions.

    d. Neither method of breaking up GDP is useful.

22. Which of the following is *not* counted in GDP?

    a. Medicaid payments

    b. illegal narcotics sales

    c. volunteering at Habitat for Humanity

    d. None of these is counted in GDP.

## Short-Answer Questions

**23.** Are the following included in U.S. GDP? Briefly explain why or why not.
 a. used books sold at a bookstore
 b. hip hop music made in the U.S. but sold to Canadians
 c. cars made in the United States at a Toyota factory
 d. cars made in Germany at a General Motors factory
 e. the price paid by a German tourist when staying at a New York hotel
 f. the price paid by an American tourist staying at a hotel in Cancun, Mexico
 g. used textbooks

**24.** Explain how GDP can be measured by counting either expenditures or income.

**25.** A country produces 5 million music players that sell for $50 each and 1 million flat screen TV's that sell for $400. What is the total amount of GDP that is added from these two goods?

**26.** Imagine that your country sells only pizza and pretzels. Last year pizza cost $20 and pretzels cost $1. This year pizza costs $22 and pretzels cost $1.10. If last year your country produced 100,000 pizzas and 1,000,000 pretzels and this year your country produced 110,000 pizzas and 1,100,000 pretzels, how much did your GDP increase in *real* terms?

**27.** Imagine that your country made tubas and bikinis (a strange country!). In 2007, it sold 500 tubas at $400 each and 1,000 bikinis at $35 each. In 2008, it sold 525 tubas at $425 and 1,200 bikinis at $36. Find the change in nominal GDP and real GDP.

**28.** Imagine that your country discovers new technology that lets it produce the exact same amount of output with a 20-hour workweek instead of a 40-hour workweek. Instead of producing even more goods and services though, the people of your country spend time reading library books, chatting with friends, napping, and watching sunsets. What would happen to GDP and overall happiness?

**29.** Why does GDP matter? Why is higher per capita GDP useful?

**30.** Imagine that your country produces only coal and cotton. In 2007, it sold 1,500 tons of coal at $300 each and 10,000 bushels of cotton at $3.50 each. In 2008, it sold 1,800 tons of coal at $425 and 12,000 bushels of cotton at $4.10. Find the change in nominal GDP and real GDP.

**31.** Using the previous question about coal and cotton, state how much is GDP reduced by the pollution from the coal and its extraction? How much is GDP reduced in total? How much is GDP reduced by the fact that there is now less coal in the ground to be used later?

**32.** Why would ordinary Americans prefer to have a long economic expansion and no recession?

**33.** List the things that GDP doesn't count.

不包括：
國外の本國人の生產值 ✗

a. 非法商品の銷售
b. 不付費の工作（在家工作或志願工）
c. 政府經費
d. 基金の买卖
e. leisure ?

# Answer Key

## Answers to Practice Exercises: Learning by Doing

1. $10,000

   **Topic: What Is GDP?**

2. Normal consumption of all sorts is counted in GDP. So is investment by firms in new equipment. Government purchases of new goods and services are counted. Goods and services that we export are counted after we subtract our imports. Taxes and transfers aren't counted. When the government sends out social security or unemployment checks those are called transfers and aren't counted. The black market (illegal market) isn't counted. Illegal narcotics purchases aren't counted. Work at home isn't counted either. When you wash the dishes at your house that isn't counted even though washing dishes at a restaurant for pay would be counted. Leisure time isn't counted.

   **Topic: What Is GDP?**

3. $(4.3 - 4)/4 = .075$. (Remember that you divide by the earlier year.)

   **Topic: Growth Rates**

4. $1012.2 - 948.6/948.6 = .067 = >6.7\%$.

   **Topic: Growth Rates**

5. Nominal values are not adjusted for changing prices. Real values are adjusted for changing prices.

   **Topic: Nominal vs. Real GDP**

6. It is hard to figure out how to convert nominal into real because some goods didn't exist before. You can ask your granddad how much he made per hour in 1970, but he couldn't buy an iPod. There are also quality adjustments. The computer you buy now might be cheaper than a computer your parents bought in the 1980's but it is surely better.

   **Topic: Nominal vs. Real GDP**

7. No, significant decline across the economy means geographically and across other sectors. But if construction, banking, retail, and manufacturing were suffering in many areas of the country, that would fit the NBER definition.

   **Topic: Cyclical and Short-Run Changes in GDP**

8. GNP counts the earnings of a country's citizens, so Anuradha's earnings are counted in India's GNP. But her earnings are counted in US GDP because GDP measures what is created within a country's borders.

   **Topic: The National Income Approach: $Y = C + I + G + NX$**

9. These purchases are counted in GDP, but be careful small goods like this are counted as consumption not investment. It seems like they should be counted as investment, but it would be too hard to know if a small cable is being used in a home or small office. For that reason, we count these little things as consumption.

**Topic: The National Income Approach:** $Y = C + I + G + NX$

## Answers to Multiple-Choice Questions

1. c, Topic: What Is GDP?
2. a, Topic: What Is GDP?
3. c, Topic: What is GDP?
4. d, Topic: What Is GDP
5. b, Make sure you know the difference between GNP and GDP. Topic: What is GDP?
6. d, Topic: What Is GDP?
7. c, Topic: What Is GDP?
8. a, Topic: What Is GDP?
9. d, Topic: What Is GDP?
10. b, The difference between national wealth and GDP is pretty easy, but it is easy to miss in a big chapter. Topic: What Is GDP?
11. c, Topic: What Is GDP?
12. b, Topic: What Is GDP?
13. a, Topic: What Is GDP?
14. b, Topic: Real GDP Growth
15. b, Topic: Real GDP Growth
16. d, This question looks hard but isn't. Inflation (as measured by the GDP deflator) is nominal GDP divided by real GDP minus 1. Then to get percentages, you multiply by 100. So it is 12/10 = 1.2. Subtract 1 = .2. Multiplying by 100 gets you 20%. Topic: Real GDP Growth
17. b, Topic: Cyclical and Short-Run Changes in GDP
18. d, Topic: Cyclical and Short-Run Changes in GDP
19. b, Topic: Cyclical and Short-Run Changes in GDP
20. a, Topic: Problems with GDP as a Measure of Output and Welfare
21. a, Topic: The Ways of Splitting GDP
22. d, Topic: Problems with GDP as a Measure of Output and Welfare

## Answers to Short-Answer Questions

**23.** a: No. Used items aren't "produced" during that year, so they don't count.

b: Yes. Hip hop made in America and sold to Canadians is counted as an export.

c: Yes. What matters is where it's made, not whether an American company owns the factory.

d: No. What matters is where it's made, not whether an American company owns the factory.

e: Yes. It's made in the USA! Technically, it counts as an "exported service."

f: No. GDP is about production inside the U.S. border. This service is produced in Mexico.

g: No. Used book sales are not counted.

**Topic: What Is GDP?**

**24.** Since every transaction has both a buyer and a seller, the amount of income equals the amount of expenditures. The income for one person is the expenditure for the other. Since GDP adds up all of these transactions, we can count either but not both.

**Topic: What Is GDP?**

**25.** 5 million × $50 AND 1 million × 400 = 250,000,000 + 400,000,000 = $650,000,000.

**Topic: What Is GDP?**

**26.** This looks really complicated but is actually really easy.

|  | Value from Pizza | Value from Pretzels | GDP in last year's dollars |
|---|---|---|---|
| Last year | $20 × 100,000 = $2,000,000 | $1 × 1,000,000 = $1,000,000 | $2,000,000 + $1,000,000 = $3,000,000 |
| This year | $20 × 110,000 = $2,200,000 | $1 × 1,100,000 = $1,100,000 | $2,200,000 + $1,100,000 = $3,300,000 |

> Make sure that you realize that when you want to see growth in *real terms* you use the same year's prices but each year's output. See the arrows pointing to $20 for both years in the pizza column. But see that the quantities do change. Again you hold the prices constant but change the output. That lets you see how output changed without being confused by changing prices too.

After you find the GDP in constant dollars (constant dollars just means that the prices are held constant), you need to find the percentage change.

(3,300,000 − 3,000,000)/3,000,000 = 300,000/ 3,000,000 = .10 = >10%

**Topic: Real GDP Growth**

**27.** The change in nominal GDP and real GDP is

|  | **Value from Tubas** | **Value from Bikinis** | **GDP in nominal dollars** |
|---|---|---|---|
| 2007 | $400 × 500 = $200,000 | $35 × 1,000 = $35,000 | $235,000 |
| 2008 | $425 × 525 = $223,125 | $36 × 1,200 = $43,200 | $223,125 + $43,200 = $266,325 |

Growth in nominal GDP = ($266,325 − $235,000)/$235,000 = .133 = >13.3%.

|  | **Value from Tubas** | **Value from Bikinis** | **GDP in real dollars** |
|---|---|---|---|
| 2007 | $400 × 500 = $200,000 | $35 × 1,000 = $35,000 | $235,000 |
| 2008 | $400 × 525 = $210,000 | $35 × 1,200 = $42,000 | $210,000 + $42,000 = $252,000 |

Growth in real GDP = ($252,000 − $235,000) / $235,000 = .072 = >7.2%.

Notice that when you hold the prices the same, the growth rate is smaller.

**Topic Real GDP Growth**

**28.** People chatting with friends and watching sunsets wouldn't increase GDP even though your countrymen are clearly better off with more leisure time. GDP stays the same.

**Topic: Problems with GDP as a Measure of Output and Welfare**

**29.** GDP matters because it tells us how much a country can produce. Some of the things it can produce are merely for pleasure such as video games and iPods. But some of the things are hospitals, cleaner water, and better medicines. Per capita GDP helps us make sure that we haven't been fooled by a big GDP that is produced by lots of people. Some countries have a big GDP because they have so many people. But the actual wealth produced per person isn't very high. These countries don't get as many hospitals per person. Countries with low GDP per capita have lower life expectancy and higher infant mortality rates.

**Topic: Real GDP Growth per Capita and Real GDP Growth**

**30.** Imagine that your country produces only coal and cotton. In 2007, it sold 1,500 tons of coal at $300 each and 10,000 bushels of cotton at $3.50 each. In 2008, it sold 1,800 tons of coal at $425 and 12,000 bushels of cotton at $4.10. Find the change in nominal GDP and real GDP.

|      | Value from Coal | Value from Cotton | GDP in nominal dollars |
|------|-----------------|-------------------|------------------------|
| 2007 | $300 × 1500 = $450,000 | $3.50 × 10,000 = $35,000 | $485,000 |
| 2008 | $425 × 1800 = $765,000 | $4.10 × 12,000 = $49,200 | $765,000 + $49,200 = $814,200 |

Growth in nominal GDP = ($814,200 − $485,000)/$485,000 = .678 = >67.8%.

|      | Value from Coal | Value from Cotton | GDP in real dollars |
|------|-----------------|-------------------|---------------------|
| 2007 | $300 × 1500 = $450,000 | $3.50 × 10,000 = $35,000 | $485,000 |
| 2008 | $300 × 1800 = $540,000 | $3.50 × 12,000 = $42,000 | $540,000 + $42,000 = $582,000 |

Growth in real GDP = ($582,000 − $485,000) / $485,000 = .2 = >20%.

Notice that when you hold the prices the same, the growth rate is smaller.

**Topic: Real GDP Growth**

**31.** In the previous question about coal and cotton, GDP is unaffected by the costs of pollution and by the fact that there is less coal to extract later.

**Topic: Problems with GDP as a Measure of Output**

**32.** Ordinary Americans like to be able to find jobs, which are easier to find during an expansion than during a recession. Also, people are richer during an expansion.

**Topic: Cyclical and Short-Run Changes in GDP**

**33.** GDP doesn't count
   a. sales of illegal goods,
   b. unpaid work either at home or as a volunteer,
   c. government transfers,
   d. sales of used goods,
   e. sales of stocks and bonds, and
   f. leisure.

**Topic: What is GDP?** *and* **Problems with GDP as a Measure of Output**

# 6 (21)
# The Wealth of Nations and Economic Growth

## Why Learn about Economic Growth?

The question of why some countries grow to be rich and some don't is one of the fundamental questions in macroeconomics. Students who are trying to understand which countries will be good for investment and increasing market share will be interested in economic growth. Students who are interested in helping and caring for people will also be interested because increasing GDP provides people with better lives across a wide variety of measures. Thinking about GDP is also a way to think about bigger questions such as how important institutions, good government, and market incentives are.

## Summary

There is a wide range of wealth for countries. Some countries are very rich and others are very poor. But all countries *were* poor by today's standards. Rich countries that were poor changed their position by experiencing **economic growth**. Economic growth is when a country's GDP and specifically its per capita GDP go up. Of course, some countries have not gotten richer; they've gotten poorer. (Make sure that you understand that while people tend to talk about GDP going up, they really mean GDP per capita.)

While economic growth gets a bad rap it is also associated with lower infant mortality, higher life expectancy, and better nutrition.

Sometimes students are under the impression that poor countries will always be poor. That makes sense since many poor countries have always been poor, but some countries were poor and aren't anymore. One example is South Korea. South Korea used to be one of the poorest countries in the world, but is now quite rich. But some countries have the opposite experience. Argentina is richer now than it was in 1900, but Argentina has lost ground compared to other countries. Argentina has had a low growth rate. Nigeria has had little or negative growth.

The *Rule of 70* is an easy way to see when a growth rate will lead to doubling the base. That sounds confusing but if your country is growing at 5%, the Rule of 70 tells you that your country will be twice as rich in 14 years. For example, it tells you that if you put $1,000 in the bank earning 7%, you will have $2,000 in 10 years.

Traditionally we think of countries getting richer through **physical capital**. Physical capital consists of factories, machines, computers, and such physical things that make workers more productive. But **human capital** or people's knowledge matters. The invention and adaption of new technology or **technological knowledge** is important. Human capital is the tools of the mind.

**Institutions** or the overarching rules are important too. Countries with honest government, institutions that protect property rights, encourage competition, and encouraging economies of scale tend to grow, while those that do not have those attributes do not grow. *Property rights* just means that when you figure out a way to do something new and more valuable with something you own, you get the benefits. This can be something as physical as converting an empty lot into apartments or as intangible as creating new software. **Free riders** are people who take the benefit without paying. They see someone else's technology and copy it without paying as an example. **Economies of scale** is just the idea that it is often cheaper to make goods with a large factory than with many small factories. For a while, India had rules against large textile factories.

Institutions are important because they help answer the "why" question. Sure South Korea is richer than North Korea because it has more physical and human capital. But why don't North Koreans invest and work the way that South Koreans do? South Korea has institutions that encourage investment and good organization. South Korea has the right incentives. Work and saving lead to more wealth. North Korea doesn't have those incentives.

# Key Terms

**economic growth** is the growth rate of real GDP per capita

**physical capital** is the stock of tools including machines, structures, and equipment

**human capital** is the productive knowledge and skills that workers acquire through education, training, and experience

**technological knowledge** is knowledge about how the world works that is used to produce goods and services

**institutions** are the "rules of the game" that structure economic incentives

**free rider** is someone who consumes a resource without working or contributing to the resource's upkeep

**economies of scale** are the advantages of large-scale production that reduce average cost as quantity increases

## Traps, Hints, and Reminders

When using the Rule of 70 it is easy to use the wrong number in the equation. If GDP is growing at 10%, the correct way to determine how quickly GDP will double is to divide 70 by 10. That gives you 7 years for GDP to double. But is easy to get confused and divide by .10. That would make sense, but it gives you the wrong answer: 700 years.

Be careful about the word *institutions*. Sometimes students think that institutions are things like banks or big companies. That's not what macroeconomists mean when they say institutions. Economists mean things like the rule of law, constitutions, democracy, and property rights.

Physical capital doesn't happen by accident. When someone buys physical capital, whether it is tractors or software, they are buying the capital to produce more in the future. Countries with corruption, little competition, no property rights, and generally bad institutions don't encourage people to invest in the future. This is a main point of the chapter: good institutions lead to good incentives, good incentives lead to good organizations and lots of physical capital, good organization and physical capital lead to economic growth.

## Practice Exercises: Learning by Doing

1. What evidence do your textbook authors present to suggest that it is better to live in a wealthy country?

2. Draw the "Understanding the Wealth of Nations" graph that illustrates how institutions lead to high per capita GDP.

3. When China experimented with its "leaps forward" what happened to the incentive to work?

4. How does corruption make a country poorer? Can corruption lead to a poverty trap?

5. List four of the most corrupt countries and four of the least corrupt countries.

6. Three different countries have three different per capita GDP growth rates. The rates are 1%, 3%, and 9%. How long will it take for these countries to double their per capita GDP?

7. Why are U.S. workers able to produce more than Indian workers?

8. Why are property rights important?

9. Why do economists like the examples of North Korea and South Korea when they talk about the importance of institutions?

10. When discussing economic growth, why is it important to remember that all countries used to be poor, even though many are rich now?

# Multiple-Choice Questions

1. Low per capita GDP is likely to be associated with which problems?
   a. high childhood mortality
   b. low childhood mortality
   c. high life expectancy
   d. good nutrition

2. Countries with high per capita GDP are more likely to have all *but* which of the following?
   a. iPods
   b. death by infant diarrhea
   c. better education
   d. life expectancy

3. When economists talk about economic growth they mean
   a. increasing the overall GDP of a country.
   b. increasing the per-capita GDP of a country.
   c. increasing the geographic size of a country.
   d. increasing the number of colonies a country has.

4. If per capita GDP was $32,000 last year and is $34,000 this year, what was the economic growth rate?
   a. $2,000
   b. 8.25%
   c. 6.25%
   d. 5.88%

5. The idea of growth miracles and growth disasters is best illustrated by looking at one country that grew rich and another that stagnated or got poorer. Which of the following is an appropriate example?
   a. Nigeria and Argentina
   b. The United States and Japan
   c. The United States and South Korea
   d. South Korea and Nigeria

6. Which of the following is true about economic growth?
   a. All countries eventually grow rich.
   b. If a country starts on the path towards growth, it will continue to grow.
   d. A country can become wealthy, fail to even get on the path toward growth, or get off the path to growth.
   d. Growth is a random process; in some years a country grows, and in other years it doesn't.

7. Factors of production are
   a. the factories that produce things.
   b. the inputs to productions such as labor and capital.
   c. the outputs of production such as tractors and satellites.
   d. None of the answers is correct.

8. Physical capital includes
   a. knowledge.
   b. people.
   d. factories.
   e. All of the answers are correct.

9. Human capital includes
   a. stocks and bonds.
   b. cash or checking accounts.
   c. tool and die machines.
   d. knowledge.

9. Technological knowledge is
   a. the same as human capital.
   b. the ability to use human capital efficiently.
   c. the knowledge to make complex goods instead of simple goods.
   d. All of the answers are correct.

10. When economists talk about institutions they mean
    a. banks and stock markets.
    b. old colleges such as William and Mary.
    c. the rules of the game.
    d. wisdom and intelligence.

11. Which of the following is *not* included in the institutions of economic growth?
    a. property rights
    b. honest government
    c. competitive and open markets
    d. labor unions

12. Good institutions provide the incentive to
    a. get rich and quickly.
    b. take advantage of your neighbors.
    c. share everything with your neighbors.
    d. work hard and invest.

13. When China collectivized farming, what happened to agricultural output?
    a. It increased exponentially.
    b. It increased slightly.
    c. It decreased.
    d. It stayed the same because economic organization isn't important.

14. A free rider is someone who
    a. earns interest from others.
    b. drives an energy efficient car.
    c. consumes a resources without working or contributing to the resource's upkeep.
    d. dislikes capitalism.

15. Property rights
    a. are rules that let people profit from their own property.
    b. are rules that split the profits from property equally among a whole community.
    c. are special courts for property disputes involving land or water.
    d. are judges who oversee cases involving land or water.

16. Which of the following countries is on the list of ten most corrupt countries?
    a. Finland
    b. United Kingdom
    c. Singapore
    d. Liberia

17. Economies of scale are
    a. the way that lots of overweight people can lose more weight than a few overweight people.
    b. the idea that increased output can lower average costs.
    c. the idea that decreased output can raise average costs.
    d. the idea that preventing large factories can increase employment in a country.

18. A country with many many regulations is
    a. more likely to have competitive and open markets.
    b. less likely to have competitive and open markets.
    c. more likely to have less corruption.
    d. more likely to have strong property rights.

19. China increased its agricultural production by more than 50% in ten years. What was the cause?
    a. giving people the proper incentives to produce
    b. using collective agriculture
    c. allowing bureaucrats to take bribes
    d. preventing bureaucrats from taking bribes

## Short-Answer Questions

20. Why does corruption make it so hard for a country to grow?

21. Imagine that you win $4,000. If your investments pay an inflation adjusted interest rate of 5%, how long would it take for your money to increase to $8,000? $16,000?

22. Why are institutions important to economic growth?

23. Your roommate suggests that the way to end infant diarrhea is to confiscate everyone's wealth and share the wealth equally. Why might that not work?

24. How was China's Great Leap Forward a free rider problem?

25. If a country goes from $50,000 per capita GDP to $59,550 per capita GDP in one year, what is the country's growth rate?

26. Imagine two similar countries in the Caribbean. One has relatively stable government but the other one is war torn. Why is the war torn country less likely to be wealthy?

27. What do economists mean when they talk about the factors of production?

28. What are some of the advantages of living in a country with high per capita GDP?

29. What do economists mean by growth disasters? Do they mean that a country has never experienced growth or that it quit growing?

# Answer Key

## Answers to Practice Exercises: Learning by Doing

1. Wealthy countries have longer life expectancy, lower infant mortality, better nutrition, more consumption, better education, and fewer children die from curable diseases such as infant diarrhea.

   **Topic: Introduction**

2. 

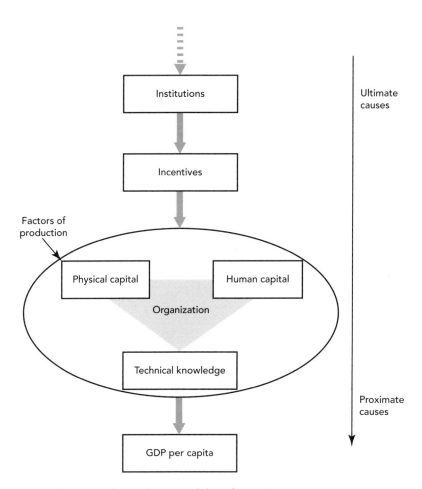

   **Topic: Understanding the Wealth of Nations**

3. The various Chinese "leap forward" programs collectivized agriculture. This meant that everyone worked together and for each other. But when everyone shares all the benefits of work, there isn't much incentive to work.

   **Topic: Incentives and Institutions**

4. Corruption makes people less likely to invest and work hard because they have to not only pay for labor and capital, but they also have to pay bribes. Not only that, but corruption encourages people to become bribe takers instead of producers. That means that nothing is being produced.

   **Topic: Honest Government**

5. The top four corrupt countries are Myanmar, Haiti, Iraq, and Angola. The top four least corrupt countries are Finland, Singapore, Sweden, and Iceland.

   **Topic: Honest Government**

6. 1% doubles in 70 years.

   3% doubles in 23.3 years.

   9% doubles in 7.77 years.

   **Topic: Key Facts about the Wealth of Nations and Economic Growth**

7. U.S. workers have about 10 times more physical capital to work with than Indian workers. U.S. workers also tend to have more human capital and more technological knowledge.

   **Topic: The Factors of Production**

8. Property rights ensure that people who work hard and invest will get to keep any profits that they make. This means that people are more likely to work hard and invest. Hard work and investing lead to wealth. If everyone free rides and refuses to invest, the country will be poor.

   **Topic: Property Rights**

9. Economists use the examples of North and South Korea when they talk about institutions because North and South Korea are similar except for their institutions. South Korea has capitalism as an institution. North Korea has communism. North Korea is much poorer than South Korea.

   **Topic: Incentives and Institutions**

10. It is important to remember that all countries used to be poor because that allows us to ask why some countries remain poor but others were able to become rich.

    **Topic: Institutions and Growth Miracles Revisited**

## Answers to Multiple-Choice Questions

1. a, Topic: Introduction
2. b, Topic: Introduction
3. c, Topic: Growth Rates
4. d, Topic: Growth Rates
5. c, Topic: Good and Bad News
6. b, Topic: Factors of Production
7. c, Topic: Factors of Production
8. d, Topic: Factors of Production
9. b, Topic: Factors of Production
10. c, Topic: Incentives and Institutions

11. d, Topic: Incentives and Institutions
12. d, Topic: Incentives and Institutions
13. c, Topic: Institutions
14. c, Topic: Institutions
15. a, Topic: Institutions
16. d, Topic: Institutions
17. b or c, Topic: Institutions (notice that the answers are two ways of asking the same question—unfair but designed to help you *think*.)
18. b, Topic: Institutions
19. a, Topic: Institutions and Growth Miracles Revisited

## Answers to Short-Answer Questions

20. Corruption makes it hard for a country to grow because it encourages productive people to avoid being productive and take jobs accepting bribes instead. It also raises the cost of being productive because entrepreneurs have to pay for labor, capital, and bribes instead of just labor and capital.

    **Topic: Honest Government**

21. It would take 14 years to increase to $8,000 and 28 years to increase to $16,000.

    **Topic: Key Facts about the Wealth of Nations and Economic Growth**

22. Institutions are important to economic growth because good institutions encourage people to save and invest in both human and physical capital. Good institutions also encourage people to organize production efficiently. With these three things, a country is on its way towards high production or GDP.

    **Topic: Institutions**

23. Your roommate's idea to confiscate everyone's wealth would solve certain problems in the short run. But in a world where everyone's wealth is shared, there would be no incentive to work or save. Everyone will free ride.

    **Topic: Incentives and Institutions**

24. China's "Great Leap Forward" removed the incentive for people to work. If you worked hard, then everyone got the benefit even though you did all the work. So people didn't work and agricultural production fell.

    **Topic: Incentives and Institutions**

25. If a country goes from $50,000 per capita GDP to $59,550 per capita GDP in one year, then the country's growth rate would be

    $$(\$59{,}550 - \$50{,}000)/\$50{,}000 = .191 = >19.1\%.$$

    **Topic: Key Facts about the Wealth of Nations and Economic Growth**

26. The war torn country will have lost physical capital from the war, but also people will be less inclined to invest because war increases uncertainty. The right workers will be harder to find because physical capital is more likely to be destroyed.

   **Topic: Political Stability**

27. The factors of production are just the things that are used in production. They include land, labor, and capital. Tractors are just one example used in the text.

   **Topic: The Factors of Production**

28. Some of the advantages of living in a country with high per capita GDP are lower infant mortality rates, higher life expectancy, better nutrition, and better education.

   **Topic: Introduction**

29. When economists talk about growth disasters they mean countries that missed an opportunity for their citizens to be rich. Sometimes that means that a country never got on the growth path and is no richer now than it was before. While some countries got richer, that country didn't. An example of this is Nigeria. Sometimes economists mean a country that was growing but then stagnated. The country started to grow but then failed to continue for some reason. A good example of this is Argentina.

   **Topic: Fact Three: There Are Growth Miracles and Growth Disasters**

# 7 (22)

# Growth, Capital Accumulation, and the Economics of Ideas: Catching Up vs. the Cutting Edge

## Why Learn about Growth, Capital Accumulation, and the Economics of Ideas?

**Business major in the back of the room:** "Hey why do we have to learn this?"

**Irritated and haughty professor:** "Growth in itself is good for investment. If you know what causes growth, you can make better international investments. The student who thinks that resources make countries rich is going to invest in the wrong places or at least make the wrong investments."

**Political science and nursing majors:** "Why do we have to learn this stuff? We aren't money grubbing business majors!"

**Even more haughty and condescending professor:** A political science major might be interested in this because she can really find out how good institutions relate to the economy. It is an opportunity to look at which is more important—democracy or economic freedom. And, regarding its relevance to nursing, economic growth is highly related to health. If you care about people, you want them to be wealthier.

## Summary

There is a wide disparity between the economic growth of different countries. Some countries are rich and others are poor. This chapter asks how countries can get wealthier. The first point is that to have more wealth, a country has to be able to produce more. In order for a country to have income, it has to produce.

The chapter then provides a simple production function. Production is a function of land, labor, capital, and technology. Land and labor are fixed. Technology has to be invented. Capital can be produced by reducing consumption. Capital is extremely important for wealth because it allows countries to produce more. Recall that this production leads to wealth.

Growth: There are only a few ways that a country could grow. It could grow by getting more land, more labor, more capital, or more technology. It's tough to get more land or labor quickly. New technology or new capital is tough to get too, but easier. (More people can make the country wealthier, but in this model, that doesn't help per capita wealth.)

The Solow Model: The Solow model is just a simple function that describes production. The Solow model just says that if you want to produce things, you need Capital (K), Labor (L), and Ideas (A), such as the idea of an internal combustion engine or the assembly line. More capital leads to more output but at a decreasing rate. But the greater output will stabilize so that the growth rate won't change.

**Incredulous student:** "Wait, this guy Solow got a Nobel Prize because he figured out that you need capital, labor, and ideas to produce things? My grandmother could have told you that. AND she makes really good chocolate chip cookies."

**Somewhat less haughty professor:** "We'll see that there is more to it than that. But I like your chocolate chip cookie example."

*Convergence:* countries with stable institutions that respect property rights (recall Chapter 6 /21) should be able to copy other countries technology and encourage savings. Diminishing marginal productivity of capital suggests that capital should move from countries with lots of capital to countries with little capital. Poor countries should be able to catch up to wealthy countries. This is called convergence. Each country has diminishing marginal productivity of capital. Countries with lots of capital like the United States should be sending their capital to other countries where it will earn a higher return. We don't see that. American entrepreneurs aren't sending their capital to Haiti to get the higher return. There must be a missing element in our explanation of growth. They either don't use capital effectively or they don't *utilize* technology for some reason.

### *An Easy Example: Your Grandma's Chocolate Chip Cookie Factory*

Think of the simplest model you can for production: your grandmother's chocolate chip cookie factory. She has her house, her knowledge, and her oven. In our simple example, we assume that your grandmother can't do much about anything but her capital. She can't reproduce herself (just as countries can't easily get more people). She can't easily invent a new idea for production technology. She could, however, save some of her money and buy a second oven. Savings is really important in this model because savings leads to *investment*. (In the most basic model, savings = investment.) Investment leads to more capital and therefore more wealth.

*"What about ingredients?"*

Ingredients are normally counted as short-lived $K$. We already know that capital depreciates; typically we think about this as wear and tear, but it is equally valid to think of depreciated capital as going *into* the final output. Thus, we can think of chocolate chips depreciating as they are turned into cookies.

**Lone alert and precocious student:** "Excuse me, professor, but you have all sorts of capital lumped in together. It looks like you have chocolate chips and ovens counted as the same thing. And you've left the function so vague that it looks like you could add more labor if you don't have enough capital. No matter how fast my grandmother rubs her hands together she can't make enough heat to bake the cookies."

**Professor:** You are exactly right. But remember that we are simplifying the model so we can understand why poor countries can catch up with rich countries relatively easily by adding capital, but rich countries can't get richer simply by adding more capital. Remember that we want to do this for several reasons:

1. We want to understand the world.
2. We want to know where to expect high growth rates.
3. We want to know what the best policy is for growth.

We don't want to get bogged down in how easy it is to substitute different goods for each other (although you grandmother might be able to make an oven if she doesn't have one; so to some extent you can get more $K$ with more $L$). If we could help your grandmother save and invest in more capital this year, we could have more chocolate chip cookies next year.

## Catching Up

Countries that have good institutions can quickly catch up to the developed countries. But once a country is a developed country, achieving more growth is tough. In order to continue to grow after it has become developed, a country must invent new technology. New technology comes from *R&D*.

Two common methods for promoting R&D are tax credits and *patents*. Patents reduce *spillovers*. A firm that spends lots of money on R&D may find that its competitors get much of the benefit. Patents can make the private benefit closer to the social marginal benefit. The new optimum is found by just looking where *social benefit* equals *marginal cost*.

Ideas are **non-rivalrous,** which means that two or more people can consume them at the same time. This makes it very difficult for the company that invented the idea to keep other people from using it. When other people use your idea for their own benefit without paying you for their use of it, that is a spillover.

## Spillovers and New Technology

We know that countries need new technology to continue to grow. New technology comes from research and development. (There are occasional lucky breaks, but mostly new technology comes from R&D.) Patents help reduce spillovers.

Companies are able to see and copy other firm's technology. Even if they don't directly copy new technology, they may still be able to benefit. Make sure you can draw the spillover graph and that you understand what the difference between the private optimum (for the individual firm doing R&D) and the social optimum. (That includes everyone.) The private optimum is the amount of R&D a firm will produce because it thinks that other firms will benefit too. If it thinks it can keep all the benefits, then it will produce at the social optimum.

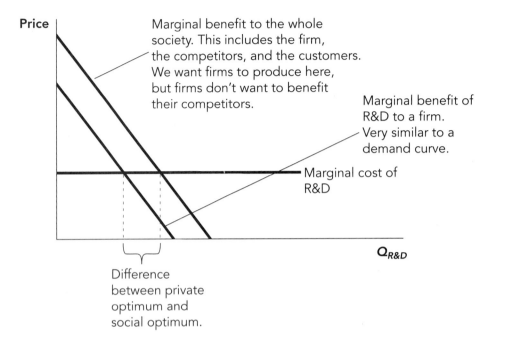

## Key Terms

**marginal product of capital** is the increase in output caused by the addition of one more unit of capital. The marginal product of capital diminishes as more and more capital is added

**steady state** is when the capital stock is neither increasing nor decreasing

**conditional convergence** is the tendency—among countries with similar steady state levels of output—for poorer countries to grow faster than richer countries and thus for poor and rich countries to converge in income

**non-rivalrous** is if two or more people can consume it at the same time. Ideas are non-rivalrous goods

## Traps, Hints, and Reminders

The graphs in this chapter are very difficult for students. Drawing them in color with colored pencils, markers, etc., is highly recommended. This is especially true for visual learners. Draw the graphs several times, and draw them big.

Keep in mind that graphing questions is very common on exams—especially questions about shifting the graph. If you can understand and show on the graph what happens when technology increases, you are on your way to doing well on this section.

Make sure that you can answer questions about when one curve is above or below another curve. These are common questions and are best dealt with by drawing the graph in the margin of your exam.

Make sure you understand "Increasing at a decreasing rate."[1]

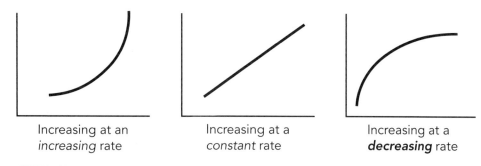

Increasing at an *increasing* rate

Increasing at a *constant* rate

Increasing at a **decreasing** rate

Increasing at a decreasing rate: while this sounds confusing, it just means that something is increasing, but it increases slower and slower as more and more inputs are added.

Students are sometimes confused by spillovers because they can't imagine why a billion-dollar company would worry about losing a bit of money to someone else. Students can't imagine that in a world without spillovers, the inventors of Google would be even richer. The chance to be even richer would make firms fund more R&D. More funding for R&D would make countries grow even more.

*Crazy Greek letters:* There are some Greek letters in this chapter that look scary at first, but are actually really easy.

δ: lowercase delta—depreciation

γ: lowercase gamma—the amount of output that is invested instead of being consumed

*Square root:* "What's the deal with the scary square root stuff?" Square roots give you the increasing at a decreasing rate thing that you need.

You could use other functions, but square root works pretty well. Many calculators have square root functions. That also makes using it easier.

Don't forget that a rise in the savings/investment rate will raise **steady state** output but won't permanently increase per capita *growth rate*. Make sure you understand this because it is a common test question.

Exponents: when you multiply two exponents to the same base, you simply **add** the exponents. This comes up when you are solving the math problems.

# Practice Exercises: Learning by Doing

1. Draw the graph for the Solow growth model and label the steady state of capital.

---

[1] This isn't meant to be condescending, but being confused about this will make the rest of the chapter really hard.

2. Show the effects increasing the savings rate by increasing the savings-investment line.

3. Show the effect of increasing technology. (Shift the production function upward.)

4. Compare the output effects of both savings and technology. What is the advantage of increasing technology instead of increasing savings?

5. Why are patents important to economic growth?

6. Draw and correctly label the spillover graph. Explain why it is important. What does it mean for countries that want to do more than "catch up?"

7. Imagine that the investment savings line is equal to $.3\sqrt{K}$ and the depreciation rate is $.03K$. What is the steady state of capital? If the production function is just $GDP = \sqrt{K}$, what is the output in the steady state?

8. Imagine that the investment savings line is equal to $.4\sqrt{K}$ and the depreciation rate is $.02K$. What is the steady state of capital? If the production function is GDP $= 5\sqrt{K}$, what is the output in the steady state?

9. What are the three takeaways for the Solow growth model?

# Multiple-Choice Questions

1. In the Solow growth model, if a country has capital such that the depreciation line is above the production function, then
    a. the country should use more capital.
    b. the country has too much capital.
    c. the country has the optimal amount of capital.
    d. the answer can not be determined from with this information.

2. The Solow growth model is about
    a. capital.
    b. entrepreneurship.
    c. labor.
    d. land.

3. Diminishing marginal productivity of capital suggests
    a. at some point there will be too much capital.
    b. more capital brings smaller and smaller gains.
    c. countries can never have too much capital.
    d. capital will approach infinity at the limit.

4. In the basic Solow growth model, everything is held constant in the production function *except*
    a. land.
    b. labor.
    c. capital.
    d. entrepreneurship.

5. If two countries have the same production function, but one is poor and the other is rich, what should the poor country do to increase growth?
   a. In this case, it should add more capital.
   b. There is nothing it can do.
   c. It should reduce its capital.
   d. It should fake it till it makes it.

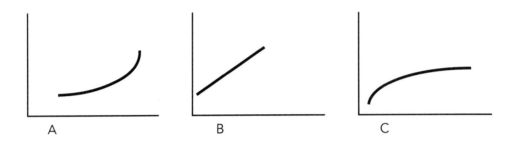

6. Which of the previous graphs shows the *y*-variable increasing at an increasing rate?
   a. A
   b. B
   c. C
   d. None of the answers is correct.

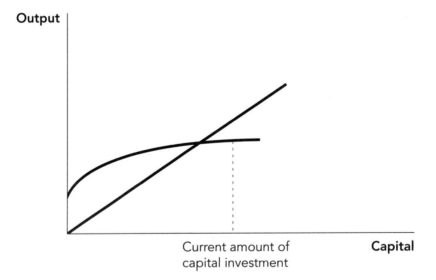

7. In the previous graph, is this country accumulating capital faster or slower than it depreciates?
   a. It is accumulating it faster.
   b. It is accumulating it slower.
   c. Investment and depreciation are equal
   d. None of the answers is correct.

8. If a country increases its savings rate, what will happen after the new steady state is reached?
   a. Growth will continue to go up.
   b. Growth will be stagnant without new technology, but output will be higher.
   c. Workers will be no better off than before.
   d. The steady state shows that the country will be no better off than before.

9. When a country increases its savings rate, the
   a. investment-savings curve shifts upward.
   b. country moves along the investment-savings curve.
   c. production function shifts upward.
   d. production function and the investment-savings curve both shift upward.

10. If a plague hits the country leaving it with much more capital *per worker* than before, then you would expect
    a. the capital would begin to depreciate faster than it is replenished.
    b. capital would increase faster.
    c. the country would have negative growth.
    d. Both (a) and (b) are correct.

11. If a country invents or copies new technology
    a. the investment-savings curve shifts upward.
    b. the production function shifts upward.
    c. the steady state of capital increases.
    d. None of the answers is correct.

12. Poorer countries should have greater growth rates than richer countries because
    a. rich countries have to invent new technology to grow and poor countries need to simply adopt it.
    b. rich countries get more benefit from additional capital.
    c. Poor countries can't adopt technology.
    d. Poor countries have too little capital for growth.

13. Poorer countries should have greater growth rates than richer countries because
    a. rich countries have to invent new technology to grow and poor countries need simply to adopt it.
    b. rich countries can't get as much output from new capital as poor countries.
    c. poor countries need to simply copy technology from rich countries instead of having to invent it themselves.
    d. All of the answers are correct.

14. In the spillover graph, what is the difference between the social benefits of R&D and the private benefits of R&D?
    a. The vertical distance between the two curves shows the spillover that is captured by people other than the company providing the R&D.
    b. The horizontal distance between the two curves shows the spillover that is captured by people other than the company providing the R&D.
    c. The difference is the amount of new technology because spillovers exist with new technology.
    d. The difference is the amount of new capital that will be provided by technology.

15. If savings in a country increases, what will happen?
    a. Steady state output will increase.
    b. The country will grow while it is attaining the new steady state.
    c. Eventually, growth will be no higher.
    d. All of the answers are correct.

16. Property rights and corruption have what effect on a country's GDP?
    a. Property rights increases GDP while corruption decreases it.
    b. Property rights and corruption increase GDP.
    c. Property rights decrease GDP while corruption increases it.
    d. Property rights and corruption both decrease GDP.

17. The Solow model says that
    a. the further a country's quantity of capital is below its steady state value, the faster it *can* grow.
    b. the further a country's quantity of capital is above its steady state value, the faster it *can* grow.
    c. the further a country's quantity of capital is below its steady state value, the faster it *must* grow.
    d. the further a country's quantity of capital is above its steady state value, the faster it *must* grow.

18. When firms decide to do R&D, which of the following is/are important?
    a. patents
    b. potential spillovers to other rivals
    c. government subsidies for scientists
    d. market size

**19.** Which of the following goods are non-rivalrous?

   a. an apple

   b. a national park

   c. the idea of penicillin

   d. a dose of penicillin

**20.** The Solow growth model tells us three important things. Which list contains those important takeaways?

   a. Getting more capital is the only way to get growth; countries with lots of natural resources have more capital; countries that are already rich have an easier time getting more capital.

   b. Having a high savings rate is the only way to get continued growth; countries with no natural resources grow faster; countries without much capital already can grow faster.

   c. It is impossible to have too much capital; growth will be faster the further away a country's capital stock is from its steady state value; capital accumulation alone can explain long run growth.

   d. Countries that devote more output to investment will be wealthier than those that don't; growth will be faster the further away a country's capital stock is from its steady state value; capital accumulation alone cannot explain long-run growth.

## Short-Answer Questions

**21.** The Solow growth model suggests that a country can grow and grow simply by adding more capital. True or false? Explain.

**22.** Find 5 problems with the following graph.

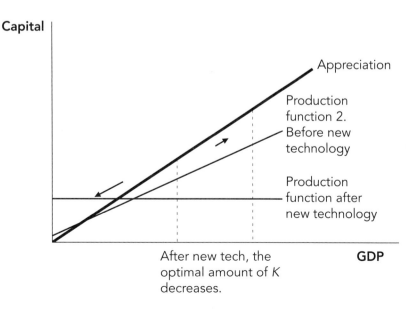

23. Why does bombing a country often lead to more reported growth?

24. Why would policies designed to encourage savings increase output? Would they increase the growth rate?

25. If the investment line $= .4\sqrt{K}$ and depreciation $= .03K$, what happens when K $= 400$?

26. If the investment line $= .4\sqrt{K}$ and depreciation $= .03K$, what happens when K $= 289$?

27. If the investment savings line is equal to $.5\sqrt{K}$ and the depreciation rate is $.01K$, what is the steady state of capital? If the production function is GDP $= 2.5$, what is the output in the steady state?

# Answer Key

## Answers to Practice Exercises: Learning by Doing

1. Drawing the scary graph with three whole lines: The Solow growth model
   For some reason, this is the scariest graph in macroeconomics. No one knows why. It's a mystery that even CSI couldn't solve. But it only has three lines. In this section, you will see how to draw the graph very easily and clearly. You should absolutely, positively practice drawing the graph while you are reading this section. You have to draw in order to actively learn this material.
   <u>The Axes</u> (not axes like lumberjacks or dwarfs, but axes—the plural of axis).
   
   A) Make sure you get that the Y-axis is (GDP). That makes sense: $Y$ = GDP, so GDP is on the Y-axis. (Don't forget to make little mnemonics for yourself.)
   
   B) The X-axis is the amount of K that a country has. This makes sense that K would be really important because the whole Solow growth model is about when more capital leads to more growth and when it doesn't.

*Curved Line #1*
That curved line thing: the one that is increasing at a decreasing rate. That's *savings for capital*. It is a percentage of how much of a country's output the country decides to invest for future capital. If your professor calls it savings–investment line, don't be shocked.

It is normally shown as the square root of K. Why is that? It is because square roots have curves that increase at a decreasing rate, just like product of capital. More capital leads to more output, but at a decreasing rate.

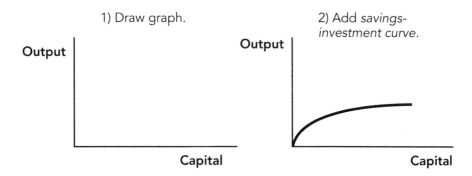

*Line #2*
A straight line. This represents depreciation rate. Remember that some capital is being used up every year. When you have more depreciation than new capital, then you are losing capital. When new capital comes in faster than it depreciates, then you are getting more capital. When your capital is depreciating faster than you replenish it, then you are getting less capital. Pretty obvious, isn't it?

118 • CHAPTER 7 (22) • Growth, Capital Accumulation, and the Economics of Ideas

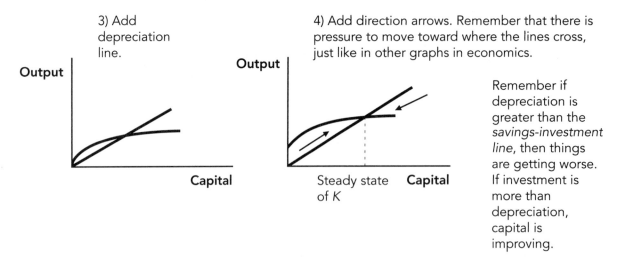

3) Add depreciation line.

4) Add direction arrows. Remember that there is pressure to move toward where the lines cross, just like in other graphs in economics.

Remember if depreciation is greater than the *savings-investment line*, then things are getting worse. If investment is more than depreciation, capital is improving.

*Steady State*
The steady state is just where depreciation and marginal capital accumulation cross in the Solow growth model. If a country tries to have more capital, the capital will depreciate too quickly. If a country has less capital, then the country could grow quickly simply by getting more capital. Make sure you label the steady state on your graphs! There should be a natural push toward the steady state. But once a country gets to the steady state, the country can't have long-term growth without either new technology or a higher savings rate.

*Curved Line #3*
The production function. This is above the savings-investment line.
It makes sense that the production function is going to be above the investment line. Capital/Investment is just part of the whole. The production function includes labor.

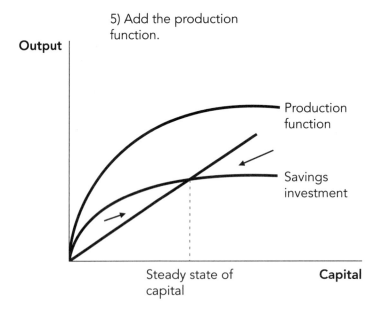

5) Add the production function.

If everything stays the same (the country's savings rate, labor, and technology don't change), then the country's output or GDP can be found by finding the point on the production function that corresponds with the steady state of capital.

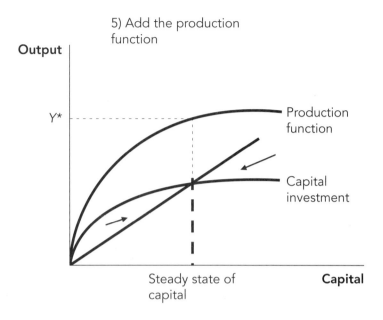

**Confused student:** "This isn't a growth model. This is an output model. There's no growth here at all. If the country doesn't change anything, we get one output, Y★."

**Completely surprised Professor:** "That's exactly right! In this model, the only way to get growth is to continually save more or add technology."

*Quick note:* Your text, and probably your professor, drew the production function and then the savings investment line, in that order. You can draw the graph in any order you like, but if you are having trouble understanding how we get to the optimal amount of capital, it might make more sense to draw the savings-capital line first. For the big picture you would draw the production function first, but to understand the optimal amount of capital, draw the savings-capital line.

### Topic: Why Capital Alone Cannot Be the Key to Economic Growth

2. Shifting the curves is one way that students show that they really understand a model. Exam questions about shifting various curves are extremely common.

*Shift 1: Increase investment*
A country that saves more will increase its investment. This shifts the investment/capital curve upward. During that change, growth will increase. After the change, the country will be in a steady state again. It will have more wealth, but no more growth. Make sure that you don't shift the production function too.
Note that in your text, you have a specific example of a country going from saving 30% of its output (and turning it into investment) to saving 40% of its capital. This study guide uses a more general savings—investment1 and savings-investment 2—just to show the actual number isn't what is important.

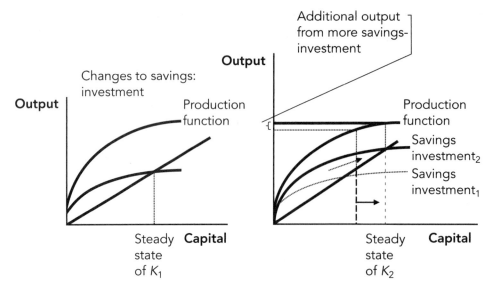

**Topic: The Solow Model and an Increase in the Investment Rate**

3. New technology increases the amount that a country can produce. So when a country increases its technology, it increases its production function. But new technology also makes the savings-investment curve shift because new technology makes capital more effective. Make sure you shift both curves.

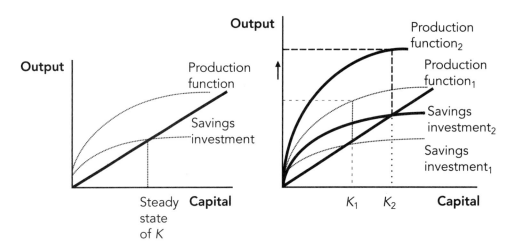

Here we see that the same amount of savings/investment leads to more output. Of course the country gets to a steady state again, but while the country is implementing the technology there is growth. Since countries can only save so much, the only way to keep growing is to keep adopting new technology.

**Topic: Better Ideas Drive Long-Run Economic Growth**

4. The advantage of increasing technology instead of increasing savings is that increasing technology doesn't mean that savings have to stay high just to keep up with greater inflation. There will still be more savings and depreciation but at a much higher level of output than would be possible with savings alone. And the amount of depreciation will be less than would be needed with savings.

**Topic: Solow and the Economics of Ideas in One Diagram**

5. Patents are important to economic growth because so much new technology comes from private R&D. Private firms won't invest in R&D unless the firms can reap the benefit.

**Topic: Research and Development Is Investment for Profit**

6. The spillover graph shows that countries that want to invent technology have real barriers because private firms won't pay for the optimal amount of new R&D. But countries that just want to catch up can use other countries' technology.

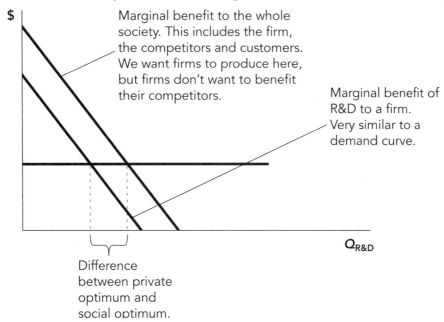

**Topic: Spillovers, and Why There Aren't Enough Good Ideas**

7. The math in this chapter can look a bit frightening, but there is no need to wet your Depends Undergarments.[2] You must work these problems. It is extremely difficult to do well on these types of problems without practicing. Recall that in the beginning of this study guide, the difference between active and passive learning is discussed. Math problems require active learning.

Don't forget the tip from the Traps, Hints, and Reminders section about using exponents. You add exponents when the base is the same.

Step 1: Solve for the steady state of capital

$.3\sqrt{K} = .03K.$
Get $K$ on one side. Divide both sides by .03
$(.3/.03) \times \sqrt{K} = K$
$.3/.03 = 10$
$10 \times \sqrt{K} = K.$

So far, so good. Hopefully, that was easy.

Now you have to remember exponents. They aren't hard, but students have often forgotten them. The square root of $K$ just equals $K^{1/2}$.

---

[2] Depends Undergarments are not sponsors of this text or this study guide.

$K$ is the same as $K^1$.

$$\sqrt{K} = K^{1/2}$$
$$K = K^1.$$

Put everything in exponent notation
$$10 \times K^{1/2} = K^1.$$

Now remember that $1/\sqrt{K} = K^{-1/2}$.

Divide both sides of the equation by $K^{1/2}$.

We get $10 = (K^1)/K^{1/2} = >10 = (K^1) \times K^{-1/2}$.

"But how do we solve $10 = K^1 \times K^{-1/2}$ ?????"

We add exponents when they have the same base. Both our exponents have the same base, $K$. So we do this.

$10 = K^1 \times K^{-1/2} = >10 = K^{1/2}$.

How did we do that? $1 - ? = ?$. We just added the exponents.

**Panicking student:** "But wait, I don't know what $K^{1/2}$ means"

**Oddly reassuring professor:** "$K^{1/2}$ just means $\sqrt{K}$."

We have $10 = \sqrt{K}$. All we have to do is square both sides.

$10^2 = 100$ and $\sqrt{K} = K$

$K = 100$. The country should have 100 units of capital.

Step 2: Solve for output. Recall that in our example, the production function was $\sqrt{K}$. This is pretty easy then. We know that the country will have 100 units of capital so output or GDP will be 10: $\sqrt{100} = 10$.

**Nearly calm student:** "How come the amount of capital is 100 but output is only 10? That doesn't really make sense."

**Condescending and snotty professor:** "Capital and output are in different units."

**Topic: Why Capital Alone Cannot Be the Key to Economic Growth**

8. Step 1: Solve for the steady state of capital

$$.4\sqrt{K} = .02K$$

Get $K$ on one side. Divide both sides by .02

$(.4/.02) \times \sqrt{K} = K$

$.4/.02 = 2$

$2 \times \sqrt{K} = K.$

Put everything in exponent notation

$2 \times K^{1/2} = K^1.$

Divide both sides of the equation by $K^{1/2}$

$2 = K^1/K^{1/2} = >2 = K^1 \times K^{-1/2}$.

Add exponents

$2 = K^{1/2}$ that just means that $2 = \sqrt{K}$.

Square both sides

$4 = K.$

This country has 4 units of capital in the steady state.
How much does it produce?
$$\text{Output} = 5\sqrt{K} => 5 \times 2 = 10.\ 10 \text{ units of output.}$$

**Topic: Why Capital Alone Cannot Be the Key to Economic Growth**

9. The three takeaways for the Solow growth model are: 1) countries that devote a larger share of GDP to investment will be wealthier, 2) the further a country is from its capital stock steady state, the faster it will grow, and 3) capital accumulation alone cannot explain long-run economic growth.

**Topic: Takeaway**

## Answers to Multiple-Choice Questions

1. b, Topic: The Solow Model and Catch-Up Growth
2. a, Topic: The Solow Model and Catch-Up Growth
3. a, Topic: The Solow Model and Catch-Up Growth
4. c, Topic: The Solow Model and Catch-Up Growth
5. b, Topic: The Solow Model and Catch-Up Growth
6. a, Topic: The Solow Model and Catch-Up Growth
7. a, Topic: The Solow Model and Catch-Up Growth
8. b , Topic: The Solow Model and Catch-Up Growth
9. b, Topic: The Solow Model and an Increase in the Investment Rate
10. a, Topic: The Solow Model and an Increase in the Investment Rate
11. d, Topic: Why Capital Alone Cannot Be the Key to Economic Growth
12. d, Topic: The Solow Model and an Increase in the Investment Rate
13. a, Topic: The Solow Model and an Increase in the Investment Rate
14. d, Topic: Better Ideas Drive Long-Run Economic Growth
15. d, Topic: The Solow Model and an Increase in the Investment Rate
16. a, Topic: Why Capital Alone Cannot Be the Key to Economic Growth
17. a, Topic: The Solow Model and an Increase in the Investment Rate
18. c, Topic: Research and Development Is Investment for Profit
19. c, Topic: Spillovers, and Why There Aren't Enough Good Ideas
20. d, Topic: Takeaway

### Notes to the Answers to Multiple-Choice Questions

1. This is a really counterintuitive answer. But in this odd case, the country would have more capital than it could actually use. To get these questions right, it is really important to draw the graph. It is difficult to see what the answer is without the graph.

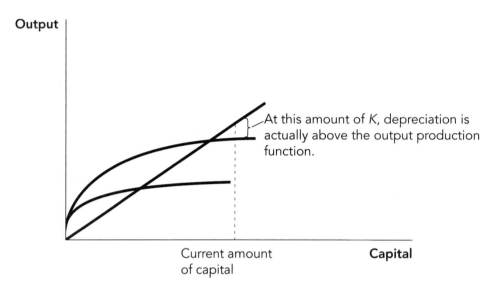

7. Make sure that you read the question carefully. If you circled (c), that means you were expecting a question about the Solow growth model instead of a question about functions.

8. The depreciation curve is above the investment curve. Make sure that you draw or at least picture the graph when answering these questions.

11. Think about this one carefully. If there are significantly fewer people, then the marginal value of capital is going to go way down. There will be more capital than people could easily use. That country will let the capital depreciate. We will also see the countries output decline, since there are fewer workers. This means that overall growth will decline.

## Answers to Short-Answer Questions

21. Five (and several more) problems are:
    - It is depreciation not appreciation.
    - GDP and Capital axis labels are flipped.
    - Arrows are pointing the wrong way.
    - Production functions cross.
    - Investment capital line is missing.
    - Steady state is not properly labeled
    - Production functions are not increasing at a decreasing rate.

    **Topic: Why Capital Alone Cannot Be the Key to Economic Growth**

22. Bombing a country destroys its capital, but may not destroy its technology. The bombed country is poorer, but while it is returning to its pre-bombed level, it is growing as it catches up.

    **Topic: Solow and the Economics of Ideas in One Diagram**

23. When countries save more they use more capital, and capital leads to more output. When the country first encourages investment the growth rate will increase. But once it reaches the steady state, the growth rate will stabilize **unless** some of that new investment is in R&D. More R&D leads to better technology.

    **Topic: Why Bombing a Country Can Raise Its Growth Rate**

24. Investment line $= .4\sqrt{400} = .4 \times 20 = 8$.

    $$\text{Depreciation} = .03(400) = 12.$$

    Depreciation is greater than capital investment, so capital is decreasing in this example.

    **Topic: Capital Growth Equals Investment Minus Depreciation**

25. All of the following will occur:
    1. Steady state will increase.
    2. The country will grow while it is attaining the new steady state.
    3. Eventual growth will be no higher.

    **Topic: Why Capital Alone Cannot Be the Key to Economic Growth**

26. Investment line $= .4\sqrt{289} = >.4 \times 17 = 6.8$.

    Depreciation $= .03(289) = 12$.

    Depreciation is greater than capital investment, so capital is decreasing in this example

    **Topic: Why Capital Alone Cannot Be the Key to Economic Growth**

27. Put $K$ on only one side of the equation: $.5\sqrt{K} = .01K => 5/.01\sqrt{K} = K$. Simplify: $50\sqrt{K} = K$.

    Express with exponents and divide both sides by $50\sqrt{K}$: $50K^{1/2} = K^1 => 50 = K^1 \times K^{-1/2}$.

    Add exponents: $50 = K^{1/2} => 50 = \sqrt{K}$.

    Square both sides: $2500 = K$.

    Multiply steady state amount of $K$ by 2.5 (from the production function). Output $= 6250$.

    **Topic: Why Capital Alone Cannot Be the Key to Economic Growth**

# 8 (23)

# Saving, Investment, and the Financial System

## Why Learn about the Financial System?

The financial system does two very important things: it allows individuals to smooth their consumption over time and it allows people to invest for the future. When countries can borrow and invest they can grow much easier. It is easier for countries to make large investments if they can borrow. Investing is important because growth (why some countries have gotten rich and others haven't) is a fundamental issue in macroeconomics.

Anyone interested in finance in general (business, finance, economics majors) will be interested in this chapter. Students who want to know in detail why some countries are filled with poor people will want to understand the financial system well enough to understand why financial markets don't work in some countries. In addition, students in all fields will be interested in how the workings and failures of the financial system make the economy boom and bust. If you've watched the news lately, you'll be interested in how financial markets help everyone find a job during some years and make sure that almost no one finds a job during other times.

## Summary

Financial markets just means that borrowers and lenders are coming together. Lenders have **savings,** which is income (money) that is not spent on consumption. Borrowers can use the money for **investment,** which is the purchase of new capital goods. The most basic way to think about the financial system is to think of the supply and demand for money. This is very similar to basic supply and demand that you have already learned.

There is a **market for loanable funds.** This market is just the supply and demand for money that can be borrowed or lent. It has a supply curve and a demand curve just like other markets.

The supply of savings is produced by people who want to delay some consumption for later. People want to save some of the money they earn while working so they have money for retirement. One way that the supply and demand for money is different from the supply and demand that you already learned about is that the interest rate rather than price is on the *y*-axis. This makes sense because the interest rate is the *price of borrowing*.

Borrowers have to pay interest because savers have time preference. **Time preference** means that people desire to have goods and services now rather than later. If you want people to delay getting goods and services, you have to pay them in the form of interest.

The demand for borrowing also comes from people who want to smooth their consumption. College students borrow because they want to have some enjoyment during their college years. Later, they will repay loans with the increased income they earn. Firms also need to borrow but firms borrow to pay for big investment projects. Some big investment projects are so big that one firm cannot come up with enough money to do them. Borrowing allows the firm to do big projects. The more potentially profitable big projects there are, the more people will want to borrow.

The theory that people smooth consumption by borrowing and saving to even out the amount they can consume over time is called the *lifecycle theory*.

People will also want to borrow more when the interest rate is low. This is the same as a downward sloping demand curve just like that described in earlier chapters. People will lend more when the interest rate goes up. That is why the supply curve for loanable funds slopes upward.

The demand for loanable funds will shift inward when there are fewer good projects to invest in. See Figure 8.8. A shift inward of the demand for loanable funds pushes the interest rate down and the quantity of loans down.

Banks, stock markets, and bond markets are **financial institutions**. Financial institutions help borrowers and lenders find each other more easily. Financial institutions also evaluate risks and spread risk. If there were no financial institutions to help people like Fred Smith, then he might have had to knock on every door in the world and ask people if they had any money to lend him. That would not be very efficient, and we wouldn't have FedEx because Fred Smith would still be knocking on doors.

A **bond** is a sophisticated IOU that documents who owes how much and when the payment must be made. Many individuals can buy bonds in small amounts that add up to large amounts, which allow companies to make big investments.

Bonds are rated by ratings agencies. Being rated just means that some company has graded the bonds by how risky they are. AAA is safe and D is in default. Default means that the company is not paying its debts. Risky companies have to pay a higher interest rate than safe companies.

Companies that have lots of collateral pay lower interest rates than firms that don't have collateral. **Collateral** is something of value that by agreement becomes the property of the lender if the borrower defaults.

If you have a car loan, the car is probably the collateral. If you don't pay off your car, the bank or lending company can take your car. This makes you safer to lend to. If you don't pay your debt, the lender gets your car, which is worth something.

Governments are also in the market for loanable funds. That means that governments borrow money just like companies do. Governments can crowd out private investment. **Crowding out** is the decrease in the private consumption and investment that occurs when government borrows more. If the government borrows $100 billion, that is $100 billion that cannot be borrowed by private investors.

Government borrowing shifts the demand for loanable funds outward. This raises the interest rate that all borrowers have to pay AND it reduces the amount of borrowing that private firms can borrow.

When the government borrows money it borrows in many ways. It borrows money that it will only repay in 30 years, which are called T-bonds ("T" because the U.S. Treasury does the borrowing.) T-notes are paid off between 2 and ten years later. T-bills are bonds that are paid off a few days and 26 weeks later. U.S. government bonds are considered to be very safe.

If you know the face value and the rate of return for a bond, then you can easily figure the current price. If you know the face value of the bond and the current price, you can easily figure the rate of return.

*Zero coupon bonds* are bonds that do not pay interest during the life of the bonds. The lender only gets the face value of the bond at the maturity or end. Because the borrower only gets money at the maturity, the price for the bond is much lower.

$$\text{Rate of Return for a zero-coupon bond} = \frac{FV - \text{Price}}{\text{Price}} \times 100$$

**Arbitrage,** which is the buying and selling of equally risky assets, ensures that equally risky assets earn equal returns. That just means that if there are two similar assets, then they should sell for the same price. Otherwise, people will buy the cheaper one until its price equals the more expensive one.

Savers don't have to just buy bonds. They can buy stocks too. **Stocks** are ownership in a corporation. Stock owners or stockholders get paid with the profit from the firm. Stock exchanges are places (either physical places or Online) where stocks are bought and sold.

**Initial public offerings (IPO)** are special types of stock sales. An IPO is the first time a corporation sells stock to the public in order to raise capital. IPO's allow firms to raise money in order to invest in big projects. If a firm does not want to issue bonds, it can do an IPO to raise money.

Sometimes *financial intermediation* fails. Financial intermediation is just the process of financial intermediaries (banks, stock markets, bond markets) working.

There are many ways that financial intermediaries can fail: 1) insecure property rights, 2) controls on interest rates and inflation, 3) politicized lending, and 4) massive bank failures and panics.

Insecure property rights means that the government won't protect your property, including your bank deposits, bonds, and/or stocks. If the government says you can't use your savings account, you do not have secure property rights.

Controls on interest are just like price ceilings described earlier in the book. Remember that a price ceiling means that a price can't go above a certain number. Interest controls or usury laws are the same thing. These laws say that an interest rate can't go above some amount. Usury laws lead to a shortage of loanable funds. The quantity supplied is lower than the quantity demanded.

Inflation causes people's savings to be worth less. Imagine that you earn 5% on your savings but that the inflation rate is 10%. You are worse off at the end of the year for saving.

$$\text{The } \textit{real} \text{ rate of return} = \textit{nominal} \text{ rate} - \text{inflation rate.}$$

If the real interest rate goes negative (nominal rate is less than the inflation rate), people won't save or they will only save in other countries.

Politicized lending is when the government makes or strongly encourages lending *not* to the best risk but to the most politically connected risk. For example, you may have a great idea, but the dictator's cousin has more clout and the cousin gets the loan instead of you.

Major bank failures or panics mean that people won't lend because they don't know if the bank will fail. If no one will lend to or through banks, then almost no one can borrow.

## Key Terms

**saving** is income that is not spent on consumption goods

**investment** is the purchase of new capital goods

**time preference** is the desire to have goods and services sooner rather than later (all else being equal)

**market for loanable funds** is where suppliers of loanable funds (savers) trade with demanders of loanable funds (borrowers). Trading in the market for loanable funds determines the equilibrium interest rate

**financial institutions** such as banks, bond markets, and stock markets reduce the costs of moving savings from savers to borrowers and investors

**bond** is a sophisticated IOU that documents who owes how much and when payment must be made.

**collateral** is something of value that by agreement becomes the property of the lender if the borrower defaults

**crowding out** is the decrease in private consumption and investment that occurs when government borrows more

**arbitrage**, the buying and selling of equally risky assets, ensures that equally risky assets earn equal returns

**stock** or a share is a certificate of ownership in a corporation

**initial public offering (IPO)** is the first time a corporation sells stock to the public in order to raise capital

## Traps, Hints, and Reminders

Be careful about the definition of investment. Remember that in macroeconomics investment means new equipment, factories, roads, and education. Investment does *not* mean buying stocks. But the money that a firm gets from an IPO often goes to new equipment or factories.

Make sure that you don't confuse shifting the demand for borrowing with movements along the demand curve for borrowing. If the interest rate (the price for funds) changes, that is *a movement along the demand curve*. If the number of good projects changes, that would *shift the demand curve*.

In Chapter 7 *institutions* meant the overall rules in a society. Chapter 8 describes *financial institutions*, which are organizations.

Interest rates and bond prices move in opposite directions. For some reason, this is very hard to remember even though it is a common test question. One good way to think about this is to imagine that you buy a bond for $1,000 that pays 10% interest. What would happen if the interest rate went to 15%? Would people want to buy your bond for $1,000 paying 10% or a different bond for $1,000 paying 15%? People would rather buy the other bond. Your bond would have to sell for less.

# Practice Exercises: Learning by Doing

1. Why is finance in a *macroeconomics* course?

2. Draw the market for loanable funds.

3. Show the effect on the market for loanable funds when government does lots of borrowing. Use colored pencils if that helps you.

4. Imagine that you have a very safe zero-coupon bond that will have paid $1,000 in 1 year. The rate of return is 5%. What is the price of the bond?

5. Calculate the *real* interest rate in the following cases.
   a. nominal interest rate = 22%, inflation = 18%
   b. nominal interest rate = 35%, inflation = 36%
   c. nominal interest rate = 5%, inflation = 3%
   d. nominal interest rate = 14%, inflation = 7%

6. What is a logical effect on the loanable fund market if life expectancy, but not the retirement age, increases by 20 years?

7. What would happen to the ability of entrepreneurs to borrow money if the government makes it illegal for a bank to seize a person's house?

8. Imagine that the federal government borrows several hundred billion dollars more than normal. What would happen to the ability of private business to borrow? What would happen to the real interest rate?

9. Better than Twitter is a brand new company that is issuing stock for the first time ever. The stock will probably sell for around $10, which is much less than Google shares currently sell for on NASDAQ. Is there any reason to believe that buying Better than Twitter might increase investment more than buying Google?

**10.** Jimmy and Joey both average $50,000 per year. Jimmy has a very stable income and always makes $50,000. Joey has a very unstable income. Sometimes he makes much more than $50,000 and sometimes much less. Which one needs functioning financial markets more?

# Multiple-Choice Questions

1. Which of the following is a list of financial institutions?
    a. banks, stock markets, bond markets
    b. Congress, the Fed, the Treasury, the Supreme Court
    c. Wall Street, Main Street, Beale Street.
    d. property rights, democracy, The Constitution

2. Venture Capitalists are
    a. borrowers.
    b. savers.
    c. financial intermediaries.
    d. markets.

3. In macroeconomics, investment includes
    a. buying stock from your friend.
    b. buying bonds from your parish priest.
    c. buying new equipment for your business.
    d. burying money in coffee cans in the back yard.

4. The lifecycle theory says that
    a. what goes around comes around, even in economics.
    b. people try to save when they are making lots of money so they can consume when they are making less money.
    c. all banks will eventually be purchased by one large bank.
    d. venture capitalists buy small companies, those companies prosper, and the venture capitalists eventually sell them and buy new companies.

5. Large investments such as Fred Smith's FedEx often require the firm to
    a. borrow.
    b. save.
    c. depreciate.
    d. reassess.

6. If the interest rate increases (all else remains the same), what is likely to happen to the number of people who want to borrow?
   a. It will stay the same.
   b. It will increase.
   c. It will decrease.
   d. It will shift.

7. If the interest rate decreases (all else the same), what is likely to happen to the amount of money that people want to save?
   a. It will stay the same.
   b. It will increase.
   c. It will decrease.
   d. It will shift.

8. If life expectancy in a poor country suddenly increases, savings will
   a. shift outward.
   b. shift inward.
   c. increase in quantity.
   d. decrease in quantity.

9. If the government gets rid of an investment tax credit, then what would happen to the market for loanable funds?
   a. Demand would shift outward.
   b. Supply would shift outward.
   c. Demand would shift inward.
   d. Supply would shift inward.

10. Coupon bonds are bonds that give
    a. buyers a discount whenever they buy a bond.
    b. sellers a discount whenever they sell a bond.
    c. the owner coupons, which can be redeemed for interest payments before the maturity of the bond.
    d. the owner coupons, which can be redeemed for discounts on future bond purchases.

11. Two bonds with the same risk and same maturity should sell at the same price because of
    a. the permanent income hypothesis.
    b. arbitrage.
    c. stock markets.
    d. initial public offerings.

**12.** Which of the following would *not* be owners of a company?
   a. bond holders
   b. stock holders
   c. people who buy in the IPO
   d. venture capitalists

**13.** When the government freezes bank accounts this is an example of
   a. price controls.
   b. insecure property rights.
   c. inflation.
   d. bank panics.

**14.** Which of the following does *not* break the bridge between bank borrowers and savers?
   a. politicized lending
   b. inflation
   c. bank failures
   d. interest

**15.** Usury laws are a type of
   a. price ceiling.
   b. price floor.
   c. credit shortage prevention rule.
   d. I.P.O.

**16.** Forcing banks to lend to politically well-connected groups and people is an example of
   a. price ceilings.
   b. inflation.
   c. politicized lending.
   d. bank panic.

**17.** Imagine that everyone is unsure of which banks are sound and which ones are unsound. That could have which effect on the banking system?
   a. Savers would not want to deposit their money in certain banks.
   b. Savers would not want to deposit their money in any banks.
   c. Savers would want to deposit their money in all financial intermediaries.
   d. Savers would want to make sure they put all their deposits into banks.

18. Jim just passed away at the age of 90. While he was alive he had student loans to pay for college. He paid the loans off and saved for retirement during his working years. During retirement he lived off of his savings. He died with no assets and no debt. Jim was very successful at

    a. smoothing his consumption.

    b. acting as a venture capitalist.

    c. delaying gratification.

    d. understanding time preference.

19. If the economy falls into a recession, what will happen to the market for loanable funds?

    a. Supply will shift outward.

    b. Supply will shift inward.

    c. Demand will shift inward.

    d. Demand will shift outward.

20. When government increases its borrowing, there are less funds available for other borrowers. This is known as

    a. collateral.

    b. crowding out.

    c. stock.

    d. initial public offerings.

21. If the interest rate increases, then the price of current bonds will

    a. go up.

    b. go down.

    c. not change.

    d. shift outward.

## Short-Answer Questions

22. Sometimes banks make mistakes about which projects to invest in. Does that mean that we should not use banks as financial intermediaries?

**23.** What macro consequences could insecure banking have?

**24.** Why do bond prices move in the opposite direction of interest rates?

**25.** Why are loanable funds markets important to firms?

**26.** What would happen to overall investment if it becomes illegal to check someone's credit report before lending him or her money?

**27.** Currently mortgage interest is deductible on income taxes. What would happen to the supply and demand for loanable funds if mortgage interest was not deductible?

**28.** Many people get a tax refund at the end of the year. In effect, they lent the government money for free. What would happen to the number of people who would be willing to get a tax refund if the real rate of interest increased?

29. Imagine you are considering purchasing General Motors bonds. What would happen to the price and yield if the chance that GM will go bankrupt again increases?

30. Micro loans in developing countries occasionally charge very high interest rates by western standards. But these loans seem to make the borrowers better off. How could this be?

31. There is currently a world market for loanable funds. How could this help some borrowers and some lenders when compared to a purely domestic market for loanable funds?

# Answer Key

## Answers to Practice Exercises: Learning by Doing

1. Countries that have good financial markets, in which people are rewarded for saving, are the same countries where people can borrow to smooth their consumption or invest in big projects. Investment is a major cause of economic growth. Economic growth (or how to get economic growth and why some countries fail at that) is one of the main issues that macroeconomists try to resolve.

   **Topic: Introduction**

2. When a test question asks you to draw a market, the question normally means draw the supply and demand for the good in the question. Make sure that you remember to label the *y*-axis as "interest rate" instead of price.

   **Topic: Equilibrium in the Market for Loanable Funds**

   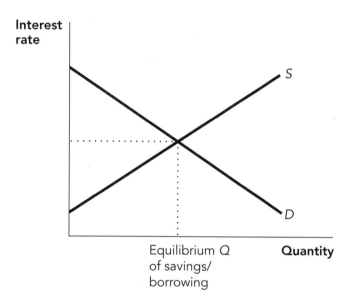

3. See Figure 8.10 from the text.

   **Topic: Shifts in Supply and Demand**

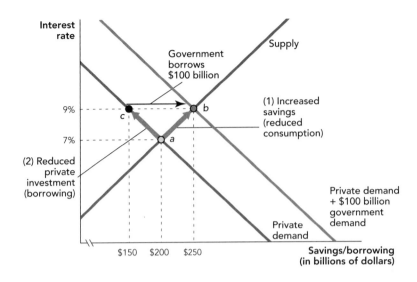

4. Rate of Return for a zero-coupon bond = $\dfrac{FV - \text{Price}}{\text{Price}} \times 100$  5 = ((1000 − Price)/Price) × 100.

Make sure that you don't put .05 on the left-hand side. Multiplying by 100 on the right-hand side of the equation takes care of conversion.

.05 = (1,000 − Price)/Price
.05 × Price = (1,000-Price)
.05 × Price + Price = 1,000
Price(.05 + 1) = 1,000
Price = 1,000/1.05
Price = $952.38

**Topic: Banks, Bonds, and Stock Markets**

5.

a. 4%

b. −1%

c. 2%

d. 7%

**Topic: What Happens When Intermediation Fails**

6. The logical effect on the loanable fund market if life expectancy, but *not* the retirement age, increases by 20 years is that more people would save. People know that they are more likely to live longer and to need more money. The supply of loanable funds should increase.

**Topic: Shifts in Supply and Demand**

7. If the government makes it illegal for a bank to seize a person's house when that person doesn't pay his or her debt, banks would be less likely to lend people money. That would hurt entrepreneurs' ability to borrow money.

**Topic: What Happens When Intermediation Fails?**

8. If the federal government borrows several hundred billion dollars more than normal, that would shift the demand for loanable funds outward. This would raise the real interest rate and make it harder for private businesses to be able to borrow.

   **Topic: Shifts in Supply and Demand**

9. Unless Google is issuing new stock, buying Google is just moving ownership from person to another. Buying Better than Twitter is helping (investing in) a new company.

   **Topic: The Demand to Borrow *and* The Role of Intermediaries**

10. Joey needs functioning financial markets more than Jimmy because Joey needs to be able to borrow when his income is low and lend when his income is high.

    **Topics: The Supply of Savings *and* The Demand to Borrow**

## Answers to Multiple-Choice Questions

1. a, Topic: Introduction
2. b, Topic: The Demand to Borrow
3. c, Topic: The Supply of Savings
4. b, Topic: The Supply of Savings
5. a, Topic: Large Investments
6. c, Topic: The Demand to Borrow
7. c, Topic: The Supply of Savings
8. a, Topic: The Supply of Savings
9. c, Topic: The Demand to Borrow
10. c, Topic: Banks, Bonds, and Stock Markets
11. b, Topic: Banks, Bonds, and Stock Markets
12. a, Topic: Banks, Bonds, and Stock Markets
13. b, Topic: Insecure Property Rights
14. d, Topic: What Happens When Intermediation Fails *and* Equilibrium in the Market for Loanable Funds
15. a, Topic: What Happens When Intermediation Fails?
16. c, Topic: What Happens When Intermediation Fails
17. b, Topic: What Happens When Intermediation Fails
18. a, Topic: The Supply of Savings *and* The Demand to Borrow
19. c, Topic: Equilibrium in the Market for Loanable Funds

20. b, Topic: Banks, Bonds, and Stock Markets

21. b, Topic: Banks, Bonds, and Stock Markets

## Answers to Short-Answer Questions

22. No, this doesn't mean that we should not use banks as financial intermediaries. Banks specialize in picking good investment projects. People who aren't specialized in this will make even more mistakes. Also, it doesn't make sense to have thousands and thousands of people evaluating the same risks. Using intermediaries reduces the number of people who need to evaluate the investment projects.

    **Topic: Introduction**

23. Insecure banking means that people don't have a good way to save their money. They can not smooth their consumption over time as easily. Also, if there are no savers, there can be no borrowers. This matters for the macroeconomy because borrowing is how firms acquire money for investment projects. Those investment projects will make workers more productive. More productive workers earn more. Countries that produce more are richer.

    **Topic: What Happens When Intermediation Fails?**

24. Bond prices move in the opposite direction of interest rates because when the current interest rate decreases, older bonds with the old interest rate are more valuable. When the interest rate increases, older bonds with the old interest rate are less valuable.

    **Topic: Banks, Bonds, and Stock Markets**

25. Loanable funds markets are important to firms because these markets allow firms to borrow money for big investment projects. They also allow firms to have more than one project at a time. Finally, some firms have more cash than good projects. Loanable funds markets allow those firms to invest in other companies' projects.

    **Topic: The Demand to Borrow**

26. If it was illegal to check someone's credit report before lending him or her money, lenders would be more wary of lending. They wouldn't know if they were making a wise investment or not. This would shift the supply curve inward.

    **Topic: The Supply of Savings**

27. People would want to borrow less money for their big investment, a house, and this would shift the demand for loanable funds inward.

    **Topic: The Demand to Borrow**

28. If the real rate of interest increases, then lending the government money becomes more expensive. You give up more when you do it. We expect fewer people to be willing to get a tax refund if the real interest rate increases.

    **Topic: The Supply of Savings**

29. If you are considering purchasing a bond from GM and you think there is a chance that GM will go bankrupt, that makes you less likely to want to purchase it. The price will come down, and the yield will increase. Remember that bond prices and bond yields move in opposite directions.

    **Topic: Banks, Bonds, and Stock Markets**

30. The high rates of return still make borrowers better because borrowers' other options (not investing or borrowing at an even higher rate) are worse than high rates on microloans.

    **Topic: The Demand to Borrow**

31. Borrowers who can borrow more cheaply abroad than they could domestically, benefit. Lenders who can lend for a higher interest rate abroad than they could domestically, benefit.

    **Topic: The Demand to Borrow**

# 9 (16)
# Stock Markets and Personal Finance

## Why Learn about Stock Markets?

**Business Student:** Why should we learn about stock markets and personal finance from you? If you know so much, wouldn't you be too rich to teach economics?
**Professor**: Oddly, that is a very good question. You would think that I ought to be able to get rich quick just like those guys on late night TV. I will show you why that doesn't work and what you can do to get rich slowly.

Who will be interested in stock markets? Any student who is at all interested in personal finance, building wealth, or avoiding scams will be interested in knowing more about the stock market.

## Summary

This chapter illustrates the idea that there is no free lunch, even in personal finance. Knowing that there is no free lunch can help you avoid big mistakes in your personal finances. If an investment provides any benefit beyond its value as an investment, then that investment should provide a lower rate of return. Think of it this way: Imagine you were trying to decide whether to buy classic cars or stocks as investments. If they were both about as safe and both paid the same rate of return, you would always buy the classic cars. It would be fun to own classic cars. However, as lots of people buy classic cars, the price is pushed up and the rate of return is pushed down. You cannot have the free lunch of fun and high rate of return.

Similarly, there is a **risk-return trade-off**, which just means that safer financial assets have a lower return.

There are two basic types of investing: active and passive. Active investing is when you pay a manager to actively buy and sell stocks for you. Passive investing is when you purchase an index fund and then **buy and hold**. Index funds are collections of stocks that are in one of the main indices such as the Dow Jones Industrial Average, the Standard and Poor's 500 (S&P 500), or the NASDAQ (which stands for the National Association of Securities Dealers Automated Quotations). Passive funds and random stock picking beat active stock picking most of the time. Active fund managers have to know more than everyone else and be able to buy and sell stocks without everyone else catching on. Also, if fund managers start to do well, others will catch on and copy them. When all the other investors start following them, they have to pay more for stocks. Before you know it, the active managers cannot beat the market anymore. Even great stock managers might just be lucky. See graphic 16.2 to see how this would work. The **efficient markets hypothesis** is the idea that as soon as new information about a stock or bond becomes available, buyers and sellers very, very quickly use that information, and asset prices adjust very quickly. Very quickly (sometimes within minutes!) no one can use that information to make extra profits.

The other reason that passive funds are preferable to active funds is that active funds tend to have higher costs. Over time, those costs really add up. In the example in the text, the fund with higher fees cost an extra $16,582.

Other than watching fees, diversification is one of the few things that an individual can do to increase their wealth. Diversification is just the idea that spreading your wealth among many different investments is more successful than "putting all of your eggs in one basket."

## Key Terms

**efficient markets hypothesis** the prices of traded assets reflect all publicly available information

**buy and hold** buying stocks and then holding them for the long run, regardless of what prices do in the short run

**risk-return trade-off** higher returns come at the price of higher risk

## Traps, Hints, and Reminders

Sometimes students get confused about the trade-off between risk and return. They do not understand why the relationship exists. Imagine that there were two bonds you could buy. One is more risky than the other. Which would you pay more for? The less risky one, of course. But paying more for the less risky bond means that bond has a lower return.

The efficient markets hypothesis is similar to the idea that there is no such thing as a free lunch. If you could easily gather special information on stocks and make money, everyone would do that. That would get rid of your advantage.

Bubbles misallocate resources. For example, if there is a real estate bubble, then resources that would have gone to produce something else are drawn into real estate.

This does not mean that investing in housing is bad; it means that consumers valued something else more, and that investors were confused.

The authors do suggest ways to get rich slow. For example, by using the power of compounding, the longer your money is invested, the bigger it will be at the end. Small amounts of money saved over a long period of time can be much bigger than large amounts of money invested for a short period of time. Another way to get rich slow is by diversifying your portfolio to protect yourself against the risk from single stocks. It also helps build your wealth when you can avoid high fees when choosing stocks.

## Practice Exercises: Learning by Doing

1. Briefly explain the difference between active and passive investing.

2. Imagine that your stock broker recommends a stock that will make a lot of money when some event everyone knows will happen happens. Your broker says this stock is sure to make lots of money. Explain why this analysis is incorrect.

3. What is the advantage of diversifying your portfolio?

4. Humberto is saving to send his children to college next year. Ling Ling is saving for her retirement in 30 years. Why should Humberto invest in more bonds than Ling Ling?

5. Imagine that a certain beer company provides free beer and free parties to all stock holders. Why would that stock be likely to have a lower rate of return?

6. Explain why it is hard to make money on the stock market or other asset bubbles.

7. Explain why the authors discuss getting rich slow.

# Multiple-Choice Questions

1. According to Burton Malkeil, who could do as well as a stock guru at picking stocks?
    a. a bond guru
    b. the average citizen
    c. highly paid news reporters
    d. a blindfolded monkey with darts and the financial pages

2. If you pay someone to pick individual stocks for you instead of buying a broad index of stocks you are
    a. active investing.
    b. assuming efficient markets.
    c. exuberant.
    d. foregoing the risk-return trade-off.

3. What is the S&P 500?
    a. a NASCAR event
    b. a basket of 500 large firms that broadly mimic the United States economy
    c. a basket of 500 small tech firms
    d. a basket of 500 firms in Switzerland and the Philippines

4. In any given year about how many mutual funds beat the S&P 500?
    a. 40%
    b. 50%
    c. 1%
    d. 100%

5. If 3,000 stock market analysts flip a coin each year to see if a firm's price will go up or down, how many analysts will be expected to be correct every time after 6 years?
   a. just 1
   b. 0
   c. 500
   d. 47

6. The efficient markets hypothesis says that
   a. big firms are more efficient so they make all the money in stock markets.
   b. you cannot get rich buying and selling stocks based on public information.
   c. big firms are more efficient at picking stocks than individual investors.
   d. individuals are better at picking stocks than big firms.

7. Your stock broker tells you that today's news means that Google will make much more money next year than anyone had predicted. He recommends a buy. Why might this be poor advice?
   a. He is just trying to unload his own stock.
   b. If it was in today's news the price has already increased.
   c. Newspapers usually try to manipulate the stock market for their own gain.
   d. None of the answers is correct.

8. After the nuclear power plant in Chernobyl melted and contaminated the Ukraine with radiation, American potato prices increased. Why?
   a. People wanted to eat more potatoes.
   b. People were afraid to buy stocks.
   c. People were afraid to buy bonds.
   d. Traders quickly realized that when Ukrainian potatoes were contaminated, American potatoes would sell for more.

9. When financial economists talk about a stock's covariance they mean
   a. how much the stock price moves up and down.
   b. how much the stock moves up or down compared to its previous amount.
   c. how the stock moves up or down along with the rest of the market.
   d. how the price of the stock is.

10. When a stock price falls that means that
    a. the stock is undervalued and will rise.
    b. the stock will continue to fall.
    c. most buyers and sellers negatively reevaluated their opinion of the stock.
    d. the stock will suddenly have more variance.

11. The evidence for "technical analysis" is
    a. very strong; it works.
    b. mildly strong; it usually works.
    c. a mix of strong and weak.
    d. weak; it does not work.

12. According to diversification, if you work in the auto industry you should
    a. invest heavily in auto stocks.
    b. split your portfolio equally between auto stocks and non-auto stocks.
    c. have relatively few auto stocks.
    d. buy companies that supply auto companies.

13. Rank the following asset categories from lowest risk to highest risk (standard deviation).
    a. United States T-bills, small stocks, S&P 500, sorporate bonds
    b. Corporate bonds, small stocks, S&P 500, T-bills
    c. United States T-bills, corporate bonds, S&P 500, small stocks
    d. United States T-bills, small stocks, corporate bonds, S&P 500

14. According to finance economists, the riskiest stocks are
    a. stocks that move opposite of the overall economy.
    b. stocks that move with the overall economy.
    c. stocks that do well when the economy is doing well.
    d. stocks that do not do well when the economy is in a downturn.

15. The riskiest stocks are those with
    a. the least covariance with the market as a whole.
    b. the most covariance with the market as a whole.
    c. the most variance with the market as a whole.
    d. the least variance with the market as a whole.

16. An old family friend comes to you with a "can't fail" investment strategy. He has been making 5% more than the market for the past ten years and as a favor he will let you invest with him. You should
    a. remember the efficient market hypothesis and invest before everyone else does.
    b. be especially wary of your friend because there is no such thing as a free lunch.
    c. assume that your friend has found a bubble and ride it out before it bursts.
    d. use your friend as one of your assets.

17. Why is the stock market a better place to gamble than Las Vegas roulette tables?
    a. They actually have the same risk.
    b. Las Vegas is actually a safer place to gamble.
    c. The odds actually favor the stock investor while the odds are against the roulette gambler.
    d. The odds actually favor the roulette gambler while the odds are against the stock investor.

18. When economists talk about bubbles they mean
    a. you never know what will happen to the economy.
    b. sometimes investors bid up the price of an asset well above what the price should be.
    c. sometimes investors spend too much time focusing on core competencies.
    d. sometimes stock prices float back and forth like soap bubbles.

19. Right around the year 2000 there was a bubble in which market?
    a. real estate
    b. large stocks
    c. T-bills
    d. tech stocks

20. Bubbles and their bursts are painful to economies because
    a. they cause economies to invest in the wrong areas.
    b. people do not like to let asset prices get too high.
    c. bubbles are not actually painful. Paper profits go up then down. But only on paper.
    d. random stock pickers seem like geniuses when they just got lucky.

## Short-Answer Questions

21. What is the difference between active and passive investing?

22. Why does your text recommend passive investing?

**23.** Some stock market analysts beat the market for many years in a row. If markets are efficient how is this possible?

**24.** Why is it hard for Warren Buffet to beat the market?

**25.** What are some simple ways to diversify?

**26.** What is meant by "technical analysis"?

**27.** Explain why you should be skeptical when your stock broker calls you with the "deal of a lifetime."

**28.** Explain why riskier stocks have higher returns.

**29.** If your economics professor says that housing prices will be at their very lowest next January, why might you be skeptical?

**30.** How do bubbles cause misallocation in markets?

# Answer Key

## Answers to Practice Exercises: Learning by Doing

1. Active investing is when you try to pick individual stocks and bonds. Passive investing is when you just pick a diversified portfolio and leave it alone.

   **Topic: Passive vs. Active Investing**

2. If the stock will make lots of money when global warming causes mass flooding and if the efficient market hypothesis is correct, then everyone would already know this information. Thus the stock price already includes this information.

   **Topic: Why Is It Hard to Beat the Market?**

3. Diversifying your portfolio protects investors from events that affect single stocks. If you own only XYZ company and XYZ goes bankrupt, you lose your entire portfolio.

   **Topic: How to Really Pick Stocks, Seriously**

4. Humberto does not have much time to get the benefit of earning higher returns and he needs to have safety. He cannot afford to have the stock market fall in the next year. Humberto needs bonds. Ling Ling has much more time to take advantage of the additional rate of return from stocks. Also, Ling Ling has time to weather the ups and downs of the stock market.

   **Topic: Compound Returns Build Wealth**

5. The beer company stock provides lots of extras in addition to the rate of return. People will be more likely to want to own that stock. As they bid up the price of the stock, the return will come down. If that were not the case, you could get better than a free lunch; you could have high stock returns and free beer.

   **Topic: The No Free Lunch Principle or No Return Without Risk**

6. It is hard to make money on bubbles because when you buy the asset to watch the price go up, you never know when the burst will come. When you bet on the burst coming, you could be wrong about the stock being a bubble or you could mistime the burst.

   **Topic: Bubble, Bubble, Toil, and Trouble**

7. The authors discuss getting rich slowly because efficient markets mean that ways of getting rich quickly are either non-existent (scams) or they are very risky. There is no free lunch.

   **Topic: Introduction**

## Answers to Multiple-Choice Questions

1. d, Topic: Introduction
2. a, Topic: Passive vs. Active Investing
3. b, Topic: How to Really Pick Stocks, Seriously

4. a, Topics: Passive vs. Active Investing; How to Really Pick Stocks, Seriously
5. d, Topic: Passive vs. Active Investing
6. b, Topic: Why Is It Hard to Beat the Market?
7. b, Topic: Why Is It Hard to Beat the Market?
8. d, Topic: Why Is It Hard to Beat the Market?
9. c, Topic: How to Really Pick Stocks, Seriously
10. c, Topic: How to Really Pick Stocks, Seriously
11. d, Topic: How to Really Pick Stocks, Seriously
12. c, Topic: How to Really Pick Stocks, Seriously
13. c, Topic: The No Free Lunch Principle or No Return Without Risk
14. b, Topics: How to Really Pick Stocks, Seriously; The No Free Lunch Principle or No Return Without Risk
15. b, Topics: How to Really Pick Stocks, Seriously; The No Free Lunch Principle or No Return Without Risk
16. b, Topic: The No Free Lunch Principle or No Return Without Risk
17. c, Topic: The No Free Lunch Principle or No Return Without Risk
18. b, Topic: Bubble, Bubble, Toil, and Trouble
19. d, Topic: Bubble, Bubble, Toil, and Trouble
20. a, Topic: Bubble, Bubble, Toil, and Trouble

## Answers to Short-Answer Questions

21. Active investing is trying to pick particular winners and losers whether they are stocks or some other asset. Passive is when you pick a diversified portfolio, not knowing which assets will be winners and losers. Passive investors hope that the majority of their portfolio will increase in value.

    **Topic: Passive vs. Active Investing**

22. The text recommends passive investing because fees are lower and it is very difficult to beat the market. Information is quickly adopted by the market. Further, diversifying your portfolio as a passive investor protects you from events that affect individual stocks. Remember that the S&P 500 beats most mutual funds most years.

    **Topics: Why Is It Hard to Beat the Market?** *and* **Avoid High Fees**

23. While it is possible that some stock analysts are smarter than the market as a whole, another explanation is that if there are enough stock pickers some of them will be super lucky. The text provides a simple example of how this could work.

    **Topics: Why Is It Hard to Beat the Market?** and **How to Really Pick Stocks, Seriously**

24. It is hard for Warren Buffet to beat the market because it is hard for anyone to have more knowledge than or to outwork the entire market. Buffet also has the difficulty that lots of people watch him. When Buffet buys a certain stock, lots of people want to buy that stock, and that pushes the stock price up.

    **Topics: Why Is It Hard to Beat the Market?** and **How to Really Pick Stocks, Seriously**

25. A really simple way to diversify is to buy index funds. Pick something like the S&P 500. That is a broad collection of 500 different stocks.

    **Topic: How to Really Pick Stocks, Seriously**

26. "Technical analysis" is when stock pickers look at the past up and down pattern of stock prices to determine when they should buy and when they should sell. Unfortunately, it does not have very good results.

    **Topics: How to Really Pick Stocks, Seriously** and **The No Free Lunch Principle or No Return Without Risk**

27. When your broker calls you with the "deal of a lifetime" you should be skeptical because if it was such a great deal the broker would buy all of the stock. Also, as soon as new information is available, the information is incorporated into the price. By the time your broker figures out a great deal and then calls you, it is not a great deal anymore.

    **Topic: The No Free Lunch Principle or No Return Without Risk**

28. Riskier stocks have higher returns because the less risky stocks have had their returns bid down. People would not buy a risky stock unless the risky stock had a higher return. People would rather buy the safer stock. When people buy the safer stock they bid safe stock returns downward.

    **Topic: The No Free Lunch Principle or No Return Without Risk**

29. How does your professor have this knowledge? Is he doing "technical analysis?" Is he making money off it? "Lowest in January" means that prices will start rising in February. If that is the case, is it not true that other people will figure this out too and be able to profit from this knowledge?

    **Topic: The No Free Lunch Principle or No Return Without Risk**

30. Bubbles encourage people to make mistakes regarding where they should invest. People see some asset prices rising and keep investing in that asset because they think that consumers want that asset. When the bubble pops, investors realize that they should have invested in something else.

    **Topic: Bubble, Bubble, Toil, and Trouble**

# 10 (24)

# Unemployment and Labor Force Participation

## Why Learn about Labor Markets?

Most people's wealth is actually an income stream from selling their labor. For that reason alone, most students will find something interesting in labor markets. Policy students will be interested in what causes long-term unemployment and why some countries have permanently higher unemployment rates. International business majors will want to be able to think about which countries are best for investment. All students will be concerned with what happens to people when their career ceases to exist.

## Summary

The **unemployment rate** is the number of people who are unemployed divided by the **labor force** multiplied by 100. The labor force is people who are either working or *actively* looking for work. **Discouraged workers** are people who are not working but no longer looking for work. They are not counted as being in the labor force.

There are three types of unemployment: **Frictional unemployment** is short-term unemployment caused by the ordinary difficulty of matching employee to employer. **Structural unemployment** is persistent, long-term (more than a year) unemployment caused by long-lasting shocks or permanent features of the economy. **Cyclical unemployment** is unemployment correlated with the business cycle.

The **natural unemployment rate** is defined as the rate of structural plus frictional unemployment.

Countries with lots of rules, regulations, and wage requirements that are supposed to protect workers often have the *unintended consequence* of employers not wanting to hire workers. This leads to long-term structural unemployment. Better unemployment insurance also leads to more unemployment. Much of the big picture in this chapter is that labor laws designed to help workers lead to unemployment.

**Active labor market policies** are policies that encourage the unemployed to rejoin the workforce. These policies include work tests (to get unemployment benefits, you must prove that you are looking for a job), job skills training, and job search assistance.

Other countries, such as the United States, have the **employment at-will doctrine**. This means that employees may be fired at any time. While this may be cruel, it encourages firms to want to hire workers.

**Labor force participation rate** is just the percentage of people who are either employed or looking for work divided by the number of adults multiplied by 100.

The unemployment rate is a less than perfect indicator of how a country is doing because it does not count people who are underemployed, working less than full time, or discouraged.

The birth control pill greatly increased labor force participation for women. The pill lets women delay pregnancy while they work or invest in human capital.

## Key Terms

**unemployed** workers are adults who do not have a job but who are looking for work

**labor force** is all workers, employed plus unemployed

**unemployment rate** is the percentage of the labor force without a job

**labor force participation rate** is the percentage of adults in the labor force

**discouraged workers** are workers who have given up looking for work but who would still like a job

**frictional unemployment** is short-term unemployment caused by the ordinary difficulties of matching employee to employer

**structural unemployment** is persistent, long-term unemployment caused by long-lasting shocks or permanent features of an economy that make it more difficult for some workers to find jobs

**median wage** is the wage such that one-half of all workers earn wages below the median and one-half of all workers earn wages above the median

**union** is an association of workers that bargains collectively with employers over wages, benefits, and working conditions

**employment at-will doctrine** says an employee may quit and an employer may fire an employee at any time and for any reason. There are many exceptions to the at-will doctrine but it is the most basic U.S. employment law

**active labor market policies** like work tests, job search assistance and job retraining programs focus on getting unemployed workers back to work

**cyclical unemployment** is unemployment correlated with the business cycle

**natural unemployment rate** is the rate of structural plus frictional unemployment

**baby boomers** are the people born during the high-birth rate years, 1946–1964

# Tips, Traps, and Hints

People who are unemployed and not looking are not counted as unemployed. This is a common problem for students who look at someone who isn't working and want to count him or her as unemployed. People who are not working are only unemployed if they are actively looking for a job. Your retired grandmother isn't unemployed unless she is actively looking for a new job.

Any time that wages are above the equilibrium wage (look at Chapter 4) there will be unemployment because $Q_d$ will not equal $Q_s$. Countries with high union or higher minimum wages have more long-term unemployment.

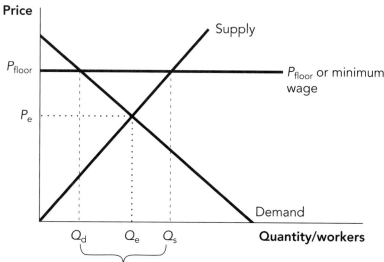

Quantity demanded is less than quantity supplied → Surplus. A surplus of workers is unemployment.

Lower growth is accompanied with higher unemployment for two reasons: 1) downturns in the economy cause firms to lay off workers, and 2) unemployed workers can't produce goods. Make sure you know both reasons why unemployment and lower growth (decreasing new amounts of goods and services) go together.

Higher taxes on work lead to less work. Women and older people are especially likely to exit the labor market. If you think about it, this makes sense. If taxes go up, the benefits of working go down. If you also have to pay commuting costs and child care, then it really makes sense to quit work. Read the section in the chapter about how the elderly are double taxed if they keep working in some countries.

On exams, make sure that you are careful about unemployment and employment rates. Sometimes students make mistakes simply by misreading the question.

Finally, make sure that you understand that while labor unions and minimum wage regulations cause unemployment directly by keeping $Q_s$ from equaling $Q_d$ in the labor market; such laws are also associated with economies that are less dynamic and able to change. That means that when there is a big change to the economy, whether from oil shocks, globalization, or new technology, less dynamic economies are unable to adjust. Structural unemployment lasts longer in such countries.

# Practice Exercises: Learning by Doing

1. What is the difference between frictional, structural, and cyclical unemployment?

2. What are the unintended consequences of labor laws designed to protect workers?

3. If the adult population is 200 million, and 100 million are working and 10 million are actively looking for a job, but not working, what is the unemployment rate?

4. If the adult population is 200 million, and 100 million are working and 10 million are actively looking for a job but not working, what is the labor force participation rate?

5. Why is long-term unemployment so high in so many European countries?

6. If a country with very rigid labor laws like Portugal switched to employment at will, what do you predict would happen in the labor market there?

7. What factors affect structural unemployment?

*8. What policies can countries implement to reduce structural employment?[1]

9. Why do countries have rigid labor laws if such laws lead to more unemployment?

10. How did the birth control pill affect labor participation rates?

# Multiple-Choice Questions

1. If there are 105 million people in the labor force and 95 million of them have jobs, what is the <u>un</u>employment rate?
    a. 95%
    b. 9.52%
    c. 100%
    d. 90.4%

---

[1] Questions marked with a ★ are also end-of-chapter questions.

2. If there are 200 million adults, and 170 million are in the labor force and 8 million are actively looking for a job but not currently working, then what is the labor force participation rate?
   a. 4.7%
   b. 8.5%
   c. 95.3%
   d. 85%

3. Esther is currently working for income but also looking for a job on monster.com. Esther is
   a. employed.
   b. not in the labor force.
   c. unemployed.
   d. discouraged.

4. Raquel was working at the local mill, but soon after it closed she got discouraged and quit looking for a job. Raquel is
   a. employed.
   b. not in the labor force.
   c. unemployed.
   d. underemployed.

5. Michael has a PhD in English literature but is forced to work at an oyster shelling plant. According to the official statistics from the Bureau of Labor Statistics, Michael is
   a. employed.
   b. not in the labor force.
   c. unemployed.
   d. underemployed.

6. If a country enacts new unemployment insurance that provides the unemployed with more money for a longer period, we would expect
   a. people to quickly find jobs.
   b. people to never lose employment.
   c. the employment rate to go up.
   d. the unemployment rate to go up.

7. Which of the following is a list of countries with very rigid labor laws?
   a. France, Germany, Italy, Spain
   b. France, New Zealand, United States
   c. France, Canada, United Kingdom
   d. France, United States, United Kingdom, Australia

8. Which of the following are examples of active labor market policies?
   a. paying a bonus to people who find a job
   b. forcing people who get unemployment insurance to prove that they are actively looking for a job
   c. providing job training and job search assistance
   d. All of the answers are correct.

9. Which groups of people protested and burned tires in France over labor rules?
   a. African immigrants who are outsiders and can't get jobs
   b. students from elite universities who are insiders who want to keep their privileges
   c. farm workers who want cushy government jobs
   d. Both (a) and (b) are correct.

10. Employment at will means that you can be fired
    a. for good reasons only.
    b. for any reason at any time.
    c. be fired only if you agree.
    d. be fired only under certain circumstances, such as when employers and union organizers agree.

11. The United States has employment at will but some restrictions do exist. Which of the following are U.S. restrictions?
    a. You may not fire someone simply because the economy is bad.
    b. You may not fire someone simply because of his or her race or religion.
    c. You may not fire someone simply because that person don't show up for work on time.
    d. You may not fire someone simply because you want to.

12. Keith just graduated and is in the process of looking for a job. Keith is
    a. structurally unemployed.
    b. cyclically unemployed.
    c. not in the labor market.
    d. frictionally unemployed.

13. Grace works as a framer for a construction company. During the recent downturn, she got laid off. If she is actively looking for employment, she is
    a. structurally unemployed.
    b. cyclically unemployed.
    c. not in the labor market.
    d. frictionally unemployed.

14. Byron lost his job as a travel agent when everyone switched to purchasing their own airline tickets on the Internet. Even though Byron is still looking for a job, Byron is
    a. structurally unemployed.
    b. cyclically unemployed
    c. not in the labor market.
    d. frictionally unemployed.

15. When people lose their jobs because technology made those jobs obsolete, the economy is permanently poorer. Is this true or false?
    a. It's true because those people will never find new jobs.
    b. It's true because those people will be forced to become unpaid servants.
    c. It's false because countries that adopt new technology are more dynamic; typewriter repairmen are gone but GeekSquad is here.
    d. It's false because those people never deserved jobs in the first place.

16. What happens to the unemployment rate during an economic boom?
    a. Unemployment increases.
    b. Unemployment increases but the unemployment rate decreases.
    c. Unemployment decreases.
    d. Unemployment decreases but the unemployment rate increases.

17. Labor force participation differs, depending on people's ages. Which group has the lowest labor force participation rate?
    a. 16–19
    b. 25–54
    c. 65+
    d. None of the answers is correct.

18. Higher income tax rates do what to labor force participation?
    a. They increase it because people have to work more just to survive.
    b. They increase it because people know that their hard work is going to benefit society.
    c. They decrease it because people won't know whether their work is valuable.
    d. They decrease it because people will find other things more valuable when work pays less.

19. Which of the following is credited with encouraging the participation of U.S. women in the labor force?
    a. the change from a manufacturing to a service economy
    b. the invention of the birth control pill
    c. social and cultural changes
    d. All of the answers are correct.

20. According to the text, what is one of the biggest reasons why women's labor force participation has increased?
    a. New laws allowed women to work.
    b. The birth control pill allowed women to easily control their fertility.
    c. Women finally got the vote in 1964.
    d. The new economy finally had jobs that women could perform.

**Short-Answer Questions**

21. What type of unemployment do each of the following people have?
    - Jim lost his job as a machinist when the recession hit.
    - Omar quit his job a corporate attorney to look for a job with a better quality of life.
    - Nancy lost her job in light manufacturing when it was outsourced to Mexico.

22. If a country has 10 million civilians between the age of 16 and 64 but only 8.2 million of them are working or looking for work, what is the labor force participation rate?

23. A country has 200 million people. Of these, 90 million are civilians between the ages of 16 and 64, 70 million of those people are working, 10 million more are actively looking for work, but 3 million of the employed are underemployed. What is the employment rate?

24. Why do some countries have persistent long-term unemployment while others do not?

**25.** What policies could you recommend to European nations that have persistent long-term unemployment?

**26.** What factors affect structural unemployment?

**27.** What happens to unemployment when the economy is more productive?

**28.** Even in an economic boom there is some unemployment. Why might there be some *natural* unemployment?

**29.** What happens to labor force participation for older men when taxes increase?

**30.** How did the birth control pill affect women's labor force participation?

# Answer Key

## Answers to Practice Exercises: Learning by Doing

1. Frictional unemployment is short-term unemployment caused by the ordinary difficultly of matching employee to employer. When people first graduate or reenter the job market they are frictionally unemployed. Structural unemployment is persistent unemployment caused by shocks to the economy. These shocks include things like new technology, making the career irrelevant, or new trade patterns. A new trade pattern might mean that your job has been outsourced. Cyclical unemployment is when demand for your services closely matches the business cycle. When the economy is in a recession, you lose your job. When the economy is booming, your services are needed again. Construction and manufacturing are cyclical work.

   **Topic: Defining Unemployment**

2. Labor laws designed to protect workers often have the unintended consequence of making firms reluctant to hire workers in the first place. This can make it hard for people to find jobs.

   **Topic: Labor Regulations and Structural Unemployment**

3. The employment rate is: (100 million working) /(100 million working + 10 million looking) = 100/110 = .909. .909×100 = 90.9% employed. (1 −.909) ×100 = 9.1% *un*employment.

   **Topic: Defining Unemployment**

4. The labor force participation rate is 100 million working + 10 million looking divided by the adult population. 110 million/200 million = 110/200 = .55. .55×100 = 55% labor force participation rate.

   **Topic: Labor Force Participation**

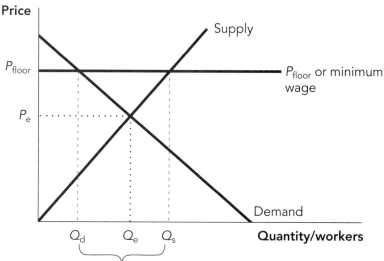

Quantity demanded is less than quantity supplied→Surplus. A surplus of workers is unemployment.

5. Long-term unemployment is high in those countries that have rigid labor laws. Looking at the previous figure of unemployment and labor rigidity, we see a strong positive relationship. In countries where firms cannot easily fire workers, firms are reluctant to ever hire workers.
   **Topic: Labor Regulations and Structural Unemployment**

6. If a country with rigid labor laws switched to employment at will, firms would be more likely to hire workers. We would also see firms taking on riskier workers such as "outsiders" or immigrants who might not be well-known and established.
   **Topic: Labor Regulations and Structural Unemployment**

7. Structural unemployment is affected by oil shocks, the shift from services to manufacturing, globalization and global competition, fundamental technology shocks like computers, and the Internet. Structural unemployment is made more lasting by labor rigidity.
   **Topic: Structural Unemployment**

8. Countries can reduce structural unemployment by doing two things 1) reducing labor market rigidity such as allowing employment at will, and 2) implementing active labor market policies such as job search assistance, job skill retraining, and bonuses for early employment.
   **Topic Labor Regulations to Reduce Structural Unemployment**

9. Countries have counterproductive labor laws because they benefit *some* workers. Certain labor laws increase unemployment but for the employed they provide benefits. Insiders who have jobs are pleased by labor protections.
   **Topic: Labor Regulations and Structural Unemployment**

10. The birth control pill affects the labor force participation rate because the **female labor force** is directly affected by it. Women are more likely to work if they can control their own fertility. Also, women are much more likely to invest in job skills or in jobs that require lots of experience if they know they can delay pregnancy.
    **Topic: How the Pill Increased Female Labor Force Participation**

## Answers to Multiple-Choice Questions

1. b, Topic: Introduction
2. d, Topic: Introduction
3. a, Topic: Defining Unemployment
4. b, Topic: Defining Unemployment
5. a, Topic: How Good of an Indicator Is the Employment Rate?
6. d, Topic: Labor Regulations and Structural Unemployment

7. a, Topic: Labor Regulations and Structural Unemployment
8. d, Topic: Labor Regulations and Structural Unemployment
9. d, Topic: Structural Unemployment
10. b, Topic: Structural Unemployment.
11. b, Topic: Structural Unemployment
12. d, Topic: Frictional Unemployment
13. a , Topic: Structural Unemployment
14. a, Topic: Structural Unemployment
15. c, Topic: Structural Unemployment
16. c, Topic: Cyclical Unemployment
17. c, Topic: Lifecycle Effects and Demographics
18. d, Topic: Life Cycle Effects and Demographics *and* Incentives
19. b, Topic: Incentives
20. b, Topic: Incentives

## Answers to Short-Answer Questions

21. Jim has cyclical unemployment because his unemployment is so closely related to fluctuations in the economy. Omar is trying to find a better job match for himself; so he is an example of frictional unemployment. If Nancy has had *persistent* unemployment because her job was outsourced, then she has structural unemployment. If Nancy is unemployed for a short period and will soon be working again, then it would suggest that she is just having the normal trouble of finding a new job. That would mean she is undergoing frictional unemployment.

    **Topic: Defining Unemployment**

22. There are 10 million people and 8.2 are working or looking for work, which means that the labor force participation rate is 8.2/10 = .82. .82 ★100 = 82% labor force participation rate.

    **Topic: Labor Force Participation**

23. If there are 90 million civilians who could be working and 70 million of them are working and another 10 million are looking for work, then the following formula tells you the employment rate: 70 million / 80 million. 80 million people are in the labor force (working plus actively looking) and 70 million are employed. 70/80 = .875. .875★ 100 = 87.5%

    **Topic: Defining Unemployment**

24. Persistent unemployment is closely correlated with rigid labor laws. Those countries that have very rigid labor laws have firms that are unwilling to hire more workers.

    **Topic: Labor Regulations and Structural Unemployment**

25. European countries that want to reduce persistent long-term unemployment could try two things: 1) reduce the rigidity in their labor laws by allowing employment at will or reducing union power, and 2) use active labor policies such as paying bonuses to people who find jobs quickly.

    **Topic: Labor Regulations to Reduce Structural Unemployment**

26. Large, long-lasting shocks that require the economy to restructure affect structural unemployment. Examples include oil shocks or other shocks to major input prices, the shift from manufacturing to services, or globalization. But some labor regulations such as high unemployment benefits, minimum wages, powerful unions, and employment protection laws make economies less dynamic and less able to change after a long-lasting shock. These labor regulations prolong structural unemployment.

    **Topic: Structural Unemployment**

27. When the economy is more productive, firms are more interested in hiring workers, and so unemployment goes down. At the same time if unemployment goes down, workers produce more.

    **Topic: Cyclical Unemployment**

28. There is a natural rate of unemployment even when the economy is booming because it is hard for firms and workers to match up. They have to search for and find each other. Since people and firms are always looking, there is a natural rate of unemployment that is unrelated to the business cycle.

    **Topic: The Natural Unemployment Rate**

29. When taxes increase for older men, they are less likely to work. They drop out of the labor force.

    **Topic: Labor Force Participation**

30. The birth control pill affected women's labor force participation by allowing them to control their fertility. Since women are getting pregnant less, they can work more. Also, because they can plan their pregnancies, they can invest in human capital such as professional degrees.

    **Topic: Labor Force Participation**

# 11 (25)

# Inflation and the Quantity Theory of Money

## Why Learn about Inflation?

Inflation is about the value of money. How much you can buy with your dollars depends on the amount of inflation. Students as consumers will be interested in inflation. But inflation also affects interest rates, which appeals to business majors and investors. Printing money, which leads to inflation, is used as policy to pay for various government programs, which should intrigue political science majors. Finally, inflation can have an effect on business cycles.

## Summary

**Inflation** is the increase in the average level of price. It isn't an increase in the price of one good. **Inflation Rate** $= \dfrac{P_2 - P_1}{P_1} \times 100$. This is a useful formula to know because it is just the formula for percentage change, and finding the percentage increase or decrease comes up often in economics. **Deflation** is the opposite of inflation and occurs when the average level of prices is falling.

There are multiple price indices. The most commonly heard price index is the *CPI*, which measures the average price for a basket of final goods bought by the average American consumer. There is also the *PPI*, which measures the average price of a basket of goods purchased by producers. The PPI is a also different in that it measures some intermediate goods as well as final goods. The third price index is the *GDP deflator*, which measures the cost of all final goods and services not just final goods and services purchased by consumers. A **real price** is a price that has been adjusted for inflation.

Inflation varies greatly over time and across countries. The U.S. average inflation rate from 1950 to 2005 is 3.9% but was over 10% in the 1970s. From 2002–2007, the United States experienced 3% inflation, but Zimbabwe experienced 735% inflation and Japan only .03% inflation.

$MV = PY + P_R$. $M$ = Money supply. $V$ is the **velocity of money,** which is how often the money is spent. If people stop spending and investing, velocity goes down. If they start, velocity goes up. Most of the time velocity is constant. $Y_R$ is the real GDP, which is stable compared to the money supply.

Inflation has an effect on real interest rates. If the nominal interest rate is 10% and the inflation rate is 5%, then the real interest rate is 5%. $r_{actual} = i - \pi$. $r_{actual}$ is the actual or *real* rate of interest. $i$ is the nominal interest rate and $\pi$ is the inflation rate. You can see that if a bank wants the real rate of interest to equal 3% and the inflation rate is going to be 9%, then the bank needs to charge 12%.

Of course, when people expect inflation, they adjust prices and interest rates accordingly. But it is hard to know what inflation to expect. There is often **money illusion.** Money illusion is when people are fooled by changes in *nominal* price, thinking that the changes are *real* price increases. More people come into your shop to buy things and you don't realize that they are coming in because of inflation. You think customers are coming in because they like your products. You get fooled by what is going on.

*Inflation redistributes wealth* if you borrow money from the bank and both of you expect 5% inflation but your country gets 15% inflation, and you as a borrower benefited. The dollars you repay are much less valuable then the dollars you borrowed. Similarly, if you sign a one year work contract and you and the boss both expect inflation to be 5% but instead it is 15%, you are worse off. At the end of the year, you are being paid with dollars that are much less valuable than you expected them to be.

**Monetizing the debt** is when a government reduces the value of its debts by raising the inflation rate. Imagine that that the United States owes 1 billion dollars. If the government has 100% inflation, then the real amount of the debt falls in half. Prices would rise but since the debt is in nominal terms, it doesn't change. The United States would be able to pay its debts back with less valuable currency.

## Key Terms

**inflation** is an increase in the average level of prices

**inflation rate** is the percentage change in the average level of prices (as measured by a price index) over a period of time

**real price** is a price that has been corrected for inflation. Real prices are used to compare the prices of goods over time

***v*, velocity of money,** is the average number of times a dollar is spent on final goods and services in a year

**the Quantity Theory of Money** is when $v$ and $Y$ are fixed (indicated by a top bar), increases in $M$ must cause increases in $P$

**deflation** is a decrease in the average level of prices

**disinflation** is a reduction in the inflation rate

**money illusion** is when people mistake changes in nominal prices for changes in real prices

**Fisher effect** is the tendency of nominal interest rates to rise with expected inflation rates

**monetizing the debt** is when the government pays off its debts by printing money

## Traps, Hints, and Reminders

Make sure that you don't confuse one price rising with price<u>s</u> rising. Inflation is about the overall price level rising.

In the consumer price index and the GDP deflator, only final goods and services are counted. In the producer price index, some intermediate goods and services are counted too.

Hyperinflation is out of control inflation. Different people have different definitions of when it starts, but very high monthly inflation is hyperinflation. Hyperinflation makes currency worthless. It is important to remember that hyperinflation breaks down financial intermediation. When there is very high inflation, lenders don't want to lend and businesspeople can't get investment loans.

Even though any of the variables in the $MV = PY_R$ could change, prices and money are the most volatile. When prices rise it is almost always the quantity of money. In the long run, we expect money supply to cause inflation. This is true even though $v$ does sometimes change.

When you see a variable with a little arrow over it, the arrow means that it is a growth rate for that variable.

## Practice Exercises: Learning by Doing

1. If the price level is 134 in 2008 and 149 in 2009, what is the inflation rate?

2. If the nominal rate of interest was 7% last year and the inflation rate was 6%, what was the real rate of interest?

3. Why does volatility in the inflation rate make it harder for businesses to get loans?

4. Why do economists think that increases in the money supply cause prices to rise instead of changes to other variables?

5. If you see that computer prices have increased by 3% but your professor argues that real prices of computers have fallen, what could your professor's argument be?

6. Provide three historical examples of incredible hyperinflation.

| Year | CPI-U. Seasonally Adjusted. January |
|---|---|
| 1999 | 164.70 |
| 2000 | 169.30 |
| 2001 | 175.60 |
| 2002 | 177.70 |
| 2003 | 182.60 |
| 2004 | 186.30 |
| 2005 | 191.80 |
| 2006 | 199.40 |
| 2007 | 203.574 |
| 2008 | 212.495 |
| 2009 | 212.174 |

7. If your older brother paid $27,000 for 1 year of college in 1999, what is the real price of his college in 2009? (Use the data in the previous table.)

8. The price of pocket calculators has fallen from $375 in 1972 to just a few dollars in 2009. Why doesn't that prove that the United States has had deflation instead of inflation?

9. What does the policy maker have to do to the money supply if velocity has doubled and he wants to keep price constant?

10. Why is it hard to stop inflation?

# Multiple-Choice Questions

1. Inflation is an increase in the _____.
   a. price of food and energy
   b. price of the most important goods
   c. price of some goods
   d. average level of prices

2. The formula for the inflation rate is _____.
   a. $(P_2 - P_1)/P_1$
   b. $(P_1 - P_2)/P_1$
   c. $(P_1 - P_2)/P_2$
   d. $(P_2 - P_1)/P_2$

3. Which of the following is *not* a price index?
   a. CPI
   b. GDP deflator
   c. bond index
   d. PPI

4. Which of the following price indices measures the prices of not only final goods but also intermediate goods?
   a. CPI
   b. GDP deflator
   c. PPI
   d. Government Services Index

5. What is the difference between real and nominal interest rates?
   a. Real interest rates are on loans for which the borrower has put up collateral. Nominal interest rates aren't.
   b. Real interest rates adjust for changes in GDP. Nominal interest rates don't.
   c. Real interest rates are adjusted for inflation. Nominal interest rates aren't.
   d. Real interest rates are for loans between the Fed and banks. Nominal interest rates are between individuals and banks.

6. If you borrowed money with at a 12% *nominal* interest rate and the inflation rate is 7%, what is your *real* interest rate?
   a. 12%
   b. 5%
   c. 19%
   d. 5%

7. Which of the following countries had very high inflation rates between 2002 and 2007?
   a. Zimbabwe, Japan, China
   b. Zimbabwe, Angola, Guinea
   c. Zimbabwe, Kiribati, Japan
   d. Zimbabwe, Angola, China

8. One reason that economists posit (say) that inflation is caused by the growth of the money supply is _____.
   a. the price level and the money supply correlate very well
   b. price are inversely related to the money supply
   c. money growth rates don't correlate to the inflation rate
   d. countries that print lots of money don't always have inflation

9. If there is inflation, then *all* prices will increase.
    a. True
    b. False

10. Commodity money is _____.
    a. money that is backed by some commodity such as gold or silver
    b. money that can be used to buy a commodity such as gold or silver
    c. money that is *not* backed by a commodity such as gold or silver
    d. money that has nothing to do with gold or silver

11. Normally velocity is pretty constant, but if people are worried about inflation and begin spending even faster, what would happen to velocity?
    a. Velocity is still unchanged.
    b. Velocity only changes when interest rates change.
    c. Velocity increases.
    d. Velocity decreases.

12. The idea that in the long run "money is neutral" means _____.
    a. money isn't very important to people in the long run
    b. in the long run, changes in money supply don't affect how much a country produces
    c. changes in the inflation rate do not affect the interest rate
    d. debt, interest, inflation, and the money supply are all unrelated

13. Money illusion refers to the idea that _____.
    a. people don't know how happy they will be when they make more money
    b. people can't tell the difference between U.S., Canadian, and New Zealand dollars
    c. people can confuse inflation with increases in demand for their products
    d. carpenters never know when they are getting ripped off by tailors and vice versa

14. If there is 10% inflation and Susie gets a 10% raise but acts as if she has *real* wage increase, then she has _____.
    a. performance anxiety
    b. fiscal illusion
    c. money illusion
    d. risk aversion

15. When a country uses inflation to reduce the real value of its debts this is known as _____.
    a. deflating the debt
    b. monetizing the debt
    c. listing the debt
    d. distributing the debt

16. Volatile inflation redistributes wealth and also _____.
    a. surprises policy makers at the Fed
    b. surprises no one
    c. makes people want to hold more cash
    d. makes it difficult to borrow and lend money

17. When inflation gets high and volatile it is more difficult to borrow and lend money. This is important because _____.
    a. people can't smooth consumption
    b. people can't invest for the future
    c. people can't buy goods that are too expensive to pay for without loans (houses and such)
    d. All of the answers are correct.

18. If you have $1,000 hidden under your mattress (gained from under the table earnings) and there is 10% inflation, was this money taxed this year?
    a. Yes, it was taxed because inflation ate away your spending power.
    b. Yes, it was taxed because the government will find your money anyway.
    c. No, it wasn't taxed because inflation isn't a tax.
    d. No, it wasn't taxed because government can't find this money.

19. Imagine that you buy a stock for $100. The price level doubles and your stock price doubles. Which of the following is correct?
    a. The real value of your stock doubled, and you pay no taxes on your stock.
    b. The real value of your stock stayed the same and you pay no taxes on your stock.
    c. The real value of your stock doubled and you pay taxes on your stock holdings.
    d. The real value of your stock stayed the same and you pay taxes on the inflated price.

20. When governments realize that inflation has gotten out of control, the inflation
    a. is easy to stop.
    b. is not painful to stop.
    c. is painful to stop.
    d. is expected to stop.

## Short-Answer Questions

21. If the price level is 200 in year 1 and 205.7 in year 2, what is the inflation rate?

22. Using the following table, find the *real* rate of interest.

| Nominal Rate | Inflation Rate | Real Rate |
|---|---|---|
| 22 | 25 | |
| 1 | .01 | |
| .5 | 2 | |
| 17 | 12 | |

23. In December 2005, the CPI was 197.7. In January 1975, the CPI 52.3. If your dad made $2.25 an hour in January 1975, what would his real wage be in December 2005?

24. Fill out the following table. The government is trying to keep prices stable, what does the money supply need to be in both cases?

| Year | M | V | P | Y |
|---|---|---|---|---|
| 1 | | 2 | 100 | 1,000 |
| 2 | | 3 | 100 | 1,200 |

25. Why do we normally expect velocity to be pretty constant or at least only slowly changing?

26. How does unexpected inflation differ from expected inflation?

27. Who gets hurt in the cases shown in the following table regarding long-term loans?

| E($\pi$) | $\pi$ | Who gets hurt |
|---|---|---|
| 12 | 8 | |
| 5 | 8 | |
| 13 | 13 | |

28. Inflation isn't painful if everyone knows the rate. Why wouldn't everyone know the rate?

29. What does the policy maker have to do to the money supply if velocity has halved and she wants to keep price constant?

**30.** Stopping inflation is painful for both businesses and workers. Why is this?

**31.** If you see that a country has only short-term loans, what would you expect that the inflation rate is and why?

# Answer Key

## Answers to Practice Exercises: Learning by Doing

1. $(149 - 134)/134 = .11194 \times 100 = 11.194\%$.

   **Topic: Defining and Measuring Inflation**

2. Real rate of interest $= 7\% - 6\% = 1\%$.

   **Topic: Inflation Redistributes Wealth**

3. Volatility in the inflation rate makes it difficult for businesses to get loans because it makes it difficult to predict the real rate of inflation. Both borrowers and lenders want to make sure that they don't get hurt by changes in the inflation rate, but they can't make the prediction.

   **Topic: Inflation Redistributes Wealth**

4. Economists think that changes to the money supply are the main cause of inflation because changes to the money supply track very closely to the inflation rate, and velocity is based on very slow changing things such as how easy it is to find ATM or how often workers get paid.

   **Topic: The Cause of Inflation**

5. The price of computers may have increased by 3%, but the computer you purchase today is very different from a computer purchased even a few years ago. Newer computers are faster, have more memory, more features, and the batteries on the laptops last much longer.

   **Topic: Price Confusion and Money Illusion**

6. Zimbabwe, Hungary, and Germany have all had serious hyperinflation.

   **Topic: Inflation in the United States and Around the World**

7. $(212.174/164.70) \times \$27,000 = \$34,782.62$. Remember that when you are converting past prices to current prices, the number is probably getting bigger. That means that the bigger number is in the denominator and the smaller one in the numerator. Then just multiply by the original price.

   **Topic: Defining and Measuring Inflation**

8. The fall in the price of pocket calculators doesn't mean that the United States has experienced deflation. Pocket calculators are just one item. Inflation measures *lots* of prices.

   **Topic: Defining and Measuring Inflation**

9. You would want to halve the money supply.

   **Topic: The Quantity Theory of Money**

10. Inflation is tough to stop because individuals and firms are expecting inflation to continue. Governments have some interest in keeping inflation high so they can monetize the debt. Therefore, wage contracts, pricing contracts, and new debt contracts are all written with the expectation of inflation. When the inflation doesn't occur there is a redistribution of wealth, and some firms may mistake the *disinflation* as decreased demand for their products. That would mean that those firms would lay off workers.

**Topic: Inflation Is Painful to Stop**

## Answers to Multiple-Choice Questions

1. **d, Topic: Defining and Measuring Inflation**
2. **a, Topic: Defining and Measuring Inflation**
3. **c, Topic: Price Indexes**
4. **c, Topic: Price Indexes**
5. **c, Topic: Inflation Redistributes Wealth**
6. **d, Topic: Inflation Redistributes Wealth**
7. **b, Topic: Inflation in the United States and Around the World**
8. **a, Topic: The Cause of Inflation**
9. **b, Topic: Defining and Measuring Inflation**
10. **a, Topic: The Cause of Inflation**
11. **c, Topic: The Quantity Theory of Money**
12. **b, Topic: The Quantity Theory of Money**
13. **c, Topic: Price Confusion and Money Illusion**
14. **c, Topic: Price Confusion and Money Illusion**
15. **b, Topic: Inflation Redistributes Wealth**
16. **d, Topic: Inflation Redistributes Wealth**
17. **d, Topic: Inflation Redistributes Wealth**
18. **a, Topic: Inflation Redistributes Wealth**
19. **d, Topic: Inflation Interacts with Other Taxes**
20. **c, Topic: Inflation Is Painful to Stop**

## Answers to Short-Answer Questions

21. $(205.7 - 200)/200 = .0285 \times 100 = 2.85\%$.

    **Topic: Defining and Measuring Inflation**

**22.**

| Nominal Rate | Inflation Rate | Real Rate |
|---|---|---|
| 22 | 25 | –3% |
| 1 | .01 | .99% |
| .5 | 2 | –1.5% |
| 17 | 12 | 5% |

**Topic: Inflation Redistributes Wealth**

**23.** (197.7/52.3) × $2.25 = $8.50.

**Topic: Defining and Measuring Inflation**

**24.**

| Year | M | V | P | Y |
|---|---|---|---|---|
| 1 | 50,000 | 2 | 100 | 1,000 |
| 2 | 40,000 | 3 | 100 | 1,200 |

**Topic: The Quantity Theory of Money**

**25.** The number of ATM's, how often workers get paid, and other slowly changing things affect velocity. Changes to money supply affect prices quickly.

**Topic: The Cause of Inflation**

**26.** Unexpected inflation causes wealth redistribution as long-term contracts are thrown off by the difference in real and nominal interest rates. Also, unexpected inflation is easy to confuse with changes in demand for a firm's products.

**Topic: Inflation Redistributes Wealth**

**27.**

| $E(\pi)$ | $\pi$ | Who gets hurt |
|---|---|---|
| 12 | 8 | *Borrowers* thought that inflation would make their real debt payments go down, but that didn't happen. |
| 5 | 8 | Lenders receive *real* payments that are below what was agreed to. |
| 13 | 13 | No one gets hurt in this case. Inflation is what it was expected to be. |

**Topic: Inflation Redistributes Wealth**

28. People might not know the rate of inflation because there are other business variables that are important. Demand for business's products or a person's work might be changing at the same time as the inflation rate. Also, not everyone takes macroeconomics.

   **Topic: Price Confusion and Money Illusion**

29. If velocity halved, then you would need to double the money supply.

   **Topic: The Quantity Theory of Money**

30. Stopping inflation is painful for both businesses and workers because long-term contracts have been written with inflation expectations. Also, firms may confuse disinflation (a reduction in the inflation rate, not deflation) as reduced demand for their goods. That would cause firms to cut back production and lay off workers.

   **Topic: Inflation Is Painful to Stop**

31. A country that has only short-term loans probably has high and variable interest rates. These high and variable interest rates make it difficult for lenders to figure out the real rate of interest, so they are wary of lending for long periods.

   **Topic: Inflation Redistributes Wealth**

# 12 (26)

# Business Fluctuations and the Dynamic Aggregate Demand–Aggregate Supply Model

## Why Learn about Business Fluctuations?

If the economy is booming, almost all college grads will easily find a job. If the economy is not booming, then even students in practical majors may have trouble getting jobs. Journalism majors and political scientists can look forward to careers in which the economy is a topic. Social justice majors will want to understand how business cycles work so they can think of effects on the disadvantaged. Social justice majors won't be able to advocate for people during recessions if they don't understand how the recessions work. Business majors will find that actually understanding business fluctuations helps them think about when to release new products and what type of products to release.

## Summary

**Business fluctuations** are fluctuations in the short-run growth rate around its long-run average. Sometimes, the economy is booming and growth is above the long-run average. Sometimes, growth is below average, or even negative. That is a recession. **Recessions** are prolonged negative growth rates or significant widespread declines in real income and employment.

There are two types of shocks that can generate business fluctuations, real shocks and *aggregate demand shocks*. Real shocks shift the Solow growth curve. Aggregate demand shocks shift the aggregate demand curve.

This chapter may seem complex, but if you remember that real shocks shift the Solow growth curve and aggregate demand shocks shift the aggregate demand curve, then everything else is learning how to read the graphs. Thus, we have provided many learning by doing questions in this chapter to give you practice with shifting the curves and reading the diagrams.

A **real shock** is any shock that affects the *potential* of an economy to produce goods and services. Recall from Chapter 6 that growth depends on capital, labor, and ideas/technology; so anything that affects these primary inputs, or how much output these inputs can create, is a real shock. If avian flu or the "swine" flu were to seriously reduce the labor force, for example, that would be a real shock. The weather, mass strikes, and dramatic new technologies are, like cell phones, other examples of real shocks.

A positive real shock increases the economy's potential ability to produce goods and services. A positive real shock shifts the Solow growth curve to the right. A negative real shock decreases the economy's potential ability to produce goods and services. A negative real shock shifts the Solow growth curve to the left. Real business cycle theory emphasizes real shocks and thus shifts in the Solow growth curve as a source of business fluctuations.

The **Solow growth rate** is an economy's potential growth rate. The *Solow growth curve* (Chapters 6 and 7) is simply a vertical line at the Solow growth rate. The curve is vertical because long-run growth is not affected by inflation. Intuitively, the Solow growth curve is just the rate (not amount) that the country can sustainably increase its production over time.

The **aggregate demand curve** is a curve or line that shows all the combinations of inflation and real growth that are consistent with a specified rate of spending growth. Intuitively, the aggregate demand curve says that if spending is growing by 10% a year this means either a) prices are rising by 10% a year and there is zero growth in the amount of real goods, b) the quantity of real goods is rising by 10% a year and prices are not rising at all, or c) there is any other combination of inflation and real growth such that the numbers add up to 10% (e.g., 5% inflation rate and 5% real growth rate).

The aggregate demand curve slopes down because if spending is growing at 10%, then the lower the inflation rate the greater real growth must be if the total of inflation plus real growth add to increasing by 10% (as it must along an *AD* curve). The aggregated demand curve shifts when the spending growth rate changes. If spending moves from increasing by 5% per year to increasing by 7% per year, then the aggregate demand curve would shift out.

An aggregate demand shock is a shift in the growth rate of consumer, business, or government spending. A positive aggregate demand shock increases the growth rate of spending and shifts the aggregate demand curve outward (to the right). A negative aggregate demand shock decreases the growth rate of spending and shifts the aggregate demand curve inward (to the left).

Aggregate demand shocks do not affect the potential growth rate of an economy (and thus do not shift the Solow growth curve) because aggregate demand shocks do not affect labor, capital, technology, or the productivity of these inputs. However, aggregate demand shocks can generate business fluctuations when prices and wages are sticky (do not adjust instantly or quickly). Thus, aggregate demand shocks can mean that, in the short run, the economy can grow slower (or even faster) than the potential growth rate.

The **short-run aggregate supply curve** shows the relationship between inflation and real growth during the period when prices are sticky. New Keynesian theory emphasizes changes to aggregate demand, sticky prices, and sticky wages as sources of business fluctuations.

**Endowment effect** is just the idea that people don't like to lose their starting position. The endowment effect is explained in the parable of the angry professor. Recall that the parable of the angry professor is a story about how both *nominal* and *real* wages matter.

*Components of AD: C + I + G + NX*. You will notice that many of the components of aggregate demand are the same as the components of GDP. (Recall Chapter 5.) This is not an accident. If the spending rate of any of these components changes, the dynamic aggregate demand curve will shift. At first glance, it will seem like all of this is unrelated to the work we did in earlier chapters with the money supply and inflation, but remember that $\vec{v}$ is the spending rate. The *AD* curve shifts outward when the consumption, investment, government, or net export *spending rates* increase.

## Key Terms

**business fluctuations** are fluctuations in the growth rate of real GDP around its trend growth rate

**recession** is a significant, widespread decline in real income and employment

**the Solow growth rate** is an economy's potential growth rate, the rate of economic growth that would occur given flexible prices and the existing real factors of production

**real shock**, also called a productivity shock, is any shock that increases or decreases the potential growth rate

**aggregate demand curve** shows all the combinations of inflation and real growth that are consistent with a specified rate of spending growth

**short-run aggregate supply (SRAS) curve** shows the positive relationship between inflation and real growth during the period when prices are sticky

**endowment effect** is when people attach special importance to their starting point and have an especially strong dislike for losing that position

**menu costs** are the costs of changing prices

## Tips, Traps, and Hints

Sometimes students are confused by the word *dynamic*. They shouldn't be confused. The word just means that things are changing. Dynamic aggregate demand is aggregate demand when things are changing. In this case, growth is changing. The changing growth is why we use growth *rates*. The arrow over a variable means growth rate. So $\overline{M}$ is just the growth rate of money. Just remember that these models are all in terms of *rates*.

Make sure that you draw the *SRAS* with a sharply upward sloping bend. If you don't draw the *SRAS* curve this way, it looks like you can easily get more output by increasing the inflation rate forever. We will see in later chapters that this is not always the case. This is a subtle point but worth knowing.

Make sure that you understand that changes to the inflation rate don't really affect the dynamic aggregate demand curve. The dynamic aggregate demand curve affects the inflation rate.

If you are a visual thinker, then you should consider practicing drawing the graphs in color. That actually helps many students who are visual thinkers.

## Practice Exercises: Learning by Doing

1. Draw the basic diagram: A Solow growth curve, a dynamic aggregate demand curve, and a short-run aggregate supply curve. (Recall that drawing this from memory multiple times will help you pass the exam.) Any graphing question about the "long-run dynamic equilibrium" for an economy will probably lead to drawing this graph.

2. Show what happens to the economy when there are real shocks to the economy. Shift the Solow growth curve. What would shift the Solow growth curve?

3. Explain what each of the following variables means: $\vec{M}, \vec{v}, \vec{P}$, and $\vec{Y}_R$.

4. Explain the parable of the angry professor. How does it relate to real and nominal wages?

5. Why is the Solow growth curve vertical in our graph?

6. Why is *AD* downward sloping? What are the factors that shift the dynamic *AD* curve?

7. Draw the long-run dynamic equilibrium for an economy twice (side by side). Show how the effect of a decrease in the Solow growth curve would provide a different recession than a decrease in the dynamic aggregate demand curve.

8. Draw the market for labor. (Draw the supply and demand graph for workers.) Shift the demand for labor inward (to the left). Are more workers hired if wages are sticky or flexible?

9. If output decreased and the inflation rate increased, did the Solow growth curve shift or did the dynamic aggregate demand curve shift?

10. Show the effect of an unexpected increase in the money growth rate.

11. How did the change in expected inflation affect the economy during the 1930's? Show this graphically.

12. Draw the basic diagram: A Solow growth curve, a dynamic aggregate demand curve, and a short-run aggregate supply curve. (Recall that drawing this from memory multiple times will help you pass the exam.) If the Solow growth curve is at 4% and the inflation rate is at 6%, what is aggregate demand?

## Multiple-Choice Questions

1. Business cycle fluctuations are
   a. up and down changes to the economy.
   b. increases and decreases in prices.
   c. increases and decreases in inflation rates.
   d. changes to the long-run growth rate *not* the long-run rate.

2. The two causes of business cycle fluctuations discussed in the text are
   a. real shocks and aggregate demand shocks.
   b. monetary shocks and real shocks.
   c. monetary shocks and demand shocks.
   d. severe shocks and demand shocks.

3. When drawing the long-run dynamic equilibrium graph, what is on the vertical (*y* axis)?
   a. prices
   b. GDP
   c. employment
   d. inflation rate

4. When drawing the long-run dynamic equilibrium graph, what is on the horizontal (*x*-axis)?
   a. inflation
   b. expected inflation
   c. GDP
   d. GDP growth rate

5. Which of the following shift(s) the Solow growth curve?
   a. drought
   b. expectations
   c. monetary policy
   d. animal spirits

6. Which of the following shift(s) the dynamic aggregate demand curve?
   a. hurricanes
   b. new technology
   c. better trading opportunities
   d. increase in confidence

7. If average growth has been 2.5%, and this year's growth is 2.5%, then the Solow growth curve will
   a. shift right by 1%.
   b. stay where it is.
   c. shift right by 2.5%.
   d. shift left by 2.5%.

8. The *SRAS* curve is upward sloping because
   a. the government can make people work more when it wants to.
   b. people don't want to work when the economy is booming.
   c. prices and wages are sticky.
   d. All of the answers are correct.

9. If nominal spending growth is 5%, and inflation is 1%, what is real growth?
   a. 6%
   b. 5%
   c. 4%
   d. 3%

10. Sticky wages and prices are emphasized
    a. in real business cycle theory.
    b. in New Keynesian theory.
    c. both in real business cycle theory and new Keynesian theory.
    d. neither in real business cycle theory nor new Keynesian theory.

11. Which of the following will lead to less employment?
    a. Aggregate demand decreases and wages are flexible.
    b. Aggregate demand decreases and wages are sticky.
    c. Aggregate demand increases and wages are flexible.
    d. Aggregate demand increases and wages are sticky.

12. What is the effect of inflation on dynamic equilibrium of the economy?
    a. Inflation shifts the SRAS rightward.
    b. Unexpected inflation shifts the *SRAS* rightward.
    c. Inflation shifts the *SRAS* leftward.
    d. Unexpected inflation shifts the SRAS leftward.

**13.** If the Fed unexpectedly increases inflation
   a. *SRAS* will temporarily shift to the left.
   b. *SRAS* will permanently shift to the left.
   c. *SRAS* will permanently shift to the right.
   d. *SRAS* will permanently shift to the right.

**14.** If the economy is in a recession that has decreased output and increased prices, that would be caused by
   a. an inward shift of the Solow growth curve.
   b. an outward shift of the Solow growth curve.
   c. an inward shift of the dynamic aggregate demand curve.
   d. an outward shift of the dynamic aggregate demand curve.

**15.** New technology has an immediate effect on which of these curves?
   a. short-run aggregate supply curve
   b. dynamic inflation
   c. Solow growth curve
   d. dynamic aggregate demand

**16.** Unexpected inflation affects
   a. the long-run ability of a country to produce goods and services.
   b. the long-run and short-run ability of a country to produce goods and services.
   c. the short-run ability of a country to produce goods and services.
   d. None of the answers is correct.

**17.** If nominal spending equals 6%, and the real growth rate equals 4%, what is the inflation rate?
   a. 4%
   b. 10%
   c. 2%
   d. 2/3%

**18.** If the inflation rate is 20%, and the real growth rate equals 12%, what is the nominal spending rate?
   a. 8%
   b. 12%
   c. 20%
   d. 32%

19. If there is a negative shock to aggregate demand, which of the following scenarios would occur in the short run?
    a. The inflation rate would increase and growth rates would decrease.
    b. The inflation rate would increase and growth rates would increase.
    c. The inflation rate would be unaffected but growth rates would decrease.
    d. The inflation rate would decrease and growth rates would decrease.

20. If there is a negative structural shift (to the Solow growth curve), which of the following scenarios would occur in the short-run?
    a. The inflation rate would increase and growth rates would decrease.
    b. The inflation rate would increase and growth rates would increase.
    c. The inflation rate would be unaffected but growth rates would decrease.
    d. The inflation rate would decrease and growth rates would decrease.

21. Imagine that output has increased and the inflation rate is down. What sort of shock is that likely to be?
    a. negative real shock
    b. positive real shock
    c. negative *AD* shock
    d. positive *AD* shock

22. The costs that firms face when they change prices is called
    a. production costs.
    b. trust costs.
    c. menu costs.
    d. unexpected costs.

23. What happens to *SRAS* when people expect the inflation rate to increase from 4% to 8%?
    a. It shifts in.
    b. It shifts out.
    c. It is unaffected by expectations.
    d. It is unclear what role expectations have in the dynamic model.

24. If fear causes individuals to spend less and firms to invest less, that would have which of the following effects?
    a. *AD* shifts in.
    b. *AD* shifts out.
    c. *SRAS* shifts in.
    d. Solow growth curve shifts in.

25. The Great Depression was the result of
    a. *neither AD* shocks nor real shocks.
    b. mostly *AD* shocks and some real shocks.
    c. *AD* shocks but not real shocks.
    d. real shocks but not *AD* shocks.

## Short-Answer Questions

26. What are the two types of causation for economic fluctuations?

27. Explain what shifts the Solow growth curve, the dynamic aggregate demand curve, and the short-run aggregate supply curve.

28. What happens to the growth rate when the Fed permanently increases the inflation rate?

29. Explain how the real business cycle leads to economic fluctuations.

30. What factors shift the dynamic *AD* curve?

31. In the real business cycle model, what do shocks to aggregate demand do?

**32.** What do economists mean by sticky wages and prices?

**33.** Why does unexpected inflation cause increased output, but expected inflation doesn't?

**34.** The following graph is purported to show the effect of a decrease in money supply, but in fact has several mistakes. Find the mistakes and don't make them on your own exam!

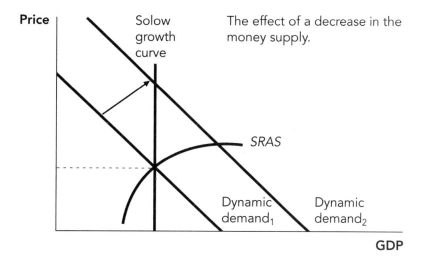

**35.** Show the effect of declining consumer confidence and decreased inflation rate during the Great Depression.

# Answer Key

## Answers to Practice Exercises: Learning by Doing

1.

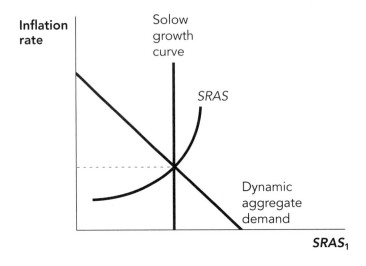

**Topic: The New Keynesian Model**

2. Real shocks to the economy shift the Solow growth curve. Recall that when the Solow growth curve shifts, so does the *SRAS*. Anything that effects an economy's ability to produce will shift the Solow growth curve. Some examples would be changing technology, drought, changes to population, education, and war.

**Topic: The Solow Growth Curve**

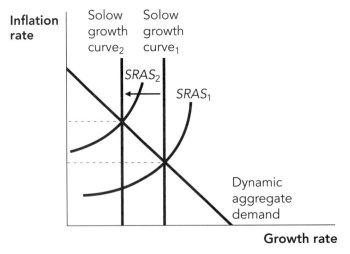

3. $\overrightarrow{M}$ is the rate of money growth; $\vec{v}$ is the rate of velocity growth or the rate of spending growth; $\overrightarrow{P}$ is the rate of price growth or inflation; and $\overrightarrow{Y}_R$ is the rate of real GDP growth.

**Topic: The Dynamic Aggregate Demand Curve**

4. The parable of the angry professor is a story about an economics professor who takes a 3% pay cut twice. The first time it happens he is really mad, but the second time it happens he isn't mad. The first time there is no inflation but his nominal salary is cut. The second time there is 6% inflation, but he gets a 3% raise. That means that the professor's salary fell by 3% both times. But the second time he feels better. This shows that both nominal and real wages matter.

**Topic: The Short-Run Aggregate Supply Curve**

5. The Solow growth curve is vertical in our graph because in the long run printing more money doesn't help an economy produce goods and services.

**Topic: The Solow Growth Curve**

6. The dynamic $AD$ is downward sloping because it shows the amount of nominal amount of goods and services that the whole economy can purchase. More inflation means that firms, individuals, and governments can purchase a higher dollar amount of goods, even though that would not be more goods in real terms. Several factors shift the dynamic $AD$ curve. They include changes to the inflation rate, the consumption rate, investment rate, government spending rate, or net exports rate.

**Topic: The Dynamic Aggregate Demand Curve**

7. See the following long-run dynamic equilibrium. New curves are in bold. Notice that when the Solow growth curve shifts inward the inflation rate increases, but when the aggregate demand curve shifts inward the inflation rate decreases.

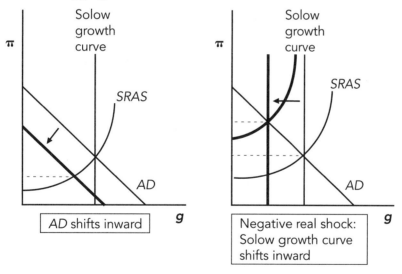

**Topic: Real Shocks and the Solow Growth Curve**

**8.**

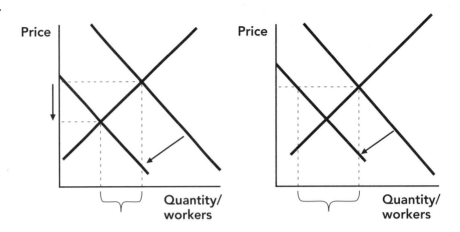

With flexible wages (Panel A), wages fall but more workers are hired (though not as many as before). With sticky wages (Panel B), $Q_s$ does not equal $Q_d$. Wages don't fall, but fewer workers are hired.

**Topic: The Solow Growth Curve**

**9.** If output decreased and the inflation rate increased, then $AD$ would have shifted in. This is shown in Panel A of the following graph. If output had decreased and the inflation rate had increased, then that would be a real shock (Panel B).

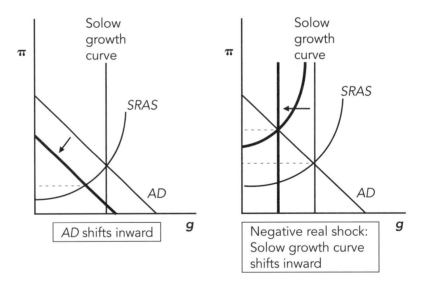

**Topic: Real Shocks and the Solow Growth Curve**

10.

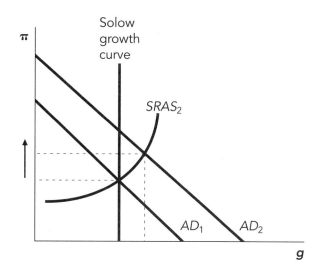

**Topic: An Increase in the New Keynesian Model**

11.

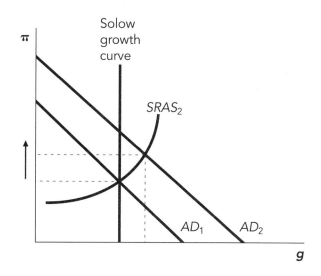

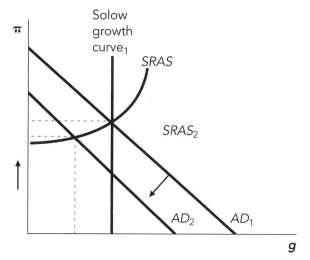

**Topic: Aggregate Demand Shocks and Real Shocks**

12.

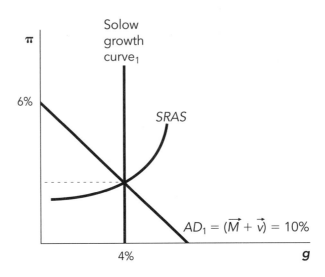

Topic: The New Keynesian Model

## Answers to Multiple-Choice Questions

1. d, Topic: Introduction *and* A Skeleton Model

2. a, Topic: A Skeleton Model *and* The Real Business Cycle Model: Real Shocks and the Solow Growth Curve *and* The New Keynesian Model

3. d, Topic: A Skeleton Model

4. d, Topic: A Skeleton Model

5. a, Topic: The Real Business Cycle Model: Real Shocks and the Solow Growth Curve

6. d, Topic: Shocks to Aggregate Demand in New Keynesian Model

7. b, Topic: The Real Business Cycle Model: Real Shocks and the Solow Growth Curve

8. c, Topic: The Short-Run Aggregate Supply Curve

9. c, Topic: The Dynamic Aggregate Demand Curve

10. b, Topic: The Short-Run Aggregate Supply Curve

11. b, The Short-Run Aggregate Supply Curve

12. d, Topic: Shocks to Aggregate Demand in the New Keynesian Model

13. d, Topic: Shocks to Aggregate Demand in the New Keynesian Model

14. a, Topic: The Real Business Cycle Model: Real Shocks and the Solow Growth Curve *and* Shocks to Aggregate Demand in the New Keynesian Model

15. c, Topic: The Real Business Cycle Model: Real Shocks and the Solow Growth Curve

16. c, Topic: The Dynamic Aggregate Demand Curve
17. c, Topic: The Dynamic Aggregate Demand Curve
18. d, Topic: The Dynamic Aggregate Demand Curve
19. d, Topic: The Dynamic Aggregate Demand Curve
20. a, Topic: The Solow Growth Curve
21. b, Topic: Real Business Cycle Model: Shifts in the Solow Growth Model *and* Shocks to Aggregate Demand in the New Keynesian Model
22. c, Topic: The New Keynesian Model
23. a, Topic: The Short-Run Aggregate Supply Curve
24. a, Topic: Shocks to Aggregate Demand in the New Keynesian Model
25. b, Topic: Understanding the Great Depression: Aggregate Demand Shocks and Real Shocks

## Answers to Short-Answer Questions

26. Economic fluctuations come in two types: Those caused by real shocks or shocks to an economy's ability to produce, and those caused by changes to aggregate demand.

    **Topic: A Skeleton Model**

27. The Solow growth curve is shifted by anything that affects an economy's ability to produce. This could include new technology or rainfall. The dynamic aggregate demand curve is shifted by changes to spending patterns—Consumption, Investment, Government, Net Exports, or the inflation rate. The short-run aggregate supply curve is affected by inflation rate and anything that affects the Solow growth curve.

    **Topic: The Solow Growth Curve *and* The Dynamic Aggregate Demand Curve**

28. When the Fed permanently increases the inflation rate, several things happen. First, if the change is *unexpected*, the *AD* curve will shift out, but the *SRAS* won't shift immediately. That means that there will be some inflation, but also some increase in output. After a while, unexpected inflation becomes expected inflation. When the new inflation rate is expected, output is no longer increased. The economy just has higher inflation.

    **Topic: An Increase in $\overline{M}$ in the New Keynesian Model**

29. Real business cycles are fluctuations in the economy's growth rate caused by fluctuations in the economy's ability to produce. For example, when India was mostly agricultural, fluctuations in rainfall affected India's growth rate.

    **Topic: The Real Business Cycle Model: Real Shocks and the Solow Growth Curve**

30. The following factors shift the dynamic AD curve.
    > Changes in the money growth rate
    > Changes in consumer / business confidence
    > Changes in taxes
    > Changes in government spending
    > Changes in export growth
    > Changes in import growth

    **Topic: The Dynamic Aggregate Demand Curve**

31. In real business cycle theory, shocks to aggregate demand are not emphasized, but shocks to the Solow growth curve are.

    **Topic: The Real Business Cycle Model: Real Shocks and the Solow Growth Curve**

32. When economists talk about sticky wages and prices, they mean that sometimes nominal wages and prices can't change easily. They will eventually change, but not right away. One reason is that there are menu costs, or costs of constantly changing prices and wages. The other reason is that there are often long-term contracts that prevent wages and prices from constantly changing.

    **Topic: The Short-Run Aggregate Supply Curve**

33. When inflation rates increase, not all prices change at the same time. Some prices are stuck. Input prices may be less than the prices on final goods. (Remember this from Chapter 11.) This causes firms to increase output. When inflation is expected, both input and final prices have already risen.

    **Topic: An Increase in $\overline{M}$ in the New Keynesian Model**

34.

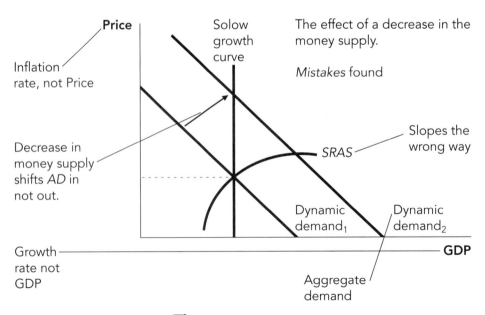

**Topic: An Increase in $\overline{M}$ in the New Keynesian Model**

35. The following graph shows the effect of declining consumer confidence and decreased inflation rate during the Great Depression.

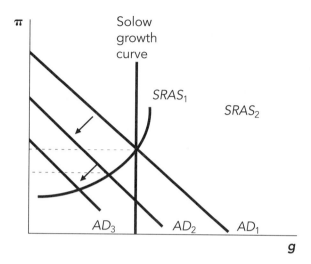

**Topic: Understanding the Great Depression: Aggregate Demand Shocks and Real Shocks: Aggregate Demand Shocks**

# 13 (27)

# The Real Business Cycle Model: Shocks and Transmission Mechanisms

## Why Learn about the Real Business Cycle?

Real Business cycle is part of a bigger explanation of why the economy fluctuates. Understanding business cycles helps students understand what is going on in the world. If the economy is booming, almost all college grads will easily find a job. If the economy is not booming, then even students in very practical majors may have trouble getting jobs. When the economy booms, summer internships are plentiful and pay well. When the economy is in recession, summer internships may be non-existent. Transmission mechanisms make these fluctuations bigger. Students interested in the economy and in policy will be interested in this chapter.

## Summary

Transmission mechanisms magnify shocks. **Transmission mechanisms** are economic forces that can amplify shocks by transmitting them across time and sectors of the economy. **Shocks** are rapid changes in economic conditions that have large effects on the productivity of capital and labor.

There are five major factors that amplify economic shocks:

1) **Intertemporal substitution** reflects how people choose to allocate consumption of goods, work, and leisure across time to maximize well-being. "Make hay when the sun shines" is a saying that reflects the idea of intertemporal substitution. People work more hours and harder when they get a bigger return. Intertemporal substitution means that we respond to negative shocks by working less and to positive shocks by working more, thus magnifying the shock.

2) **Irreversible investments** have high value only under specific conditions—they cannot be easily moved, adjusted, or reversed if conditions change. Shocks, especially

negative shocks, often increase uncertainty, and when we are uncertain we, as businesspeople and workers, are less likely to make big decisions. Thus, a negative shock can reduce investment, especially when investments are hard to reverse. Uncertainty can also cause people to delay making big changes, such as moving to a better job or selling a house.

3) **Labor adjustment costs** are the costs of shifting workers from declining sectors of the economy to growing sectors. Labor adjustment costs can also increase frictional unemployment by raising the costs of moving labor from declining sectors of the economy to growing sectors of the economy.

4) **Time bunching** is the tendency for economic activities to be coordinated at common points in time. Economic activity does not occur evenly across space or time. Every day there is a boom between 9 AM and 5 PM and a bust between 12 AM and 5 AM. Every year there is a boom around Christmas and a bust after New Year. Time bunching occurs because people work better together, and it often makes sense to coordinate production processes. Thus, when one sector of the economy is booming, say because of a positive productivity shock, other sectors tend to follow. The same is true for busts. Thus, bunching through time magnifies shocks.

5) *Sticky wages and prices* are when *nominal* wages and prices don't change quickly, leading to disequilibrium in *real* wages and prices. (Disequilibrium means *not* in equilibrium.) Sticky wages and prices can magnify real shocks. In this case, the growth rate falls because productivity is lower, *and also* because sticky wages create a mismatch between aggregate demand and the Solow growth rate.

## Key Terms

**transmission mechanisms** are economic forces that can amplify shocks by transmitting them across time and sectors of the economy

**shocks** are rapid changes in economic conditions that have large effects on the productivity of capital and labor

**intertemporal substitution** reflects how people choose to allocate consumption of goods, work, and leisure across time to maximize well-being

**irreversible investments** have high value only under specific conditions—they cannot be easily moved, adjusted, or reversed if conditions change

**labor adjustment costs** are the costs of shifting workers from declining sectors of the economy to growing sectors

**time bunching** is the tendency for economic activities to be coordinated at common points in time

## Tips, Traps, and Hints

Sometimes, students are confused by the way that shocks affect the economy. Remember that the Solow growth curve is about a growth *rate*. The rate part is really important. When the government increases spending, that pushes the Solow growth curve out for a short time. But the additional growth rate is unsustainable. Sometimes, students think that increasing government spending permanently shifts the Solow growth curve out. In reality, additional government spending can only shift the Solow growth curve out for a short while. Then the Solow growth curve and the aggregate demand curve shift inward.

Don't forget that transmission mechanisms not only amplify shocks, they transmit them through the economy. For example, if your mom is a cosmetic dentist who is thinking of retiring, but suddenly the real estate industry starts booming, your mom may delay retirement. Why? She is going to be able to sell more cosmetic procedures when other people are wealthy. So the boom in real estate is transmitted to the dental industry. This makes the boom even bigger.

Students often confuse *Time Bunching* and *Intertemporal Substitution*. They are closely related.

Short version: Robinson Crusoe intertemporally substitutes. Even though he is by himself on an island, he still does intertemporal substitution. Crusoe doesn't work and play an equal amount each day, but he works harder when it is more productive — he fishes extra hard when there are schools of fish in the water and collects fruit in season.

Time bunching is what is added to intertemporal substitution when Friday (another person) joins Crusoe on the island. If Friday is working, Crusoe has an extra reason to work hard at the same time. The same is true for play. So time bunching is the social aspect of intertemporal substitution.

Another pithy way of saying this is that intertemporal substitution says you work on some days and shop on other days. Time bunching says you work M-F and shop on Saturday-Sunday.

In other words, time bunching is what gets people to coordinate their intertemporal substitution. If there were no social coordination factor, then it would be irrelevant which days you worked and which you shopped. It's the benefits of coordination, which mean that everyone chooses their intertemporal substitution at the same time.

*I*ntertemporal substitution is about the *i*ndividual's decision. The letter "I" helps you remember it. Time *bunching* is about groups, or *bunches* of people, being together.

When this happens at business cycle time scales, it adds to booms and busts.

# Practice Exercises: Learning by Doing

1. What do economists mean by transmission mechanisms?

2. How are transmission mechanisms related to economic fluctuations?

3. What are the five transmission mechanisms?

4. Why are oil shocks less severe now than they were in the 1970's?

5. How does an increase in government spending affect both the aggregate demand curve and the Solow growth curve?

6. How does Christmas shopping explain a transmission mechanism that leads to a seasonal economic fluctuation?

7. What are some real world examples of how uncertainty in the economy caused less spending and less investment?

8. If there is a negative shock to the economy that adversely affects some industries more than others, which transmission mechanism will be most likely to come into play?

9. Show the effect of sticky wages and prices on the economy when there is a negative real shock.

10. Imagine that there is an increase in technology in the manufacturing sector, how could that affect your parent's decision to retire, even if they aren't in manufacturing?

# Multiple-Choice Questions

1. Transmission mechanisms
   a. are the economics of the automobile industry.
   b. lessen the severity of real shocks.
   c. increase the seriousness of real shocks.
   d. None of the answers is correct.

2. Which of the following is a list of the transmission mechanisms?
   a. intertemopral substitution, sticky wages and prices, production costs, irreversible investments
   b. labor adjustment costs, intertemporal substitution, sticky wages and prices, irreversible investments, time bunching
   c. monetary shocks, intertemporal substitution, flexible wages and prices, production costs, and irreversible investment
   d. demand shocks, intertemporal investment, sticky money, time bunching, and labor adjustment costs

3. If there is a transmission mechanism and a negative real shock, then the effect on the economy will be
   a. stronger than without a transmission mechanism.
   b. weaker than without a transmission mechanism.
   c. unaffected by a transmission mechanism.
   d. weakened by some transmission mechanisms but strengthened by others.

4. Everyone working at the same time is an example of which mechanism?
   a. labor adjustment costs
   b. time bunching
   c. irreversible investments
   d. intertemporal substitution

5. Bartenders wanting to work the Friday and Saturday evening shifts is an example of which mechanism?
   a. intertemporal substitution
   b. irreversible investments
   c. sticky wages and prices
   d. time bunching

6. After Hurricane Katrina hit New Orleans and the Gulf Coast, many homeowners waited to rebuild their houses until new building code rules had been enacted. This is an example of which mechanism?
   a. labor adjustment costs
   b. intertemporal substitution
   c. sticky wages and prices
   d. uncertain/irreversible investments

7. If in 2020, interstellar space travel becomes possible and the crab/fish population in Alaska dies out, workers will need to move from Alaska to Sioux Falls, SD (the headquarters of space travel). Which transmission mechanism has the most effect on the economy of losing Alaska fisheries?
   a. labor market adjustment costs
   b. intertemporal substitution
   c. irreversible investments
   d. time bunching

8. Now that you are in college, your mom is thinking of going from part-time work to full-time work outside the home. Which mechanism is at work when she considers whether there have been positive or negative shocks to the economy?
   a. labor market adjustment costs
   b. intertemporal substitution
   c. irreversible investments
   d. time bunching

9. In 2013, the L.A. Clippers (a basketball team) win back to back championships. You and your friends decide to have one giant blowout to celebrate all on one day instead of having a very tiny celebration every day for the rest of year. This would be an example of
   a. labor market adjustment costs.
   b. intertemporal substitution.
   c. irreversible investments.
   d. time bunching.

10. Sticky wages and prices affect which curve?
    a. short-run aggregate supply
    b. dynamic aggregate demand
    c. Both the Solow growth curve and the dynamic aggregate demand curve
    d. the Solow growth curve

11. What is the difference between time bunching and intertemporal substitution?
    a. Time bunching is when you decide to invest or work at the same time as other people because it makes the most sense to do this when other people are around. Intertemporal substitution is when your decision to work when the gains from working all at once are higher than working a little at a time.
    b. Intertemporal substitution is when you decide to invest or work at the same time as other people because it make the most sense to do this when other people are around. Time bunching is when your decision to work because the gains from working all at once are higher than working a little at a time.
    c. Time bunching is when individuals don't move to better positions because it is costly to do so. Intertemporal substitution is when people change their behavior because prices and wages can't change.
    d. Time bunching is when people are afraid to invest, while intertemporal substitution is when people want to work harder when the returns to working are highest.

12. If the price of oil increases by 10%, what is the total effect on the economy?
    a. Over time GDP is 10% less than what it would have been.
    b. Over time GDP is 10% more than what it would have been.
    c. Over time GDP is 1.4% less than what it would have been.
    d. Over time GDP is 1.4% more than what it would have been.

13. How has the deviation of annual rainfall (rainfall shocks) from the long-run average correlated with agricultural output and GDP in the Indian economy?
    a. Rainfall does not correlate with GDP in the Indian economy.
    b. Rainfall, GDP, and agricultural output have a strong positive correlation in India.
    c. Rainfall and GDP in India correlated very well until about 1980; then they correlated less well.
    d. Rainfall correlates negatively with Indian GDP and agricultural production.

14. How has the deviation in the price of oil (oil shocks) from the long-run average correlated with GDP in the U.S. economy?
    a. Oil shocks do not correlate with GDP in the U.S. economy.
    b. Higher oil prices have a strong positive correlation with GDP in the U.S.
    c. Oil prices correlates negatively with U.S. GDP.
    d. Economic recessions lead to oil shocks, not the other way around.

15. Imagine that there is a negative shock to the economy that causes businesses to be especially uncertain about the future. Which curve is affected by this new uncertainty?

    a. short-run aggregate supply curve

    b. nflation demand curve

    c. Solow growth curve

    d. dynamic aggregate demand

16. If there is a negative shock to the economy, firms will want to pay workers less and lower their prices. Sometimes, that is hard to do, and so firms lay workers off and sell even fewer units. This is because of

    a. time bunching.

    b. wage consistency.

    c. labor adjustment costs.

    d. sticky prices and wages.

17. Raju was just laid off from his job as a skilled carpenter. He's thinking about moving to a new city to become a pharmaceutical salesman, but he's unsure if it will really be worth it. What is this an example of?

    a. time bunching

    b. intertemporal substitution

    c. labor adjustment costs

    d. sticky wages and prices

18. Aiden decides to wait to open up his new coffee shop at the point when the economy in his hometown improves. What is this an example of?

    a. time bunching

    a. intertermporal subsitution

    b. labor adjustment costs

    c. sticky wages and prices

    d. irreversible investments

19. Malik is planning to work more hours selling ice cream at the beach in August instead of in November. What is this an example of?

    a. time bunching

    b. intertermporal subsitution

    c. labor adjustment costs

    d. sticky wages and prices

20. If the SRAS curve shifted even more than you would have expected it to when a negative shock occurred, this would probably be caused by

   a. time bunching.

   b. intertermporal subsitution.

   c. labor adjustment costs.

   d. sticky wages and prices.

## Short-Answer Questions

*21. Why would a restaurant owner prefer to open a new restaurant two years after an oil shock hits instead of one year after the oil shock hits?

*22. How is marriage like a decision to build a new factory?[1]

23. Policy in the United States encourages home ownership. How could home ownership exacerbate business cycles?

24. Explain how transmission mechanisms exacerbate economic fluctuations.

25. Draw a graph that shows how an increase in government spending affects both the aggregate demand curve and the Solow growth curve.

[1]Questions marked with a ★ are also end-of-chapter questions.

**26.** Christmas shopping leads to seasonal economic fluctuations. Why doesn't Arbor Day lead to seasonal fluctuations too?

**27.** What are some real world examples of how labor adjustment costs act as transmission mechanisms?

**28.** If there is a negative shock to the economy that adversely affects some industries more than others, which transmission mechanism will be most likely to come into play?

**29.** Show the effect of uncertain and irreversible investments on the economy when there is a negative real shock.

**30.** Imagine that there is a negative shock to the economy. How could a parent desire to return to work after maternity/paternity leave, even if his/her industry isn't directly affected?

# Answer Key

## Answers to Practice Exercises: Learning by Doing

1. Transmission mechanisms are means of making a real shock to the economy spread throughout the economy and magnify the effect of the shock.

   **Topic: Introduction**

2. Transmission mechanisms are related to economic fluctuations in that they magnify real shocks to the economy and make fluctuations bigger.

   **Topic: Introduction**

3. The five transmission mechanisms are sticky wages and prices, labor adjustment costs, intertemporal substitution, time bunching, and irreversible investment.

   **Topic: How Transmission Mechanisms Amplify and Spread Shocks**

4. Oil shocks are less severe now than in the 1970's because the United States uses less oil per $1,000 of GDP even though we use more oil. Also, firms and individuals have had a chance to get used to the idea of oil shocks and are better prepared.

   **Topic: Shocks: Oil Shocks**

5. An increase in government spending affects aggregate demand curve by increasing a main component of the aggregate curve (government spending). Increased government spending affects the Solow growth curve indirectly by encouraging workers and firms to increase effort while the effort pays off.

   **Topic: Intertemporal Substitution**

6. Seasonal fluctuations aren't so different from regular business cycle fluctuations. Christmas is a boom and January is a bust. Individuals work harder leading up to the Christmas season because whatever product you sell is more likely to sell during Christmas than January. But people also are involved in time bunching by doing their shopping when the most variety is available.

   **Topic: Intemporal Substitution *and* Time Bunching**

7. After 9/11 there was a lot of uncertainty. That meant that many firms and individuals were afraid to make irreversible investments. People didn't want to build new factories until they figured out if the terrorist attacks would continue or not.

   **Topic: Uncertainty and Irreversible Investments**

8. If there is a negative shock to the economy that adversely affects some industries more than others, labor adjustment costs are most likely to affect the economy because in this case workers need to move from the most affected industry to other industries.

   **Topic: Labor Adjustment Costs**

9. The effect of sticky wages and prices on the economy when there is a negative real shock is shown in the following graph.

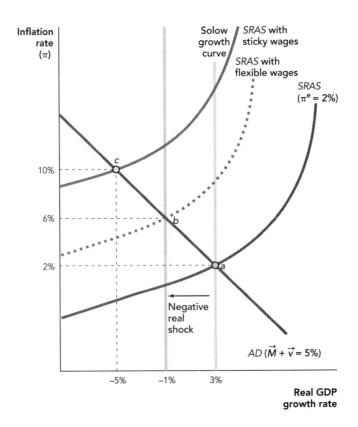

**Topic: Sticky Wages and Prices**

10. An increase in technology in the manufacturing sector, could that affect your parents' decision to retire even if they aren't in manufacturing by spurring the economy. If the economic growth is improving, then your parents' chances to make money improve. That means that they are more likely to delay retirement.

**Topic: How Transmission Mechanisms Amplify and Spread Shocks: Labor Adjustment Costs**

## Answers to Multiple-Choice Questions

1. **c,** Topic: Shocks
2. **b,** Topic: How Transmission Mechanisms Amplify and Spread Shocks
3. **a,** Topic: How Transmission Mechanisms Amplify and Spread Shocks
4. **b,** Topic: Time Bunching
5. **d,** Topic: Time Bunching
6. **d,** Topic: Uncertainty and Irreversible Investments
7. **a,** Topic: Labor Adjustment Costs

8. b, Topic: Intertemporal Substitution

9. d, Topic: Intertemporal Substitution *and* Time Bunching

10. a, Topic: Time Bunching

11. a, Topic: Time Bunching *and* Intertemporal Substitution

12. c, Topic: Oil Shocks

13. c, Topic: Shocks

14. c, Topic: Oil Shocks

15. d, Topic: Uncertainty and Irreversible Investments

16. d , Topic: Sticky Wages and Prices

17. c, Topic: Labor Adjustment Costs

18. b, Topic: Intertemporal Substitution

19. a, Topic: Time Bunching

20. d, How Sticky Wages and Prices

## Answers to Short-Answer Questions

21. A restaurant owner would prefer to open a new restaurant 2 years after an oil shock hits because the economy can be expected to have recovered in 2 years, but not in 1 year. The new restaurant is uncertain and an irreversible investment, so the owner wants to make his investment when people will be wealthy enough to go out for meals.

    **Topic: Uncertainty and Irreversible Investments**

22. Marriage is like a decision to build a new factory in that both decisions are uncertain. Neither is truly irreversible, but they are expensive to get out of. It is difficult to sell a failing factory and expensive to get divorced.

    **Topic: Uncertainty and Irreversible Investments**

23. Home ownership could exacerbate business cycles by encouraging laid off workers to stay in an area without any jobs. The longer those workers stay unemployed, the longer the recession could be.

    **Topic: Intertemporal Substitution**

24. Transmission mechanisms exacerbate economic fluctuations by making negative shocks worse and positive shocks better. They encourage people to work more when the economy is booming and less when the economy is not. They encourage firms to invest more when the economy is already booming and to invest less during recession.

    **Topic: Intertemporal Substitution**

**25.**

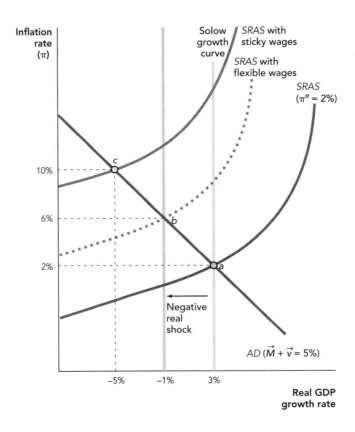

### Topic: Intertemporal Substitution

**26.** Arbor Day doesn't lead to seasonal fluctuations the way that Christmas does because not enough people celebrate Arbor Day. There is no reason for someone who doesn't celebrate Arbor Day to start working harder or investing more in order to intertemporally substitute or time bunch around Arbor Day. Christmas does provide such incentives.

### Topic: Time Bunching

**27.** When the auto industry in Detroit started failing, workers should have left quickly. However, many workers were stuck in Detroit or voluntarily stayed because they hoped that jobs would return.

### Topic: Labor Adjustment Costs

**28.** In this situation, labor market adjustment costs are the most likely transmission mechanism. Workers in the strongly affected industry should switch to the less affected industries. However, labor market adjustment costs are real and will prevent at least some workers from moving.

### Topic: Labor Adjustment Costs

29.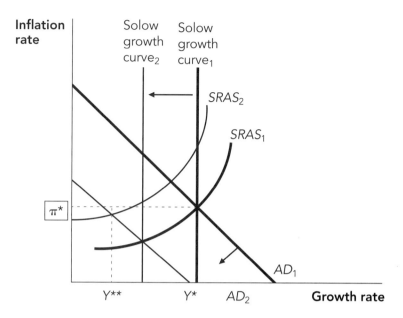

**Topic: Uncertainty and Irreversible Investments**

30. A parent's decision to return to work after maternity/paternity leave would be affected by a negative shock because the opportunities to make money will have changed. When the economy is booming there is a better market for most goods, so firms can hire more workers and pay them more. When the economy is in recession there is less opportunity for that. A parent might decide to stay home if the prevailing wages aren't very high.

**Topic: Labor Adjustment Costs**

# 14 (28)

# The Federal Reserve System and Open Market Operations

## Why Learn about the Federal Reserve System?

The Federal Reserve System is often in the news. The chairman of the Federal Reserve is one of the most powerful people in the world, but isn't elected. Anyone interested in the economy or policy will be interested in this chapter. Banking and bank insolvency have been blamed for the most recent recession. Students get to find out what happened. The Fed has the power to affect both growth rates and short-term economic fluctuations by creating money. Finally, who isn't interested in money?

## Summary

This chapter is about how the Federal Reserve controls the money supply. **Money** is a widely accepted means of payment. It is a liquid asset. A **liquid asset** is an asset that can be used for payments or quickly, and without loss of value, be converted into an asset that can be used for payments.

The money supply is broken into a few different categories.

- Monetary base: currency plus total reserves held at the Fed.
- M1: currency plus checkable deposits
- M2: M1 plus savings deposits, money market mutual funds, and small-time deposits.

Fractional reserve banking means that banks do not hold all of your deposits in their vault. They hold a fraction of your deposits in their vault (or the Fed's vault) and lend the rest of your deposit to other people. The **reserve ratio, RR,** is the ratio of reserves to deposits. The **money multiplier, MM**, is the amount the money supply expands with each dollar increase in reserves. MM = 1/RR. The money multiplier works because any new dollars injected into the economy by the Fed are lent and then lent again.

The following graphic shows how the money multiplier works. The Fed puts $1,000 into the economy. The first bank lends out most of it (all but the 10% reserves). The money ends up in other banks that keep 10% reserves and then lend that money out. You can see that it would be tedious to keep doing this until the last loan is for just a penny.

Thankfully, you can use the money multiplier equation to quickly figure out how much money is being created by the Fed and the banking system.

Explanation of the Money Multiplier: Imagine that the Fed injects $1,000 into the banking system. Assume that all banks have 10% reserves. How much money is created in total?

$1,000 injected
$900 in new loans (90% lent and 10% in reserves)
Total new money = $1,000 + $900 = $1,900

$900 deposited
$810 in new loans that end up in other banks.
Total new money = $1,000 + $900 + $810 = $2,710

$810 deposited
$729 in new loans that end up in other banks.
Total new money = $1,000 + $900 + $810 + $729 = $3,439

Ways for the Fed to control the money supply:

1. Open market operations—the buying and selling of U.S. government bonds on the open market

2. Discount rate lending and the Term Auction Facility—Federal Reserve lending to banks and other financial institutions

3. Required reserves and payment of interest on reserves—changing the minimum ratio of reserves to deposits, which is legally required of banks and other depository institutions, and paying interest on any reserves held by banks at the Fed

**Open market operations** occur when the Fed buys and sells government bonds. The **Federal Funds rate** is the overnight lending rate from one major bank to another. **Discount rate** is the interest rate banks pay when they borrow directly from the Fed.

A **lender of last resort** loans money to banks and other financial institutions when no one else will. **Required reserves** are the minimum percentage of reserves a bank is required to hold, as dictated by the Fed.

A **solvency crisis** occurs when banks become insolvent. An **insolvent bank** has liabilities that are greater than its assets. A **liquidity crisis** occurs when banks are illiquid. An **illiquid bank** has short-term liabilities that are greater than its short-term assets but overall has assets that are greater than its liabilities. It might seem unlikely that this could happen but imagine that a bank has lots of good loans to people that will pay the money back, and yet the bank doesn't have much in the way of reserves. If lots of people want to withdraw money, the bank might have a liquidity crisis even though it is solvent.

**Systemic risk** is the risk that the failure of one financial institution can bring down other institutions, as well. **Moral hazard** occurs when banks and other financial institutions take on too much risk, hoping that the Fed and regulators will bail them out later.

## Key Terms

**money** is a widely accepted means of payment

**liquid asset** is an asset that can be used for payments or, quickly and without loss of value, be converted into an asset that can be used for payments

**fractional reserve banking** is when banks hold only a fraction of deposits in reserve, lending the rest

the **reserve ratio, RR**, is the ratio of reserves to deposits

the **money multiplier, MM**, is the amount the money supply expands with each dollar increase in reserves. MM = 1/RR

**open market operations** occur when the Fed buys and sells government bonds

the **Federal Funds rate** is the overnight lending rate from one major bank to another

**lender of last resort** loans money to banks and other financial institutions when no one else will

**discount rate** is the interest rate banks pay when they borrow directly from the Fed

**solvency crisis** occurs when banks become insolvent

**insolvent bank** has liabilities that are greater than its assets

**liquidity crisis** occurs when banks are illiquid

**illiquid bank** has short-term liabilities that are greater than its short-term assets but overall has assets that are greater than its liabilities

**required reserves** are the portion of their deposits that banks are required by law to hold as reserves

**systemic risk** is the risk that the failure of one financial institution can bring down other institutions as well

**moral hazard** occurs when banks and other financial institutions take on too much risk, hoping that the Fed and regulators will later bail them out

## Tips, Traps, and Hints

There is a lot of vocabulary in this chapter. Make sure you know the vocabulary and practice the money multiplier questions.

It is very easy to confuse yourself regarding questions about open market operations. But drawing a simple picture will help. Draw a silly picture of the Fed (any building) and a person. Then you can easily show the Fed buying bonds from people, which means that the people have more money. Buying bonds increases the money supply. Or you can show the Fed selling bonds and taking money from people, which reduces the money supply. Don't be afraid to draw this graphic on your exam. It will help you make sure you don't miss questions.

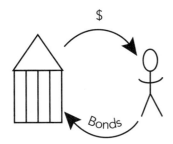

### Fed increases money supply: buying bonds

Drawing simple pictures helps you remember if the Fed's purchase of bonds increases or decreases the money supply.

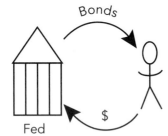

### Fed decreases money supply: sells bonds

One additional tip is that it is worth keeping in mind that credit cards are **not** money. They are short-term loans. This is a common trip-up on exams. Credit cards are not part of M1 or M2.

## Practice Exercises: Learning by Doing

1. What is a central bank? How does the U.S. central bank perform its functions?

2. What are the three most important definitions of money supply and what are they?

3. How is money created directly by the Fed?

4. How is money created indirectly by fractional reserve banking?

5. We think of the Fed as controlling the size of the money supply. Explain how the Fed controls only a small part of the money supply.

6. If the Federal Reserve credits your account with an extra $10,000 and banks have a reserve ratio of 5%, by how much does the money supply increase? Show your work.

7. Open market operations can stimulate the economy in two ways. What are those two ways?

8. How does the Fed deal with systemic risk?

9. Explain why economists think of the Fed as independent. What does it mean that a central bank is independent?

10. If the Federal Reserve increases the money supply, how will that affect the entire economy? Show the short-run and long-run effects.

# Multiple-Choice Questions

1. Which of the following can create money?
   a. the U.S. Congress
   b. the Federal Reserve Bank
   c. the U.S. Department of the Treasury
   d. the U.S. Printing Office

2. Which of the following is a demand deposit?
   a. savings accounts
   b. money market accounts
   c. currency
   d. checking accounts

3. Of the major means of payment in the United States, which is *most* liquid?
   a. currency
   b. checkable deposits
   c. savings deposits
   d. money market mutual funds

4. Of the major means of payment in the United States, which has the largest total value?
   a. currency
   b. checkable deposits
   c. savings deposits
   d. money market mutual funds

5. Which of the following countries use U.S. dollars for currency?
   a. Panama, Ecuador, El Salvador, Iraq
   b. Panama, Ecuador, El Salvador, Caicos Islands
   c. Iraq, Panama, Turkey, El Salvador
   d. None of the answers is correct.

6. Credit cards are counted in which definition of money?
   a. monetary base
   b. M1
   c. M2
   d. None of the answers is correct.

7. The Fed has the most control over which part of the money supply?
   a. M1
   b. M2
   c. monetary base
   d. None of the answers is correct.

8. Which list shows assets from most liquid to least liquid?
   a. currency, savings accounts, small-time deposits, the Mona Lisa that you stole
   b. the Mona Lisa that you stole, savings accounts, small-time deposits, currency
   c. currency, demand deposits, savings accounts, small-time deposits, bonds
   d. bonds, small-time deposits, savings accounts, gold, currency

9. The Federal Reserve has direct control over which part of the money supply?
   a. M2
   b. M1
   c. monetary base
   d. credit cards

10. If your bank has a 10% reserve ratio and you deposit $100,000, how much of your money is lent out?
    a. $10,000
    b. $90,000
    c. $100,000
    d. $0

11. If the Fed *directly* increased the money supply by $1,000 and the total effect on the money supply (after the money multiplier) was $5,000, what percent of deposits are banks keeping in reserves?
    a. 10
    b. 5
    c. 20
    d. 100

12. If the Fed puts $100,000 into your bank and the reserve ratio is 10%, how much did the money supply increase after the new money makes its way through the economy and is lent and lent again?
    a. $10,000
    b. $90,000
    c. $1,000,000
    d. $10,000,000

13. What is the Federal Funds rate?
    a. the interest rate that you pay on your car
    b. the interest rate that people with the best credit pay on their mortgage
    c. the rate that banks pay when they borrow money from the Fed
    d. the rate that banks pay when they borrow money from each other overnight

14. How does the Fed control the Federal Funds rate?
    a. The Fed simply prints the Federal Funds rate in the newspaper.
    b. The Fed changes the discount rate and that changes the Federal Funds rate.
    c. The Fed works with Congress to change the Federal Funds rate.
    d. The Fed buys and sells bonds until the Federal Funds rate changes by the desired amount.

15. If a bank has many good loans, but can not provide cash to depositors, then the bank is
    a. insolvent and illiquid.
    b. insolvent but liquid.
    c. solvent but illiquid.
    d. solvent and liquid.

16. The Term Auction Facility was designed to
    a. encourage banks to borrow money from the Fed.
    b. auction off cars from GM and Chrysler.
    c. auction off the bad debt from Citi and other big banks.
    d. discourage banks from borrowing money from the Fed.

17. Systemic risk is

    a. the risk that one financial institution's failure will lead to many other institutions failing.

    b. the risk that your bank will become illiquid just because of a rumor.

    c. the risk that your bank will make risky loans knowing that depositors will be repaid with FDIC money.

    d. the risk that aggregate demand will collapse.

18. Your bank is less conscientious about its loans because it knows that the government will bail it out. This is an example of

    a. Federal Funds rate.

    b. moral hazard.

    c. systemic risk.

    d. liquid risk.

19. Someone can become the chairperson of the Fed by being

    a. an AFL/CIO leader.

    b. on the Board of Governors and then appointed by the President.

    c. Chairman of the New York Fed.

    d. Members of the Board of Governors take turns being chairperson of the Fed.

20. If the Fed increases the growth of money in order to shift the aggregate demand curve out, the economy will improve for a short while. How does the economy get back into a long-run equilibrium?

    a. Solow growth curve shifts in.

    b. Aggregate demand curve shifts back.

    c. Solow growth curve and aggregate demand curve shift back.

    c. Short-run aggregate supply curve shifts inward.

## Short-Answer Questions

21. Why is currency considered to be the most liquid of assets?

**\*22.** Think of the "money supply" (*MS*) as equal to either M1 or M2. If banks keep 10% of any new deposits as reserves, what is the money multiplier? How much money will be created in total if the Fed adds 1 million dollars to bank reserves?[1]

**23.** What are the three ways that the Federal Reserve can affect the money supply?

**24.** Explain how the money multiplier works.

**25.** If the Federal Reserve credits your account with an extra $100,000 and banks have a reserve ratio of 10%, by how much does the money supply increase? Show your work.

**26.** Why doesn't the Fed know exactly how much money will be created through the money multiplier?

**27.** Why doesn't the Fed change the reserve requirement as a means of changing the money supply?

---

[1] Questions marked by a ★ are also end-of-chapter questions.

**28.** What problem was the Federal Reserve dealing with when it lent money to AIG (an insurance company) and Bear Stearns (an investment bank)?

**29.** If the Fed wasn't independent, what could the President make the Fed do to temporarily help the economy and boost the President's reelection chances?

**30.** If the Federal Reserve decreases the money supply growth rate, how will that affect the entire economy? Show the short-run and long-run effects.

# Answer Key

## Answers to Practice Exercises: Learning by Doing

1. A central bank is the bank that lends to other banks *and* is in charge of monetary policy. The U.S. central bank is the Federal Reserve System. It affects the money supply by acting as a lender of last resort, changing the required reserves, open market operations, and its discount lending affects the interest rate.

   **Topic: What Is the Federal Reserve System?**

2. The three most important definitions of the money supply are the *monetary base*, M1, and M2. The monetary base is currency plus total reserves held at the Fed. M1 is currency plus checkable deposits. M2 is M1 plus savings deposits, money market mutual funds, and small-time deposits.

   **Topic: The U.S. Money Supplies**

3. Money is created *directly* by the Fed when it does one of the following: It can print more money and simply scatter it around (never done). It can buy bonds, which means that money is taken out of the Fed's vaults and put into circulation. It can make loans to other banks and those banks then lend out the money.

   **Topic: How the Fed Controls the Money Supply**

4. The Fed creates money indirectly through fractional reserve banking by counting on money being put into the banking system. When people get money from the Fed through selling their bonds, they put that money into their bank, and the bank lends out much of the money. When banks start lending money out, they increase the number of times that the money is spent. This is a way that the Fed increases the money supply by more than its original infusion.

   **Topic: Fractional Reserve Banking, the Reserve Ratio, and the Money Multiplier**

5. While we think of the Fed controlling the money supply, in reality it only creates a tiny bit of the money supply. The Fed doesn't control how many people are suitable borrowers. (Banks don't want to lend to people who won't repay.) The Fed doesn't control how many people want to borrow money. But the Fed can control the monetary base. The monetary base is the amount of currency (which the Fed controls directly) and the amount of reserves that banks hold at the Fed. The rest of M1 and M2 are not controlled by the Fed.

   **Topic: The U.S. Money Supplies**

6. If the Fed increases your account by $10,000, you might spend every penny of it. But as long as the money eventually ends up as deposits in banks, they will lend most of it out (Banks keep reserves: 5% in this case). The money will continue to be lent again and again until the amount of money supply increases by $200,000.

   $$10{,}000 \times 1/RR = 10{,}000 \times 1/.05 = 10{,}000 \times 20 = \$200{,}000$$

   **Topic: Fractional Reserve Banking, the Reserve Ratio, and the Money Multiplier**

7. Open market operations can stimulate the economy in two ways. When the Fed buys bonds, it increases the demand for bonds, which pushes up the price of bonds, thus lowering the interest rate. (Remember that bond prices and interest rates are inversely related.) So, buying bonds stimulates the economy through two distinct mechanisms—higher money supplies and lower interest rates. In a sense, the increase in the money supply increases the supply of loans, and the lower interest rates increase the quantity of loans demanded.

   **Topic: How the Fed Controls the Money Supply**

8. The Fed deals with systemic risk by acting as a lender of last resort. For example, banks can borrow from the discount window if another bank's insolvency is causing problems. Banks can also borrow from the Term Auction Facility.

   **Topic: The Federal Reserve and Systemic Risk**

9. Economists think of the Fed as independent because it is not closely controlled by politicians. It is difficult for Congress or the President to make the Fed do something. Members of the Board of Governors have long terms that outlast those of the President. Being independent means that the Fed can't easily be pressured into increasing the money supply just before an election.

   **Topic: Who Controls the Fed?**

10.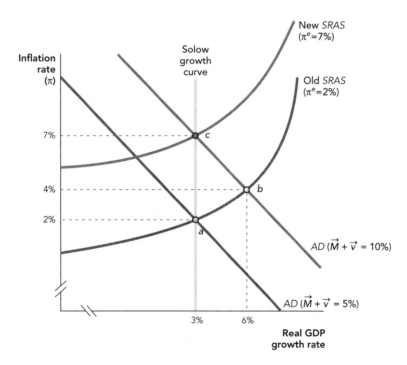

    **Topic: Revisiting Aggregate Demand and Monetary Policy**

## Answers to Multiple-Choice Questions

1. b, Topic: What is the Federal Reserve System?
2. d, Topic: The U.S. Money Supplies
3. a, Topic: The U.S. Money Supplies
3. a, Topic: The U.S. Money Supplies
4. c, Topic: The U.S. Money Supplies
4. c, Topic: The U.S. Money Supplies
5. b, Topic: The U.S. Money Supplies
6. d, Topic: The U.S. Money Supplies
7. c, Topic: How the Fed Controls the Money Supply
8. c, Topic: How the Fed Controls the Money Supply
9. c, Topic: How the Fed Controls the Money Supply
10. b, Topic: Fractional Reserve Banking, the Reserve Ratio, and the Money Multiplier
11. c, Topic: Fractional Reserve Banking, the Reserve Ratio, and the Money Multiplier
12. c, Topic: Fractional Reserve Banking, the Reserve Ratio, and the Money Multiplier
13. d, Topic: How the Fed Controls the Money Supply
14. d, Topic: How the Fed Controls the Money Supply
15. c, Topic: How the Fed Controls the Money Supply
16. a, Topic: How the Fed Controls the Money Supply
17. a, Topic: The Federal Reserve and Systemic Risk
18. b, Topic: The Federal Reserve and Systemic Risk
19. b, Topic: Who Controls the Fed?
20. d, Topic: Revisiting Aggregate Demand and Monetary Policy

## Answers to Short-Answer Questions

21. Currency is considered to be the most liquid of assets because liquidity is a measure of how easily you can pay for goods and services with an asset. You can almost always pay for things with currency. You don't need to swipe your debit card or show an I.D. You just have to hand over currency and you can buy things.
    **Topic: The U.S. Money Supplies**

22. If banks keep 10% of any new deposits, then the money multiplier will be 10. The money multiplier = 1/RR. 1/.10 = 10. If the Fed adds 1 million dollars to bank reserves, the total increase in the money supply will be 10 million dollars.

    **Topic: Fractional Reserve Banking, the Reserve Ratio, and the Money Multiplier**

23. The Fed can affect the money supply in the following ways:
    1. Open market operations—the buying and selling of U.S. government bonds on the open market
    2. Discount rate lending and the Term Auction Facility—Federal Reserve lending to banks and other financial institutions
    3. Required reserves and payment of interest on reserves—changing the minimum ratio of reserves to deposits, which is legally required of banks and other depository institutions, and paying interest on any reserves held by banks at the Fed

    **Topic: How the Fed Controls the Money Supply**

24. The money multiplier works because we have fractional reserve banking. Banks don't hold all of their deposits. Individuals decide how much of their money they are spending immediately and how much is going to be put into banks. The banks lend out a portion of this money (everything but the reserves). That money gets lent again and again as it works its way through the economy.

    **Topic: Fractional Reserve Banking, the Reserve Ratio, and the Money Multiplier**

25. $100,000 deposited into a bank account by the Fed would eventually become $1,000,000 after the money multiplier works its magic.

    $100,000 × 1/RR = $100,000 × 1/.10 = $100,000 × 10 = $1,000,000

    **Topic: Fractional Reserve Banking, the Reserve Ratio, and the Money Multiplier**

26. The Fed never knows *exactly* how much money will be created through the money multiplier because there are many possible sources of uncertainty. Banks might decide to hold larger reserves. People might not deposit their loans into banks immediately.

    **Topic: Revisiting Aggregate Demand and Monetary Policy**

27. The Fed doesn't use the reserve requirement very often as a monetary tool because it is very blunt tool. Banks might hold far more reserves than they are required to do by law. Banks need to have reserves, not just to obey the Fed rules, but also to make sure that depositors can withdraw cash. Also, banks decide to lend based on how many good loan applicants come to them. If a bank has already lent to all the good loan applicants, then lowering the reserve requirement won't make the bank lend more money.

    **Topic: Required Reserves and Payment of Interest on Reserves**

28. When the Fed lent money to AIG and Bear Stearns, it was trying to deal with systemic risk. Traditionally, the Fed didn't lend to insurance companies and investment banks, but AIG and Bear Stearns owed so much money to regular banks that if AIG and Bear Stearns failed, many regular banks would fail, too.

**Topic: The Federal Reserve and Systemic Risk**

29. If the Fed wasn't independent, then the President of the United States could insist that the Fed increase the growth rate of money. That would temporarily shift out the aggregate demand curve and boost the economy. Voters might be fooled into thinking that the President was especially good because of this short-term outcome and vote for his or her reelection. Eventually, of course, the SRAS would change and the economy would have the same growth but higher inflation.

**Topic: Who Controls the Fed?**

30. If the Fed decreases the money supply, then aggregate demand will shift inward. This will cause the economy to slow its growth until the SRAS shifts as well. The SRAS will eventually shift because eventually unexpected changes to inflation become expected changes to inflation. When SRAS shifts, then the economy will be at its Solow growth rate with lower inflation. This would be a painful period, but eventually inflation would be reduced.

**Topic: Revisiting Aggregate Demand and Monetary Policy**

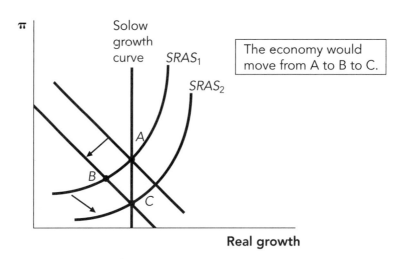

# 15 (29)
# Monetary Policy

## Why Learn about Monetary Policy?

This chapter is about whether the Fed's really can do much about the economy and when it should do something about the economy. Any business major who might be skeptical about news reports from the Fed will want to understand the details of the Fed's ability. Students with a political bent, whether liberal or conservative, may also be skeptical of the Fed and want to understand when the Fed can and can't help.

## Summary

This chapter is concerned mostly with how monetary policy might be able to return an economy *quickly* to the Solow growth rate after a shock. But as we saw in Chapter 11's "In this chapter," the text takes for granted *how* the Fed influences *AD* and turns more directly to three key practical questions:

1) When *should* the Fed try to influence *AD*?
2) When *will* the Fed be able to influence *AD*?
3) When will the influence on *AD result* in higher GDP growth rates?

The Fed has some influence over the growth rate of GDP through its influence over the money supply, and thus *AD*. An increase in (?) increases *AD* and a decrease in (?) decreases *AD*. Getting the policy "just right" is difficult. Poor monetary policy can decrease the stability of GDP. Mistakes can be hard to fix because credibility can be tough to earn. A monetary policy is **credible** when it is expected that a central bank will stick with its policy. The Fed may have to reduce the growth of money, which can be painful. A **disinflation** is a significant reduction in the rate of inflation. A **deflation** is a decrease in prices, that is, a negative inflation rate.

The Fed can, however, encourage **market confidence**. One of the Federal Reserve's most powerful tools is its influence over expectations, not its influence over the money supply.

Rules versus Discretion: Some people don't trust the Fed to act appropriately and they want strict monetary rules that the Fed must follow. The problem is that sometimes people want the Fed to be able to break the rules and follow discretion to solve problems.

## Key Terms

**disinflation** is a significant reduction in the rate of inflation

**deflation** is a decrease in prices, that is, a negative inflation rate

**credible** refers to a monetary policy in which it is expected that a central bank will stick with its policy

**market confidence** acts as one of the Federal Reserve's most powerful tools in its influence over expectations, not its influence over the money supply

## Tips, Traps, and Hints

This chapter builds on other chapters and should be one of the easier chapters. However, the graphs build on each other. Some of the graphs combine many other graphs that you already understand. Using color will help you understand the graphs here. Even using black and blue pens will help you learn these graphs.

## Practice Exercises: Learning by Doing

1. Why is it hard for the Fed to get monetary policy "just right?"

2. Show how the Fed should offset a negative shock to aggregate demand if everything can go just right.

3. If the economy as a whole is in a recession due to decreased demand, the Fed should increase the rate of monetary growth. Show (graphically) how the Fed might make a mistake in monetary policy in trying to fix things.

4. What do we mean by "Rules vs. Discretion" in central banking?

5. Graphically, show what happens if there is a negative real shock to the economy and the Fed tries to stimulate the economy.

6. Graphically show what happens to the whole economy if there is a negative shock to *SRAS, AD,* and the Solow growth curves.

7. If there is a negative shock to *SRAS, AD,* and the Solow growth curve, what happens to output and the inflation rate if the Fed tries to increase *AD?*

8. Why would it have been hard for Alan Greenspan to pop the real estate bubble?

9. Central banks and voters alike usually want higher real growth and lower inflation. What kind of shock makes that happen? (Note: This is similar to the type of shock that causes higher quantity and lower price in a simple supply and demand model.)

*10. Draw a graph showing how Fed must choose between allowing low rates of growth, excessively high rates of inflation, or some combination of both in the event of a negative real shock.

# Multiple-Choice Questions

1. What are the three primary tools that the Fed can use to influence aggregate demand through the money supply?
   a. lending to banks and other financial institutions, and changes to the reserve requirement and changes to interest paid on reserves, and changing default rules
   b. open market operations, lending to banks and other financial institutions, and changes to the reserve requirement and changes to the unemployment rate
   c. open market operations, direct lending to individuals, and changes to the reserve requirement and changes to interest paid on reserves
   d. shifting the Solow growth curve, lending to banks and other financial institutions, and changes leading to the growth of technology

2. Imagine that consumers want to borrow and spend less money thus shifting the *AD* curve inward. What is the ideal response by the Fed?
   a. Increase the money supply.
   b. Increase the rate of money growth.
   c. Increase the interest rate.
   d. Increase the rate of growth of the interest rate.

3. What are two reasons why it is difficult for the Fed to properly shift the aggregate demand curve when there is an aggregate demand-caused recession?
   a. Fed analysts don't know whether to increase or decrease the growth of the money supply *and* Fed policy must be approved by Congress.
   b. The data that the Fed need are delayed *and* all policy must be approved by the President.
   c. The Fed's control of the money supply is incomplete and subject to lags *and* the Fed's policy must be approved by the states.
   d. The Fed's control of the money supply is incomplete and subject to lags *and* the data that the Fed need are delayed.

4. Why is important data unavailable when the Fed needs the data?
   a. Data are collected by government bureaucrats who are lazy.
   b. Data take time to collect and come out monthly or quarterly.
   c. Rich banks conspire to keep the data from getting into the Fed's hands.
   d. The Fed Chairman is so powerful that he doesn't need up-to-date data.

5. What does it mean when we say that the Fed has to overshot?
   a. The Fed increased money supply growth too much.
   b. The Fed terms of employment are too long.
   c. The Fed tried to get more political power than it could attain.
   d. The Fed tried to shift the *SRAS* too much.

6. If the Fed overshoots, what will be the effect?
   a. The economy will have a higher than desirable inflation rate and a growth rate that is high, but unsustainable in the long run.
   b. Aggregate demand won't shift enough.
   c. The *SRAS* will shift too much.
   d. The *SRAS* won't shift enough.

7. If the Fed doesn't shift *AD* curve out enough, what will be the effect?
   a. Tax revenues won't be high enough.
   b. Growth will still be sluggish.
   c. Unemployment won't be high enough.
   d. Inflation won't be low enough.

8. If the Fed makes lots of mistakes with monetary policy, what will be the result?
   a. There will be more GDP volatility.
   b. There will be less GDP volatility.
   c. There will be more GDP stability.
   d. None of the answers is correct.

9. Milton Friedman was
    a. the Chairman of the Fed.
    b. the head of the Treasury.
    c. a Nobel prize winning monetary economist.
    d. head of the House Ways and Means Committee.

10. Milton Friedman favored a monetary rule instead of discretion. A typical monetary rule is
    a. a strict rule regarding the amount that either M1 or M2 can increase.
    b. a strict rule regarding the amount that the Fed can change the reserve requirement.
    c. a strict rule regarding the allowable amount of unemployment.
    d. a strict rule regarding the amount of loans the Fed can make.

11. If people are nervous and adopt a "wait and see" attitude, velocity will
    a. not be affected.
    b. increase.
    b. decrease.
    c. The rate of increase will increase.

12. An example of the bandwagon effect on investment is
    a. I delay my investments because you delay your investments.
    b. I speed up my investments because you delay your investments.
    c. You delay your investments because you want me to delay my investments.
    d. I delay my investments because I want you to delay your investments.

13. After the September 11, 2001 attacks, the Fed tried to boost confidence by doing what?
    a. It delayed loans to banks to show that it had enough cash.
    b. It raised reserve requirements.
    c. It lent more than 10 times the normal amount of money to banks.
    d. It sent TV crews to Fort Knox to show how much gold was stored there.

14. If the economy is hit by a negative real shock instead of a negative aggregate demand shock, what will be the effect of monetary policy?
    s. It will be more effective.
    b. It will be less effective.
    c. It will be no more or less effective.
    d. None of the answers is correct.

**15.** If monetary policy intended to stabilize the economy mostly leads to higher inflation, and not to more output, that means that the recession is *most* likely caused by
   a. aggregate demand shift.
   b. irrational expectation.
   c. negative real shock.
   d. money shocks.

**16.** If wages and prices are sticky, what is the result after a negative real shock?
   a. The *SRAS* will shift inward again.
   b. The *SRAS* will shift outward after moving with the Solow growth curve.
   c. The *AD* curve will shift inward because of the sticky prices.
   d. The Solow growth curve will shift further inward.

**17.** If a negative real shock makes consumers and investors nervous, what will be the *additional* effect?
   a. The aggregate demand curve will shift out.
   b. The aggregate demand curve will shift in.
   c. The *SRAS* will shift in.
   d. The *SRAS* will shift out.

**18.** How do you draw the following—a negative real shock occurs, there are sticky wages and prices, declining output makes investors and consumers decide to wait and see?
   a. Shift the Solow growth curve inward, then shift the *SRAS* outward, then shift the *AD* curve inward.
   b. Shift the Solow growth curve inward, then shift the *SRAS* inward, then shift the *AD* curve inward.
   c. Shift the Solow growth curve inward, then shift the *SRAS* inward, then shift the *AD* curve outward.
   d. Shift the Solow growth curve outward, then shift the *SRAS* inward, then shift the *AD* curve inward.

**19.** When home prices started to fall, and homeowners felt poorer, what was the effect on the macroeconomy?
   a. The Solow growth curve shifted inward.
   b. Aggregate demand shifted inward.
   c. *SRAS* shifted outward.
   d. There was no effect.

20. How did money growth decline when mortgage backed securities became worth significantly less?

   a. Banks were unable to lend as much and still keep reserves.

   b. Banks spent less money on new consumption.

   c. Investors bought less imports.

   d. None of the answers is correct.

## Short-Answer Questions

21. Explain why the Fed has a hard time getting monetary policy just right even when it knows what to do.

*22. Show the effect of the Fed increasing $\overline{M}$ after a negative real shock.

23. If the Solow growth curve shifts inward due to a negative real shock, the *SRAS* is affected by sticky wages and prices, and the aggregate demand curve shifts inward too; what is the effect of increasing $\overline{M}$? Show the effect graphically.

24. How do problems with data affect the Fed's ability to set monetary policy "just right?"

25. This chapter is concerned mostly with how monetary policy might be able to return an economy *quickly* to the Solow growth rate after a shock. But as we saw in Chapter 11's discussion of the quantity theory of money, a market economy has a correction mechanism to return itself *slowly* to the Solow growth rate after a shock: flexible prices. Let's review the quantity theory, and remember that in the quantity theory, inflation does *all* of the adjusting.

    Recall: $\vec{M} + \vec{v} = \vec{P} + \vec{Y_R}$

    a. Consider the nation of Kydland. Before the shock to Kydland's economy, $\vec{M} = 10\%, \vec{v} = 3\%, \vec{Y_R} = 4\%$. What is inflation?

    b. In Kydland, $\vec{v}$ falls to 0 %, but $\vec{M}$ stays the same. In the long run, what will inflation equal? What will real growth equal?

    c. Consider the nation of Cowen. Before the shock to Cowen's economy, $\vec{M} = 2\%, \vec{v} = 4\%, \vec{Y_R} = 3\%$. What is inflation?

26. Neither Alan Greenspan, the former Chairman of the Fed, nor Ben Bernanke, the current Chairman of the Fed, tried to pop the real estate bubble with monetary policy. Why is this?

**27.** Why did Milton Friedman argue for a strict rule of 3 % money growth per year?

**28.** How does the market's impression that the Fed will always cave in to demands from Wall Street affect the Fed's ability to set monetary policy?

**29.** Why didn't the Fed use monetary policy to burst the 1997–2006 housing bubble?

**30.** What could or should the Fed have done to deal with the 2007–2009 recession?

# Answer Key

## Answers to Practice Exercises: Learning by Doing

1. It is hard for the Fed to get monetary policy just right because the Fed gets incomplete and delayed data, but it has to make decisions right away. Also, the Fed controls only a small amount of the money supply and that control is subject to lags.

   **Topic: Monetary Policy: The Best Case**

2. If the Fed does things just right, it can increase $\vec{M}$ to perfectly offset a fall in aggregate demand.

   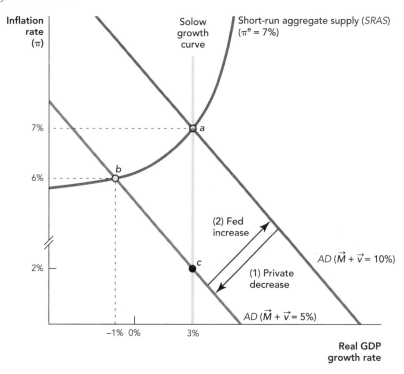

   **Topic: Monetary Policy: The Best Case**

3. It is very easy for the Fed to increase the $\vec{M}$ too much or too little.

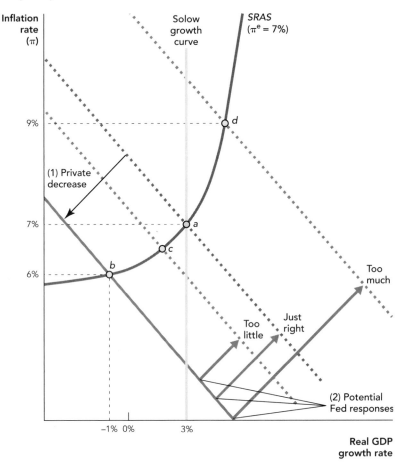

**Topic: Monetary Policy: The Best Case**

4. When we talk about Rules vs. Discretion in central banking we are asking if the Fed has to follow a strict rule such as increasing either M1 or M2 by a certain amount each year. That is a rule. Alternatively, the Fed might change whenever the Chairman and the Board think it necessary. A rule is predictable and some people think the Fed's operations add volatility. Discretion allows the Fed to make subtle or drastic changes whenever conditions demand.

**Topic: Rules vs. Discretion**

5. When there is a negative real shock and the Fed tries to increase that will lead to high inflation and only small increases to the real growth rate.

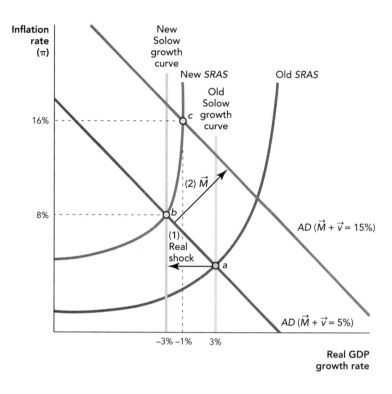

**Topic: The Negative Real Shock Dilemma**

6. If there is a negative real shock that can come with a negative shock to *SRAS* and to aggregate demand, the effect is as follows:

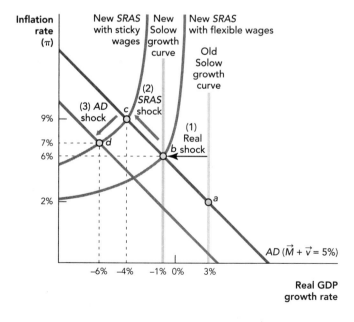

**Topic: The Negative Real Shock Dilemma**

7. If there is a negative shock to the Solow growth curve, SRAS, and to the aggregate demand curve, then the Fed's attempt to increase $\vec{M}$ will lead to higher inflation and only a small increase in real growth. In the figure from the previous question, the economy will move from point "d" to point "c." Of course the economy would only be at point "c" if the Fed increased $\vec{M}$ just right.

   **Topic: The Negative Real Shock Dilemma**

8. It would have been hard for Alan Greenspan to pop the real estate bubble for several reasons. It was not clear that there was a real estate bubble. Sometimes the value of assets increases for fundamental reasons. Data come in slowly and with mixed signals. Also changing would not have just affected real estate prices, it would have affected the whole economy.

   **Topic: The Problem with Positive Shocks: The 1997–2006 Housing Boom and Bust**

9. Positive real shocks increase real output while keeping inflation low.

   **Topic: The Problem with Positive Shocks: The 1997–2006 Housing Boom and Bust**

10. The solid lines show the negative real shock. The dashed lines show that the Fed can have low inflation with low output or somewhat higher output with high inflation.

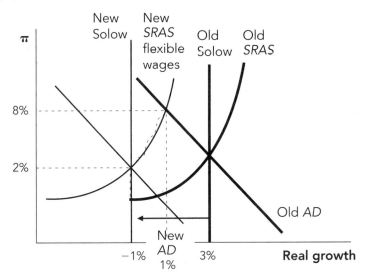

   **Topic: The Negative Real Shock Dilemma**

## Answers to Multiple-Choice Questions

1. a, Topic: Introduction
2. b, Topic: Introduction
3. d, Topic: Introduction
4. b, Topic: Monetary Policy: The Best Case
5. a, Topic: Monetary Policy: The Best Case
6. a, Topic: Monetary Policy: The Best Case
7. b, Topic: Monetary Policy: The Best Case
8. a, Topic: Rules vs. Discretion
9. c, Topic: Rules vs. Discretion
10. a, Topic: Rules vs. Discretion
11. c, Topic: The Fed as a Manager of Confidence
12. a, Topic: The Fed as a Manager of Confidence
13. c, Topic: The Fed as a Manager of Confidence
14. b, Topic: Monetary Policy: The Best Case
15. c, Topic: Reversing Course and Engineering a Decrease in *AD*
16. a Topic: The Negative Real Shock Dilemma
17. b, Topic: The Negative Real Shock Dilemma
18. b, Topic: The Negative Real Shock Dilemma
19. b, Topic: The Problem with Positive Shocks: 1997–2006 Housing Boom and Bust
20. a, Topic: The Problem with Positive Shocks: 1997–2006 Housing Boom and Bust

## Answers to Short-Answer Questions

21. The Fed has a hard time getting monetary policy just right even when it knows what to do because the Fed's data are often delayed and incomplete. Also, the Fed controls only a small part of the money supply. That control also has lags. Finally, sometimes people don't really believe in the Fed policy. If this occurs, then policy will take a long time to take effect.

    **Topic: Monetary Policy: The Best Case**

22. The following graph shows the effect of the Fed increasing $\vec{M}$ after a negative real shock. It is a best case scenario. The Fed knew how much to shift the $AD$ curve and was able to do it perfectly.

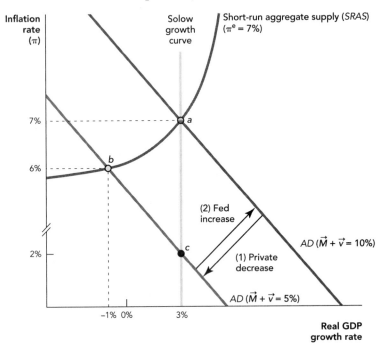

**Topic: The Negative Real Shock Dilemma**

23. In the previous graph, all three curves have shifted inward. The $SRAS$ has shifted in extra far because of sticky wages and prices. Aggregate demand has shifted in as well due to fear and less wealth. You can see that when the Fed tries monetary expansion the effect is very high inflation with only modest changes to output.

**Topic: The Negative Real Shock Dilemma**

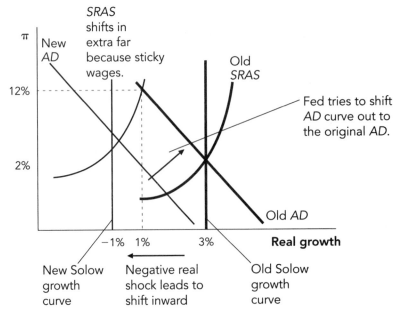

24. It is very difficult for the Fed to get monetary policy just right for several reasons. One reason is that it is often difficult for the Fed to know what to do. Several things may be affecting the economy all at once. Data are incomplete and delayed. When there is a negative real shock the Fed can slightly influence output but only by having very high inflation. Also, the Fed only influences a small part of the money supply and that influence is subject to lags.

    **Topic: Monetary Policy: The Best Case**

25. Recall: $\vec{M} + \vec{v} \equiv \vec{P} + \vec{Y_R}$.

    a. Inflation is 9%.

    b. Real growth equals 4%.

    c. Inflation is 3%.

    **Topic: Monetary Policy: The Best Case**

26. Neither Chairman of the Fed tried very hard to pop the real estate bubble with monetary policy for two main reasons. First, it is difficult to know during a bubble whether the increase in asset prices really is a bubble or something else. Second, contractionary monetary policy (reducing $\vec{M}$) wouldn't just affect real estate prices; it would affect the whole economy. Finally, the more that prices and wages are sticky instead of flexible, the more contractionary monetary policy hurts the economy.

    **Topic: The Problem with Positive Shocks: The 1997–2006 Housing Boom and Bust**

27. Milton Friedman argued for a strict rule of 3% money growth per year because that is about how much output increases per year. The quantity theory of money suggests that when money growth is the same as output growth, prices will be stable. The stability helps provide clear expectations, as well as prevent inflation. Finally, the Fed can make mistakes and misread information. A money rule prevents Fed mistakes. (Of course, it also prevents the Fed from doing the right thing when it needs to.)

    **Topic: Rules vs. Discretion**

28. The market's impression that the Fed will always cave in to demands from Wall Street affects the Fed's ability to set monetary policy by leading people to believe that the monetary policy is not credible. If people don't think that contractionary policy is credible, they won't adjust wages and prices. This means that the economy will be out of long-run equilibrium for a longer period of time. Output will be low and inflation will be high because people keep expecting monetary growth to increase.

    **Topic: The Fed as Manager of Market Confidence**

**29.** The Fed didn't use monetary policy to burst the 1997–2006 housing bubble because it wasn't sure that there was a bubble. Perhaps more importantly, the Fed worried that contractionary monetary policy would push all prices and output down, not just prices and output in the real estate market.

**Topic: The Problem with Positive Shocks: The 1997–2006 Housing Boom and Bust**

**30.** While the Fed was wary about using monetary policy to "pop" the real estate bubble because of the collateral damage, it could have used its regulator power. For example, the Fed may have been have to restrain or prevent some of the sub-prime mortgages. There were also some "no questions asked mortgages" that could have been limited by the Fed. This would have helped pop the bubble without taking down the broader economy.

**Topic: The Negative Real Shock Dilemma**

# 16 (19)

# The Federal Budget: Taxes and Spending

## Why Learn about Taxes and Spending?

Anyone who pays taxes will be interested in this chapter. Your income taxes, the taxes on businesses you own, and your social security tax are all explained in this chapter. Where did all of that money come from and where does it all go? You will also learn who really pays taxes, including social security taxes. Students who care about the fairness of taxes on the poor or on businesses or on the rich will care about this chapter. Students who wish to become financial planners will care as well. History majors may be interested in how social security changed over time and to have the economic tools to discuss changes in the government's ability to tax and spend. Accounting majors will be particularly interested in this chapter.

## Summary

The federal government takes in and spends a great deal of money. It is hard to imagine revenues and spending of over $2.5 *trillion*. The huge majority of tax revenues—over 82 percent—come from individuals in the form of individual income taxes and taxes on wages linked to Social Security and Medicare. While defense spending represents around 20 percent of spending, over one-third (36.5 percent) of the federal budget goes for Social Security and Medicare payments.

Comprehensive general transfers to the elderly represent far more money than do welfare expenditures per se. What about the future? The U.S. tax system is very complicated and not always transparent in its effects. Nevertheless, we can estimate future expenditures and revenues as a way of understanding the fiscal strength or weakness of a nation. It is very likely that federal expenditures will rise in the future, most of all because of rising Medicare expenditures. One question is whether and if so, how federal revenues will rise to keep the budget sufficiently close to balance.

## Key Terms

**marginal tax rate** is the tax rate paid on an additional dollar of income

**average tax rate** is the total tax payment divided by total income

**alternative minimum tax (AMT)** is a separate income tax code that began to operate in 1969 to prevent the rich from not paying income taxes. It was not indexed to inflation and is now an extra tax burden on many upper middle class families

**progressive tax** has higher tax rates on people with higher incomes

**flat tax** has a constant tax rate

**regressive tax** has higher tax rates on people with lower incomes

**national debt held by the public** is all federal debt held outside the United States government

**deficit** is the annual difference between federal spending and revenues

## Tips, Traps, and Hints

The trickiest part of this chapter is understanding that the law doesn't dictate who actually pays a tax. For example, the law says that employees pay half of the social security tax and employers pay the other half. In reality, employees pay most of the tax. If employers weren't required to send money to the Federal government for social security taxes, most of that money would go to employees in the form of higher wages.

Make sure that you don't believe that most federal tax money goes to welfare programs.

## Practice Exercises: Learning by Doing

1. What are the three biggest parts of the U.S. tax revenue?

2. How is it possible for your marginal tax rate to be higher than your average tax rate?

3. Provide an example in which a very high *marginal* tax rate might affect your decisions.

4. What do we mean by saying that the mortgage deduction doesn't necessarily go to the homeowner?

5. What is the alternative minimum income tax?

6. What does it mean that corporations don't really pay taxes?

7. Is the U.S. federal tax system progressive, regressive, or flat? Provide evidence.

8. What are some of the advantages and disadvantages of a flat tax?

9. Where do most state and local governments get their tax revenue? Is this progressive or regressive?

10. How does the United States rank in total government spending as a percentage of GDP? Name some countries that spend less and some that spend more.

## Multiple-Choice Questions

1. Who is the/was Ida May Fuller?
    a. the first woman to run the Social Security administration
    b. the current head of the IRS
    c. the first person to receive a social security check
    d. the first head of the IRS

2. In order from biggest to smallest, what are the three biggest parts of tax revenue?
    a. personal income tax, corporate income tax, and Social Security/Medicare taxes
    b. personal income tax, Social Security/Medicare taxes, and corporate income tax
    c. corporate income tax, excise taxes, and Social Security/Medicare taxes
    d. corporate income taxes, Social Security/Medicare taxes, tariffs

3. How does the personal income tax rank in U.S. tax receipts?
    a. It is the smallest part.
    b. It is the second smallest part.
    c. It is the second biggest part.
    d. It is the biggest part.

4. What is the FICA tax?
    a. It is a tax to fund Social Security and Medicare.
    b. It is a tax to fund the wars in Iraq and Afghanistan.
    c. It is a tax on estates.
    d. It is an excise tax on alcohol, cigarettes, and gasoline.

5. The U.S. tax codes use what type of tax rates on personal income?
   a. They use a flat rate. Everyone pays the same amount.
   b. They use an average rate. You pay a tax based on the average amount you earn.
   c. They use a marginal rate. The amount you pay on each additional dollar you earn changes.
   d. They use a geographic rate. Different parts of the country pay different federal taxes.

6. What is the difference between a tax deduction and a tax exemption?
   a. Income tax exemptions and the deductions are the same thing.
   b. Deductions apply to sales taxes and exemptions apply to income taxes.
   c. Deductions apply only to people with specific circumstances. Exemptions apply to everyone.
   d. Deductions apply to everyone. Exemptions apply only to people who do specific things.

7. Not counting deductions, what is the lowest marginal tax rate for the U.S. income tax?
   a. 1%
   b. 10%
   c. 57%
   d. 90%

8. If you have an income of $67,000 so far this year, your marginal tax rate is 15%. How much would you pay on the next dollar that you earn?
   a. none
   b. the full dollar
   c. $ 0.25
   d. $ 0.15

9. The average tax rate is
   a. the tax rate paid on an additional dollar of income.
   b. the total tax payment divided by total income.
   c. the total amount of money earned by all U.S. citizens at home and abroad divided by the total population.
   d. the total amount of money earned by all U.S. citizens at home and abroad divided by the total population *and* social security taxes divided by the population under age 65.

10. If you earned $43,000 last year and paid a total of $5,500 in taxes after all of your deductions, what is your average tax rate?
    a. 10%
    b. 12.8%
    c. 25%
    d. 91%

11. Why do economists argue that your employer doesn't really pay any of your Social Security tax?
    a. Your employer just uses it as a business write off.
    b. Your employer probably doesn't actually pay the tax anyway.
    c. This is a misconception. There are no rules whatsoever that employers should pay any of your social security. Some nice firms just pay to increase employee happiness.
    d. Your employer would just pay higher wages if she didn't have to pay the tax.

12. If Homer, with a wife and three children, makes the same as Flanders, with a wife and two children, will they pay the same income tax rate?
    a. They will only if their houses are worth the same.
    b. It is unlikely because Homer has three exemptions for children, and we don't know what sort of other exemptions and deductions these two have
    c. Yes, it would be unfair to tax people differently when they earn the same.
    d. The taxes that Homer and Flanders each pay depends on what taxes their employers pay.

13. Your text makes an interesting point about the 35% corporate income tax. What is it?
    a. The 35% corporate income tax is the lowest of any industrialized nation.
    b. The 35% corporate income tax is one of the highest of any industrialized nation.
    c. It is only fair that corporations instead of people pay the high tax.
    d. The tax rate is 35% but the actual rate that profitable companies pay tends to be far lower.

13. In the United States, how is the effective income tax rate different among different wealth groups?
    a. The poorest people pay the highest tax rate.
    b. The richest people pay the highest tax rate.
    c. The middle quintile of people pay the highest tax rate.
    d. The second, third, and fourth quintiles of people pay a far higher tax rate than either the very rich or the very poor.

14. What are the four *biggest* parts of federal government spending?
    a. unemployment insurance, welfare, foreign aid, and interest on debt
    b. welfare, aid to foreign governments, transportation, interest on debt
    c. Social Security, welfare, defense, and aid to foreign governments
    d. Social Security, defense, Medicare, and Medicaid

15. Which of the following is the way that Social Security works?
    a. Social Security taxes are deposited into the general fund and then benefits are allocated as the government sees fit.
    b. Each person has a special account and those dollars are invested in non-taxable municipal bonds.
    c. Each person has a special account with his or her Social Security taxes deposited into it.
    d. Each person has a special account with his or her Social Security taxes invested in stocks. Social Security is actually less safe than index funds.

16. How big is the interest on the U.S. national debt?
    a. 1% of the federal budget and 10% of GDP
    b. 10% of federal budget and about 10% of GDP
    c. almost half of GDP and two thirds of the federal budget
    d. 9.1% of the federal budget or about 2% of GDP

17. At the federal level, what is the main antipoverty program?
    a. Earned Income Tax Credit
    b. welfare
    c. TANF
    d. unemployment insurance

18. What percentage of the U.S. federal budget is devoted to foreign aid?
    a. about 40
    b. about 10
    c. about 20
    d. about 1

19. What did abolishing the draft and moving to an all volunteer army do to government financing?
    a. Government's share of a military went up but the country's cost of a military went down, since young men with high opportunity costs didn't become soldiers.
    b. Government's share of a military went down because only poorly skilled low-paying men became soldiers.
    c. Government's share of a military went up and the cost to the country went up too, since workers had to pay all those taxes.
    d. There was no effect on it.

## Short-Answer Questions

21. How do high *marginal* tax rates affect people's decisions to work, consume, invest, and enjoy leisure?

22. If there is an income tax deduction for certain types of clean energy, including solar panels on your house, what would it mean if economists say that the consumer doesn't get the full deduction?

23. Republican Steve Forbes and Democrat Jerry Brown have both argued for a flat tax instead of the current income tax. What are the advantages and disadvantages?

24. In this chapter, we learned that people, not corporations pay corporate income taxes. What does this mean?

**25.** Many Americans complain about the high cost of foreign aid. How big is foreign aid?

**26.** The United States has one of the highest corporate income taxes in the developed world. Why hasn't this high corporate income tax sent companies to other countries?

**27.** More and more Americans have to pay the alternative income tax. What is the alternative income tax?

**28.** Is the tax system for most state and local governments progressive, flat, or regressive?

**29.** Let's explore the difference between the average income tax rate and the marginal income tax rate. In the simple land of Rabushka, there is only one tax rate, 20 percent, but workers don't have to pay tax on the first $10,000 of their income. For every dollar they earn above $10,000, they pay 20 cents to the Lord High Mayor of Rabushka. The easy way to calculate the tax bill is the same way that America's IRS does:

Subtract $10,000 from each person's income and call the remainder "taxable income."

Multiply taxable income by 0.20, and the result is "tax due."

Fill in the following table.

| Average | Taxable Income | Tax Due | Marginal Tax Rate | Average Income Tax Rate |
|---|---|---|---|---|
| $ 1,000 | | | | |
| $ 5,000 | | | | |
| $ 10,001 | | | | |
| $150,000 | | | | |

**30.** What is the difference between the national debt and the national deficit?

# Answer Key

## Answers to Practice Exercises: Learning by Doing

1. The three biggest parts of U.S. tax revenue are: individual income tax, Social Security and Medicare taxes, and the corporate income tax.

   **Topic: Tax Revenues**

2. Your marginal tax rate will be higher than your average tax rate because the United States has a progressive tax system. Marginal rates (the rates on additional dollars of earning) increase as you make more money.

   **Topic: The Individual Income Tax**

3. If you had a very high marginal tax rate, that would mean that the next dollar you earn would be taxed very highly. This could encourage people to consume instead of invest or to take leisure time instead of working.

   **Topic: The Individual Income Tax**

4. When economists say that the mortgage deduction doesn't necessarily go to the homeowner, they mean that previous owner was able to charge a higher price because people will pay more for a house and a mortgage deduction than they will for just a house.

   **Topic: The Individual Income Tax**

5. The alternative minimum income tax is a separate income tax code that was created in 1969 to prevent the rich from not paying income taxes. It was not indexed to inflation and is now an extra tax burden on many upper middle class families.

   **Topic: The Individual Income Tax**

6. The idea that corporations don't pay taxes means that corporations are not separate entities in a real sense. Corporations are made up of owners, employees, and customers. A corporate income tax must be paid out of profits by owners, wages by employees, or prices by customers.

   **Topic: The Corporate Income Tax**

7. The U.S. federal tax system is progressive. In terms of earnings, the bottom 20 percent of Americans pay 4.3% of their incomes in taxes. The middle 20% pay 14.2% of their income in taxes. The top 1 percent have an effective tax rate of 31.2%.

   **Topic: The Bottom Line on the Distribution of Federal Taxes**

8. A flat tax is a constant tax applied to income at all levels of earning. Almost all deductions, including the deductions for mortgage interest and charitable giving, would be removed. The advantages of a flat tax are that taxes would be easier to file, loopholes would be eliminated. People would make their decisions based on good economic reasons instead of the tax code. Finally, smart people who currently work as tax preparers would go do something that *creates* wealth instead of preventing wealth from being transferred. The disadvantage of a flat tax is that moving to a flat tax would require lowering rates on the rich and raising rates on the middle class and the poor.

   **Topic: The Bottom Line on the Distribution of Federal Taxes**

9. Most states and local governments get a large percentage of their tax revenue from a sales tax. Since poor people spend more of their income than the wealthy (who save), this is regressive.

   **Topic: State and Local Taxes**

10. In the United States government spending is about 36.5% of GDP. This is more than Ireland, Switzerland, and Australia spend. But it is less than Japan, the UK, and Sweden spend.

    **Topic: The Future Is Hard to Predict**

## Answers to Multiple-Choice Questions

1. c, Topic: Introduction
2. b, Topic: Tax Revenues
3. d, Topic: Tax Revenues
4. a, Topic: The Individual Income Tax
5. c, Topic: Tax Revenues
6. c, Topic: The Individual Income Tax
7. b, Topic: The Individual Income Tax
8. d, Topic: The Individual Income Tax
9. b, Topic: The Individual Income Tax
10. b, Topic: The Individual Income Tax
11. d, Topic: Social Security and Medicare Taxes
12. b, Topic: Social Security and Medicare Taxes
13. d, Topic: The Corporate Income Tax
14. b, Topic: The Bottom Line on the Distribution of Taxes
15. d, Topic: Spending
16. a, Topic: Social Security
17. d, Topic: The National Debt, Interest on the National Debt, and Deficits
18. a, Topic: Unemployment Insurance and Welfare Spending
19. d, Topic: Everything Else
20. a, Topic: Everything Else

## Answers to Short-Answer Questions

21. A high marginal tax rate means that when people work harder or longer they get much less of the additional money. This makes them more likely to rest or consume leisure instead of work. A high marginal tax rate also reduces the incentive to invest for the future.
    **Topic: The Individual Income Tax**

22. A deduction for solar panels on your house would shift the demand for solar panels outward. That would raise the price. The increase in price would increase *producer surplus;* thus producers would get much of the benefit.
    **Topic: The Individual Income Tax**

23. Republican Steve Forbes and Democrat Jerry Brown have both argued for a flat tax instead of the current income tax because:
    - a flat tax would be easier to file,
    - loopholes would be eliminated,
    - people would make their decisions based on good economic reasons instead of the tax code, and
    - smart people who currently work as tax preparers would go do something that *creates* wealth instead of prevent wealth from being transferred.

    The disadvantage of a flat tax is that moving to a flat tax would require lowering rates on the rich and raising rates on the middle class and poor.
    **Topic: The Bottom Line on the Distribution of Federal Taxes**

24. Corporate taxes are paid out of the profits from stock owners (including elderly women who use stocks for their retirement); the wages of employees (whether they work on the line or are in the executive suite); and the prices that customers pay. The taxes are not paid by some nebulous entity.
    **Topic: The Corporate Income Tax**

25. While many Americans complain about the high cost of foreign aid, it is actually a very small part of the federal budget.
    **Topic: Spending**

26. Companies don't want to leave the United States because the United States is a big market with skilled labor and lots of capital. The reason the corporate income tax doesn't make companies move out of the United States is because the *effective* corporate income tax rate is very low. Even though the rate is high, there are lots of deductions and exemptions for companies.
    **Topic: The Corporate Income Tax**

27. The alternative minimum income tax is a different set of tax codes that apply to wealthy people. In order to make sure that wealthy people pay at least some taxes no matter how many deductions they have, it is required that they have to do their taxes the normal way and the alternative way. Then, the wealthy people have to pay whichever tax is higher. Since the alternative minimum income tax isn't adjusted for income, more and more people have to pay it each year.

   **Topic: The Alternative Minimum Tax (AMT)**

28. The tax system for most state and local governments is regressive. Large parts of the tax system for most state and local governments come from sales taxes. Wealthy people can avoid these taxes by buying in places with lower sales taxes. Also, wealthy people save more money. Saved money isn't taxes with a sales tax.

   **Topic: State and Local Taxes**

29.

| Average | Taxable Income | Tax Due | Marginal Tax Rate | Average Income Tax Rate |
|---|---|---|---|---|
| $ 1,000 | $0 | 0 | 0 | 0 |
| $ 5,000 | $0 | 0 | 0 | 0 |
| $ 10,001 | $1 | $.20 | .2 | 1.9998E-05 |
| $150,000 | $140,000 | $28,000 | .2 | 0.18666667 |

   **Topic: The Individual Income Tax**

30. The national debt is the total amount that is owed by the federal government. The national deficit is a measure how much more the government spent *this year* than it brought. The deficit is how much greater expenses were than revenue. [Keep in mind that the national debt doesn't include future obligations like promises to pay Social Security.]

   **Topic: The National Debt, Interest on the National Debt, and Deficits**

# 17 (31)

# Fiscal Policy

## Why Learn about Fiscal Policy?

Fiscal policy is the government spending that is designed to influence business fluctuations. History majors will be interested in fiscal policy so they can understand FDR's New Deal. Science majors will be interested in fiscal policy because government grants for basic research are commonly included in fiscal policy bills, which is helpful since private funding may disappear during recessions. Business majors will want to understand how to best use tax credits and tax rebates.

## Summary

**Fiscal policy** is federal government policy on taxes, spending, and borrowing that is designed to influence business fluctuations.

There are two general categories of fiscal policy used to fight a recession:

a) the government spends more money, or

b) the government cuts taxes, giving people more money to spend.

The **multiplier effect** is the additional increase in $AD$ caused when expansionary fiscal policy increases income and thus consumer spending. **Crowding out** is the decrease in private spending that occurs when government increases spending. **Ricardian equivalence** occurs when people see that lower taxes today mean higher taxes in the future, so instead of spending their tax cut they save it to pay future taxes. When Ricardian equivalence holds, a tax cut doesn't increase aggregate demand even in the short run. Ricardian equivalence is a special case of crowding out. **Automatic stabilizers** are changes in fiscal policy that stimulate $AD$ in a recession without the need for explicit action by policymakers. Welfare and unemployment insurance are examples of automatic stabilizers.

### The Limits to Fiscal Policy

There are four major limits to fiscal policy. Three of these limits have to do with the difficulty of using fiscal policy to shift aggregate demand ($AD$).

1. *Crowding out:* If government spending crowds out or leads to less private spending, then the increase in $AD$ is reduced or neutralized on net.

2. *A drop in the bucket*: The economy is so large that government can rarely increase spending enough for it to have a large impact.

3. *A matter of timing*: It can be difficult to time fiscal policy so the $AD$ curve shifts at just the right moments.

4. *AD shock instead of real shock:* Shifting $AD$ really helps only if the recession is caused by an $AD$ shift instead of a real shock.

## Key Terms

**fiscal policy** is federal government policy on taxes, spending, and borrowing that is designed to influence business fluctuations

**multiplier effect** is the additional increase in $AD$ caused when expansionary fiscal policy increases income and thus consumer spending

**crowding out** is the decrease in private spending that occurs when government increases spending

**Ricardian equivalence** occurs when people see that lower taxes today mean higher taxes in the future; so instead of spending their tax cut, they save it to pay future taxes. When Ricardian equivalence holds, a tax cut doesn't increase aggregate demand even in the short run

**automatic stabilizers** are changes in fiscal policy that stimulate $AD$ in a recession without the need for explicit action by policymakers

## Tips, Traps, and Hints

Many of the graphs in this chapter are very similar to the monetary policy graphs in Chapter 15. Make sure that you don't forget to add in crowding out. The crowding out effect is *more* likely to be stronger when the economy is already in a *long-run equilibrium*.

It is very easy for professors to ask very difficult fiscal policy questions that have very simple answers because of Ricardian equivalence. Example: Ricardia is a small country where people are forward looking and very interested in smoothing consumption. If the government of Ricardia decides to stimulate the economy with $1 billion worth of fiscal stimulus paid for by bonds. What will be the effect of the economy? Answer: There is no effect; this is a case of Ricardian equivalence.

# Practice Exercises: Learning by Doing

1. How can a fall in $\overline{C}$ lead to a fall in $\vec{v}$?

2. How is fiscal policy different from other government spending?

3. What are the two types of fiscal policy?

4. Explain how fiscal policy can work in the best case.

5. How can an increase in government spending be self-financing?

6. What are the four problems with fiscal policy?

7. What is Ricardian equivalence?

8. Why is it that a temporary tax break does not necessarily increase the consumption part of aggregate demand very much in the following year? Does a temporary investment tax credit have the same effect?

9. Show the effect of fiscal policy on aggregate demand and then show how crowding out can make fiscal policy less effective.

10. Draw a graph showing that the effect of fiscal policy on a recession was to cause lower aggregate demand, and then draw a graph next to it showing the effect of fiscal policy on a recession caused by a real shock.

## Multiple-Choice Questions

1. Fiscal policy is designed to shift which of the following curves in our macro model?
   a. aggregate demand
   b. Solow growth curve
   c. short-run aggregate supply curve
   d. None of the answers is correct.

2. Using the components of GDP, recessions are often caused by a fall in ____ and fiscal policy is designed to increase ____.
   a. $\vec{C}; \vec{I}$
   b. $\vec{C}; \vec{G}$
   c. $\vec{NX}; \vec{G}$
   d. $\vec{NX}; \vec{C}$

3. When additional government spending shifts the *AD* curve by more than the increase in government spending, that is known as the
   a. multiplier effect.
   b. additional effect.
   c. crowding out.
   d. drop in the bucket effect.

4. Which of the following lists the four limits to fiscal policy?
   a. crowding out, multiplier effect, gains from trade, real shocks instead of demand shocks
   b. crowding out, real shocks instead of demand shocks, timing, and bonds
   c. crowding out, drop in the bucket, externalities, monetary policy
   d. crowding out, drop in the bucket, timing, and real shocks instead of demand shocks

5. If $\vec{G}$ increases by 5% and *AD* shifts a total of 3%, then the economy has experienced
   a. the crowding out effect, which outweighs the multiplier effect.
   b. timing issues.
   c. the multiplier effect, which outweighs the crowding out effect.
   d. dedication.

6. If $\vec{G}$ increases by 5% and *AD* shifts a total of 7%, then the economy has experienced
   a. the crowding out effect, which outweighs the multiplier effect.
   b. timing issues.
   c. the multiplier effect, which outweighs the crowding out effect.
   d. dedication.

7. If the economy is already at the *long-run equilibrium* and the government engages in $100 million worth of fiscal policy, what will be the effect on *AD* in the short run?
   a. The *AD* curve will shift out by $100 million.
   b. The *AD* curve will shift out by more than $100 million.
   c. The *AD* curve will shift by less than $100 million.
   d. The *SRAS* curve will shift by $100 million.

8. Other than increased $\vec{G}$, the most direct effect of the government financing fiscal policy through bond sales is an decrease in_____.
   a. $\vec{C}$
   b. $\vec{I}$
   c. $\vec{M}$
   d. $\vec{v}$

# CHAPTER 17 (31) • Fiscal Policy

9. If people are consumption smoothing (Chapter 8), what will they do with a tax rebate?
    a. They will use it to pay off debt or save the amount of the tax rebate.
    b. They will spend the amount of the tax rebate.
    c. They will spend more than the amount of the tax rebate.
    d. None of the answers is correct.

10. How does a tax rebate differ from a reduction in tax rates?
    a. A reduction in tax rates discourages work; a tax rebate changes people's work decisions.
    b. A reduction in tax rates encourages work and investment; a tax rebate encourages lots of spending.
    c. A reduction in tax rates encourages work and investment; a tax rebate encourages saving or paying off debt.
    d. A reduction in tax rates encourages investment but not work; a tax rebate encourages work but not investment.

11. How does a tax rebate differ from a tax credit?
    a. A tax rebate discourages work; a tax credit changes people's work decisions.
    b. A tax rebate encourages work and investment; a tax credit encourages lots of spending.
    c. A tax rebate encourages saving; a tax credit changes the timing of investment or consumption.
    d. A tax rebate encourages investment but not work; a tax credit encourages work but not investment.

12. When the Bush administration gave tax rebates of $78 billion, what did most people do?
    a. Most people spent the money on luxury goods like flat screen TV's.
    b. Most people paid down their debt.
    c. Most people gave the money back to the government.
    d. Most people invested in gold.

13. Ricardian equivalence is a special case of
    a. crowding out.
    b. legislative delay.
    c. timing.
    d. real shocks versus aggregate demand shocks.

14. In GDP terms, how big is President Obama's fiscal stimulus per year?
    a. about 10% of GDP
    b. almost 50% of GDP
    c. slightly more than 2/3s of GDP
    d. about 2% of GDP

**15.** Which of the following is an example of an automatic stabilizer?
   a. unemployment benefits
   b. cash
   c. roads to nowhere
   d. increased highway funds

**16.** The political differences between Democrats and Republicans is sometimes shown by which of the following types of fiscal policy that they prefer?
   a. Republicans prefer more spending.
   b. Democrats prefer more spending.
   c. Republicans prefer tax rebates and Democrats prefer more spending.
   d. Democrats prefer tax rebates and Republicans prefer more spending.

**17.** What is the effect of fiscal policy when there has been a real shock?
   a. GDP growth is large while inflation increases minimally.
   b. GDP growth is large while inflation increases dramatically.
   c. GDP growth is small while inflation increases minimally.
   d. GDP growth is small while inflation increases dramatically.

**18.** How is inflation affected by fiscal policy during a recession that is caused by real shocks rather than by aggregate demand shocks?
   a. Fiscal policy causes the same amount of inflation regardless of whether a recession was caused by aggregate demand or a real shock.
   b. Inflation will be greater if there was a real shock.
   c. Inflation will be greater if there was an aggregate demand shock.
   d. Fiscal policy leads to deflation not inflation.

**19.** Which of the following scenarios would imply that fiscal policy might be successful?
   a. The country has a real shock and the national debt is already 200% of GDP.
   b. The country has a demand shock and unemployment is relatively low.
   c. The country has a demand shock and unemployment is quite high.
   d. All of the answers are correct.

**20.** Which of the following would imply that fiscal policy would *not* be successful?
   a. The country experienced a real shock instead of a demand shock.
   b. The country has low unemployment.
   c. Long-term growth is more important than short-term gain.
   d. All of the answers are correct.

## Short-Answer Questions

21. There are five lags for fiscal policy. What are they?

22. How could more government spending actually pay for itself?

23. What are the four problems with fiscal policy?

24. When is fiscal policy *most* likely to matter?

25. What is the effect of a tremendous fiscal stimulus paid through bonds, if Ricardian equivalence holds?

26. Show the effect of fiscal policy on aggregate demand, and then show how crowding out can make fiscal policy less effective.

27. How does the outcome of fiscal policy differ depending on the cause of the recession?

**28.** How would fiscal policy turn out if the economy were already at full employment?

**29.** Explain when fiscal policy can actually make matters worse.

**30.** Let's see what each of the "three demand difficulties of using fiscal policy" look like in real life. Categorize each of the three following stories as either an example of: 1) crowding out, 2) a drop in the bucket, or 3) a matter of timing.
   a. During a recession, the state of California hires 1,000 new prison guards. The legislature in Sacramento takes 6 months to pass the law and because of government rules and paperwork, the workers actually begin a full 18 months after the recession begins.
   b. During a recession, the state of Illinois hires 1,000 new police officers, but most of the officers were just people who quit their other jobs to take better paying police jobs.
   c. During the recession, the State of Florida hires 1,000 new social workers, but in the meantime 300,000 other workers lose their jobs.

# Answer Key

## Answers to Practice Exercises: Learning by Doing

1. A fall in $\vec{C}$ and a fall in $\vec{v}$ are very similar. When $\vec{C}$ falls because consumers are worried about the recession, they are spending less money. Since they are spending less money, each dollar is in fewer transactions, and so $\vec{v}$ falls too.

   **Topic: Fiscal Policy: The Best Case**

2. Fiscal policy is specific government spending designed to lessen the negative effects of the business cycle.

   **Topic: Introduction**

3. The two types of fiscal policy are increases in government spending and cuts in taxes designed to increase consumer spending.

   **Topic: Introduction**

4. In the best case, fiscal stimulus replaces lower consumption, with increased government spending to shift the aggregate demand curve outward by exactly the appropriate amount with minimal lags. In fact in an absolutely best case scenario, increased government spending can stimulate the economy enough to encourage consumption to increase as well.

   **Topic: Fiscal Policy: The Best Case**

5. An increase in government spending can be self-financing because money spent by the government goes into people's pockets. Those people spend the money allowing the fiscal stimulus to spread and increase. The more people respend the money, the more the stimulus will be self-financing.

   **Topic: Fiscal Policy: The Best Case**

6. The four problems with fiscal policy are: crowding out (the idea that government spending pushes out private consumption and investment), a drop in the bucket (the idea that government stimulus isn't very big compared to the size of the economy), timing (fiscal policy is slow so the problem may be gone before the stimulus takes effect), and fiscal stimulus is helpful when there is a aggregate demand shock but not a real shock.

   **Topic: The Limits to Fiscal Policy**

7. Ricardian equivalence is a special case of crowding out in which people reduce their consumption and investment by the same amount as the fiscal stimulus. If Ricardian equivalence holds, then a fiscal stimulus has no effect on the economy.

   **Topic: A Special Case of Crowding Out: Ricardian Equivalence**

8. A temporary tax break does not necessarily lead to much greater aggregate demand in the following year because a temporary tax cut will be smoothed by many people. People know that they are getting temporary shot of extra income and will save some of it. Therefore, a temporary tax cut has a small effect for many years instead of a big effect in one year. Thus, a temporary investment credit can encourage firms to purchase new capital now instead of later.

   **Topic: Tax Rebates and Tax Cuts as a Tool of Fiscal Policy**

**9.**

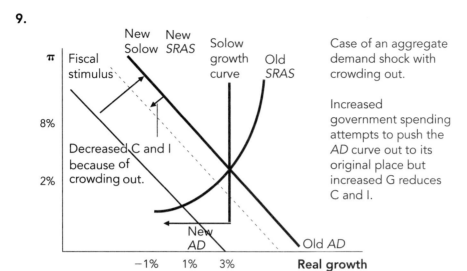

**Topic: Fiscal Policy Does Not Work Well to Combat Real Shocks**

**10.** The following graphs show the effect of fiscal policy on a recession that was caused by lower aggregate demand and the effect of fiscal policy on a recession caused by a real shock.

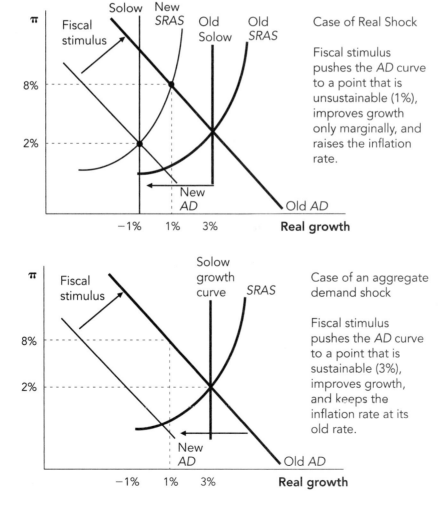

**Topic: Fiscal Policy Does Not Work Well to Combat Real Shocks**

## Answers to Multiple-Choice Questions

1. a, Topic: Introduction
2. b, Topic: Fiscal Policy: The Best Case
3. a, Topic: The Mutliplier
4. d, Topic: The Limits to Fiscal Policy
5. a, Topic: Crowding Out
6. c, Topic: The Multiplier
7. c, Topic: Crowding Out
8. b, Topic: Crowding Out
9. a, Topic: Crowding Out
10. c, Topic: Government Spending versus Tax Cuts as Expansionary Fiscal Policy
11. c, Topic: Government Spending versus Tax Cuts as Expansionary Fiscal Policy
12. b, Topic: Government Spending versus Tax Cuts as Expansionary Fiscal Policy
13. a, Topic: Crowding Out
14. d, Topic: A Drop in the Bucket: Can Government Spend Enough to Simulate Aggregate Demand?
15. a, Topic: A Matter of Timing
16. c, Topic: Government Spending versus Tax Cuts as Expansionary Fiscal Policy
17. d, Topic: Fiscal Policy Does Not Work Well to Combat Real Shocks
18. b, Topic: Fiscal Policy Does Not Work Well to Combat Real Shocks
19. c, Topic: So When Is Fiscal Policy a Good Idea?
20. d, Topic: So When Is Fiscal Policy a Good Idea?

## Answers to Short-Answer Questions

21. The five lags for fiscal policy are:
    1. Recognition lag—the problem must be recognized.
    2. Legislative lag—Congress must propose and pass a plan.
    3. Implementation lag—bureaucracies must implement the plan.
    4. Effectiveness lag—the plan takes time to work.
    5. Evaluation and adjustment lag—Did the plan work? Have conditions changed? [Return to lag 1!].

    **Topic: A Matter of Timing**

22. More government spending could actually pay for itself if there were unused resources that were spurred into use by government spending. If fiscal policy encourages private investment and private consumption enough, then growth will be large enough to pay for the government expenditures.

**Topic: Fiscal Policy: The Best Case**

23. The four problems with fiscal policy are: crowding out (the idea that government spending pushes out private consumption and investment), a drop in the bucket (the idea that government stimulus isn't very big compared to the size of the economy), timing (fiscal policy is slow so the problem may be gone before the stimulus takes effect), and fiscal stimulus is helpful when there is a aggregate demand shock but not a real shock.

**Topic: The Limits to Fiscal Policy**

24. Fiscal policy is most likely to matter when there was an aggregate demand shock instead of a real shock. It matters when there are unused resources, so that there won't be crowding out. It matters when Ricardian equivalence does not hold. Finally, fiscal policy is more likely to work when the national debt is not too large.

**Topic: So When Is Fiscal Policy a Good Idea?**

25. If Ricardian equivalence holds, then a tremendous fiscal stimulus will have no effect on aggregate demand. People will consume and invest less in order to pay for future taxes that will come about to pay off the bonds.

**Topic: A Special Case of Crowding Out: Ricardian Equivalence**

26.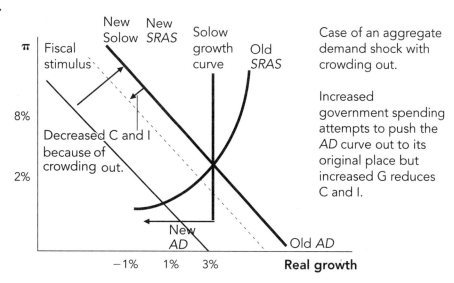

27. Fiscal policy is not very effective when the recession is caused by real shocks. In that case fiscal policy will have limited effect on real growth but a large effect on inflation. In the event of a aggregate demand caused recession, fiscal policy can be effective. In that case the aggregate demand curve can shift back to its original position with expected growth and inflation.

**Topic: Fiscal Policy Does Not Work Well to Combat Real Shocks**

28. Fiscal policy will have poor effects if the economy is at full employment. In this case, there is no opportunity for fiscal policy to hire the unemployed. Aggregate demand will not shift very much. There will be lots of crowding and the possibility of higher inflation is very real.

    **Topic: A Matter of Timing**

29. If a country already has lots of debt relative to its GDP, then people will be very aware that new fiscal policy will be very hard to achieve. People will fear that the government will monetize its existing debt in order to pay for fiscal policy. This will encourage people to convert their money into other currencies and deposit the money in other countries.

    **Topic: When Fiscal Policy Might Make Matters Worse**

30. a. 3 a matter of timing

    b. 1 crowding out

    c. 2 a drop in the bucket

    **Topic: The Limits to Fiscal Policy**

# 18 (8)

## International Trade

## Why Learn about International Trade?

As the authors say in the introductory paragraph to this chapter, asking why you should learn about international trade is a very good question. After all, trade is trade. Trade between two people is the same whether they happen to live on the same side of an artificial line drawn on a map or whether they happen to live on opposite sides of that line. So, as the authors say, this is a chapter on the economics of trade and the politics of international trade.

However, almost everyone should care about this topic because we all trade with people in our own country and other countries. So, who will be interested in international trade?

> Consumers who must make purchases, that is, trade with businesses or other people, or else become self-sufficient and make their own goods
> Businesspeople, who are generally on the other side (that is, the selling side) of trading with consumers
> Legislators, government officials, and candidates (at any level), who will be under pressure to regulate trade, would want to have a better understanding of how to proceed and what the effects of regulation will be
> Students of economics, of course, as consumers or potentially businesspeople

## Summary

The economics of trade does not vary, whether it is between two parties within a country or two parties in different countries. Trade takes place when both sides expect to gain. There are, however, political issues associated with trade between two parties in different countries.

Trade allows people to specialize in production and take advantage of division of knowledge and economies of scale. Division of knowledge is important as it allows people to specialize. The farmer need only know about farming, the attorney need only know about the law, and the chef need only know about cooking. Division of knowledge allows each individual to know more about their one specific area. Without specialization, one person running a restaurant would have to know enough about farming to grow crops, know enough about the law to set up the business enterprise, and know enough about food preparation to be the chef.

**Economies of scale** are cost per unit savings that come with the size of an enterprise. Division of knowledge allows enterprises to grow larger and take advantage of economies of scale. The farmer-attorney-chef person described above would not be growing enough wheat to take advantage of combine threshers, but a farmer that specializes in growing wheat to sell to others, could realize such economies of scale.

One has a **comparative advantage** in producing those goods that can be produced at the lowest opportunity cost. This concept can be contrasted with **absolute advantage,** which is when one can produce goods using fewer resources than other producers. Everyone will have a comparative advantage in something, even if they do not have an absolute advantage in any one good. This applies to people individually and the people of a country. Exploiting comparative advantage can be summed up as it was in the text as "sell what you can make at low cost and buy what you can make only at high cost."

Comparative and absolute advantage can be shown with the simple example in Table 18.1, where Jill can produce either pizzas or sandwiches using less of the labor input.

### Table 18.1

|  | Labor units required to produce... | | Opportunity cost of... | |
| --- | --- | --- | --- | --- |
|  | **1 Pizza** | **1 Sandwich** | **1 Pizza** | **1 Sandwich** |
| Jack | 2 | 6 | 0.33 Sandwiches | 3 Pizza |
| Jill | 1 | 2 | 0.5 Sandwiches | 2 Pizza |

Thus Jill has an absolute advantage in producing both goods as she can produce each good with few labor units. Jack does not have an absolute advantage in either good. Still Jack and Jill can trade based on comparative advantage. Notice that Jack has a lower opportunity cost of producing pizzas. He gives up only one-third of a sandwich to produce a pizza while Jill gives up half a sandwich. On the other hand, Jill has a comparative advantage in producing subs. She gives up only 2 pizzas per sandwich produced, while Jack's opportunity cost is 3 pizzas per sandwich.

If Jack and Jill each worked an 8-hour day, then we can see the benefits of free trade in Table 18.2, where the production amounts are based on labor units required from Table 18.1.

Table 18.2 Gains from Free Trade

|  |  | Pizzas | | Sandwiches | |
|---|---|---|---|---|---|
|  |  | Production | Consumption | Production | Consumption |
| No trade with an 8-hour day | Jack | 1 (2 hours) | 1 | 1 (6 hours) | 1 |
|  | Jill | 4 (4 hours) | 4 | 2 (4 hours) | 2 |
|  |  | Production | Consumption | Production | Consumption |
| Trade with an 8-hour day | Jack | 4 (8 hours) | 1.5 | 0 | 1 |
|  | Jill | 2 (2 hours) | 4.5 | 3 (6 hours) | 2 |

With no trade, Jack can produce and consume 1 pizza and 1 sandwich, while Jill can produce and consume 4 pizzas and 2 sandwiches. But remember from Table 18.1, Jack has a comparative advantage in producing pizzas, while Jill has a comparative advantage in producing sandwiches. So in our example, if Jack specializes in pizza and Jill moves toward producing more sandwiches, Jack plus Jill's total production of pizza can rise from 5 to 6 pizzas, while they are jointly able to maintain their production of sandwiches at 3. Thus in our example, Jill can trade 1 sandwich for 2.5 pizzas from Jack and both increase their consumption of pizzas by one-half pizza, while maintaining the same consumption of sandwiches. Remember, an example like this showing gains from trade can be constructed for the people of two countries just as it was for two people here.

Gains from free trade can also be seen graphically in Figure 18.1, where $5 and 100 units are the equilibrium price and quantity if there is no trade.

With no trade, consumer surplus is area A, producer surplus is area $B + F$, and total surplus is area $A + B + F$. Once this market is opened up for free trade, then con-

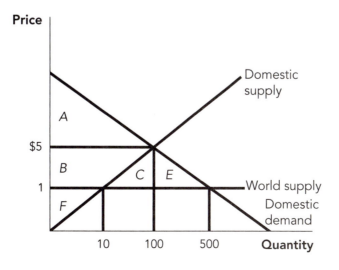

Figure 18.1

sumers can buy at the world price of $1. Then consumer surplus is $A + B + C + E$, producer surplus is $F$, and total surplus is $A + B + C + E + F$. Thus total surplus has grown by area $C + E$ or there are gains from trade of $C + E$.

Conversely, we can see what happens if the government imposes some type of protection on this market. **Protectionism** is an economic policy of restraining trade through **quotas**, **tariffs**, or other regulations that burden foreign producers but not domestic producers. A trade quota is a quantity restriction where imports greater than the quota amount are forbidden. A tariff is a tax on imports.

In Figure 18.1, if the government imposed a quota or tariff large enough that none of the good was imported and price returned to the no-trade equilibrium, where domestic supply equals domestic demand, there will be lost gains from trade. As in the no-trade situation discussed above, consumer surplus is area $A$, producer surplus is area $B + F$, and total surplus is $A + B + F$. The gains from opening up the market to free trade, area $C + E$, are lost due to the protection. Area $E$ is a consumption loss due to domestic consumers losing consumption they formerly had. Area $C$ is an efficiency loss due to relatively inefficient domestic producers replacing relatively efficient foreign producers in supplying this good to the domestic market.

The losses due to protectionism can also be described in terms of the conditions from Chapter 3, concerning why a free market is efficient. With the protection, the good is no longer sold by suppliers with the lowest costs. Since there are lost gains from trade with the protection, the sum of consumer plus producer surplus is no longer maximized.

Protectionism, in general, raises the price of imported goods by reducing supply in the domestic market. This leads to an increase in price of the domestic substitutes for the foreign good too, as the supply of the good, domestic plus foreign, will be reduced.

There are other issues associated with international trade. One concern is the effect on wages. Wages depend on productivity and by encouraging workers to move to relatively productive industries. International trade between two countries can cause wages in both countries to rise. With international trade, jobs are lost in some industries, but jobs grow in other industries. Keeping jobs via protectionism is very expensive and retraining displaced workers or somehow compensating workers who lost their jobs would be a better policy. Child labor is related to the income of the people of a country, as is free trade. So free trade, rather than restrictions on free trade, is a better policy to reduce child labor around the world. Some people argue for protection of certain strategic or national defense industries. Every industry will argue that they are strategic or important for national defense and if protected they will eventually become inefficient due to reduced competition.

Decreases in transportation costs, integration of world markets, and increased speed of communication has made the world seem smaller. This trend is sometimes called *globalization*. Some people think this is new or bad, but the world has only recently become as globalized as it was prior to World War I. To give up globalization is to give up the gains from international trade.

# Key Terms

**economies of scale** costs per unit fall with increases in production

**absolute advantage** the ability to produce the same good using fewer inputs than another producer

**comparative advantage** the ability to produce a good at a lower opportunity cost than another producer

**protectionism** the economic policy of restraining trade through quotas, tariffs, or other regulations that burden foreign producers but not domestic producers

**trade quota** a restriction on the quantity of goods that can be imported: Imports greater than the quota amount are forbidden or heavily taxed

**tariff** a tax on imports

# Traps, Hints, and Reminders

Trade takes place, whether it occurs between individuals in a country or individuals in different countries, when both individuals expect to benefit.

One has a comparative advantage when one can produce at lower opportunity costs than other producers.

A tariff is simply a tax, so it has many of the effects on a market that any other tax would.

# Practice Exercises: Learning by Doing

1. How is the economics of international trade different from trade between two people within a country?

2. What are division of knowledge and economies of scale? What is their role in trade?

3. What is comparative advantage? How does comparative advantage differ from absolute advantage?

4. Fill in the opportunity costs in the table below. Who has the comparative advantage and what is it for? Who has the absolute advantage and what is it for?

| | Labor units required to produce... | | Opportunity cost of... | |
|---|---|---|---|---|
| | 1 Barrel of Oil | 1 Movie | 1 Barrel of Oil | 1 Movie |
| United States | 1 | 2 | | |
| Canada | 2 | 8 | | |

5. In the graph below, mark out (that is, set boundaries to) the losses associated with protecting the market to such an extent that there is no trade. Calculate the value of the deadweight loss associated with the protection.

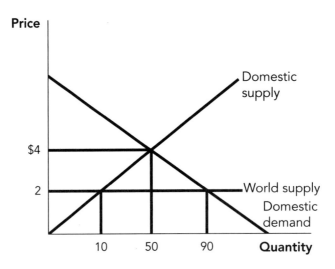

6. What is protectionism? What is a tariff? What is a quota?

7. What does specialization and trade lead to for individuals and the people of countries that trade?

*8. The Japanese people currently pay about four times the world price for rice. If Japan removed its trade barriers so that Japanese consumers could buy rice at the world price, who would be better off: Japanese consumers or Japanese rice farmers? If we added all the gains and losses to the Japanese, would there be a net gain or net loss? Who would lobby for reducing trade barriers? Explain why. Who would lobby against reducing trade barriers? Explain why.[1]

# Multiple-Choice Questions

1. You have a comparative advantage in producing goods you can produce
   a. more of.
   b. at the lowest opportunity cost.
   c. using fewer inputs.
   d. All of the answers are correct.

2. You have an absolute advantage in producing goods you can produce
   a. more of.
   b. at the lowest opportunity cost.
   c. using fewer inputs.
   d. All of the answers are correct.

3. Everyone must necessarily have
   a. a comparative advantage.
   b. an absolute advantage.
   c. a tariff.
   d. All of the answers are correct.

---

[1]Questions marked with a ★ are also end-of-chapter questions.

## Table 18.3

| | Labor units required to produce... | | Opportunity cost of... | |
|---|---|---|---|---|
| | 1 Computer | 1 Camera | 1 Computer | 1 Camera |
| United States | 3 | 5 | | |
| Japan | 2 | 2 | | |

4. According to the data in Table 18.3, the opportunity cost of a computer in the United States is

   a. 0.6 cameras.

   b. 1 camera.

   c. 1.67 cameras

   d. None of the answers is correct.

5. According to the data in Table 18.3, the opportunity cost of a camera in Japan is

   a. 0.6 computers.

   b. 1 computer.

   c. 1.67 computers.

   d. None of the answers is correct.

6. According to the data in Table 18.3, Japan has an absolute advantage in

   a. producing cameras.

   b. producing computers.

   c. producing both goods.

   d. producing neither good.

7. According to the data in Table 18.3, the United States has a comparative advantage in

   a. producing cameras.

   b. producing computers.

   c. producing both goods.

   d. producing neither good.

8. According to the data in Table 18.3, Japan has a comparative advantage in

   a. producing cameras.

   b. producing computers.

   c. producing both goods.

   d. producing neither good.

Figure 18.2

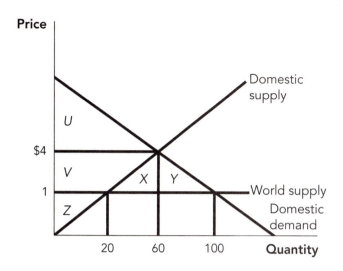

9. In Figure 18.2, with no international trade, consumer surplus is area
   a. U.
   b. U + V + X + Z.
   c. V + Z.
   d. Z.

10. In Figure 18.2, with no international trade, producer surplus is area
    a. U.
    b. U + V + X + Y.
    c. V + Z.
    d. Z.

11. In Figure 18.2, with international trade, consumer surplus is area
    a. U.
    b. U + V + X + Y.
    c. X + Y.
    d. Z.

12. In Figure 18.2, with international trade, producer surplus is area
    a. U.
    b. U + V + X + Y.
    c. X + Y.
    d. Z.

13. In Figure 18.2, the gain from international trade is area
    a. U.
    b. U + V + X + Y.
    c. X + Y.
    d. Z.

14. In Figure 18.2, if the market was protected to such an extent that all international trade stopped, then the deadweight loss would be
    a. $3.
    b. $60.
    c. $120.
    d. $240.

15. A tax on imports is called
    a. a comparative advantage.
    b. a tariff.
    c. an absolute advantage.
    d. a quota.

16. A restriction on the amount of imports to less than they would be with free trade is called
    a. a comparative advantage.
    b. a tariff.
    c. an absolute advantage.
    d. a trade quota.

17. Free international trade
    a. necessarily reduces wages in the high-wage country.
    b. potentially increases wages in both countries because workers are encouraged to enter into more productive lines of work.
    c. potentially lowers wages in the low-wage country.
    d. increases child labor.

18. Economies of scale occur
    a. due to government aid.
    b. as firm size increases.
    c. due to protectionism.
    d. All of the answers are correct.

19. Trade can take place because of
    a. specialization.
    b. economies of scale.
    c. division of knowledge.
    d. All of the answers are correct.

**20.** Among the winners with a tariff on cars are

   a. domestic producers of cars.

   b. domestic consumers of cars.

   c. the economy as a whole.

   d. All of the answers are correct.

# Short-Answer Questions

**21.** How is the economics of international trade different from trade between two people within a country?

**22.** What are division of knowledge and economies of scale? What is their role in trade?

**23.** What is comparative advantage? How does it differ from absolute advantage?

**24.** Fill in the table below and state who has absolute and comparative advantages in what good.

| | Labor Units Required to Produce... | | Opportunity cost of... | |
|---|---|---|---|---|
| | 1 salad | 1 hamburger | 1 salad | 1 hamburger |
| Bonnie | 1 | 5 | | |
| Clyde | 3 | 3 | | |

25. Refer to the graph below. What area shows the losses associated with protecting the market to such an extent that there is no trade? Calculate the value of the deadweight loss associated with the protection.

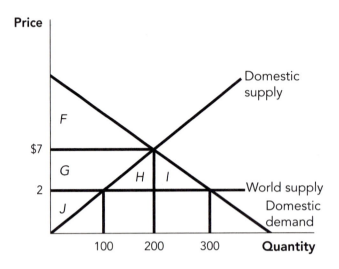

26. In the graph in Question 25, explain the sources of the lost gains from trade due to the protection eliminating any international trade.

27. What is protectionism? What is a tariff? What is a quota?

28. If protectionism makes a foreign good more expensive, what happens to the price of the domestic version of the good? Why?

**29.** What does specialization and trade lead to for individuals and the people of countries that trade?

**30.** Who are the winners and losers with a tariff?

# Answer Key

## Answers to Practice Exercises: Learning by Doing

1. The economics of trade does not vary whether it is between two parties within a country or two parties in different countries. Two parties trade when each expects to be made better off by the trade.

   **Topic: Division of Knowledge *and* Economies of Scale and Creating Competition**

2. Division of knowledge is important as it allows people to specialize. The farmer need only know about farming, the attorney need only know about the law, and the chef need only know about cooking. Division of knowledge allows each individual to know more about their specific area than if to operate a restaurant one person had to grow the crops, know enough law to set up the business enterprise, and finally know enough about food preparation to be the chef. Economies of scale are cost per unit savings that come with the size of an enterprise. Division of knowledge allows enterprises to grow larger and take advantage of economies of scale. The farmer-attorney-chef scenario described above would not be growing enough wheat to take advantage of combine threshers, but a specialist farmer that grows wheat to sell to others, can realize such economies of scale and produce at lower per unit costs. Trade allows people to specialize in production and take advantage of division of knowledge and economies of scale.

   **Topics: Division of Knowledge *and* Economies of Scale and Creating Competition**

3. One has a comparative advantage in producing those goods that one can produce for the lowest opportunity cost. This concept can be contrasted with absolute advantage, that is, when one can produce using fewer resources than other producers. Everyone will have a comparative advantage in something, even if they do not have an absolute advantage in any one good. This applies to people individually and all the people of a country. Exploiting comparative advantage can be summed up as it was in the text as "sell what you can make at low cost and buy what you can make only at high cost."

   **Topic: Comparative Advantage**

4. The table below contains the filled-in boxes.

   |  | Labor units required to produce... | | Opportunity cost of... | |
   |---|---|---|---|---|
   |  | 1 Barrel of Oil | 1 Movie | 1 Barrel of Oil | 1 Movie |
   | United States | 1 | 2 | .5 movies | 2 barrel |
   | Canada | 2 | 8 | .25 movies | 4 barrels |

The people of the United States have an absolute advantage in both oil and movie production as they can produce each with fewer labor inputs. But looking at the opportunity costs, we can see that the people of the United States have a lower opportunity cost of producing movies and thus a comparative advantage in producing movies. The people of Canada have a lower opportunity cost of producing oil and thus a comparative advantage in producing oil.

**Topic: Comparative Advantage**

5. The losses associated with protection, eliminating all international trade in this market, are marked in the graph below.

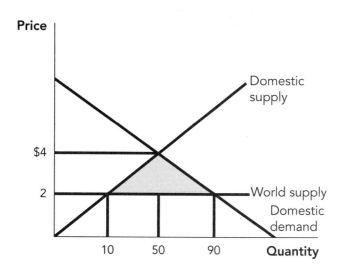

The amount of the area is $2 \times 80/2$ or $80 in deadweight loss.

**Topic: The Costs of Protectionism**

6. Protectionism is an economic policy of restraining trade through quotas, tariffs, or other regulations that burden foreign producers but not domestic producers. A tariff is a tax on imports. A trade quota is a quantity restriction where imports greater than the quota amount are forbidden.

**Topic: Analyzing Trade with Supply and Demand**

7. Trade between individuals and countries can lead to gains by both sides. Trade only takes place when both sides expect to gain. Also since wages depend on productivity, by encouraging workers to move to relatively productive industries, international trade can cause wages in both countries to rise. With international trade, jobs are lost in some industries, but jobs grow in other industries. Child labor is related to the income of the people of a country, as is free trade. So free trade can increase incomes in poorer countries and thereby reduce child labor.

**Topics: Trade and Jobs *and* Child Labor**

8. Japanese rice consumers would be better off by the removal of all Japanese barriers to rice trade. The gains of Japanese rice consumers would be greater than the losses of Japanese rice farmers, meaning that there would be a net gain from removing all barriers to rice trade in Japan. But since the costs to the farmers are concentrated on a relatively few farmers and the benefits are spread across a larger number of consumers, the farmers are likely to spend more money lobbying against this policy change than consumers would spend lobbying for it.

**Topic: Winners and Losers from Trade**

## Answers to Multiple-Choice Questions

1. b, Topic: Comparative Advantage
2. c, Topic: Comparative Advantage
3. a, Topic: Comparative Advantage
4. a, Topic: Comparative Advantage
5. b, Topic: Comparative Advantage
6. c, Topic: Comparative Advantage
7. b, Topic: Comparative Advantage
8. a, Topic: Comparative Advantage
9. a, Topic: Analyzing Trade with Supply and Demand
10. c, Topic: Analyzing Trade with Supply and Demand
11. b, Topic: Analyzing Trade with Supply and Demand
12. d, Topic: Analyzing Trade with Supply and Demand
13. c, Topic: Analyzing Trade with Supply and Demand
14. c, Topic: The Costs of Protectionism
15. b, Topic: The Costs of Protectionism
16. d, Topic: The Costs of Protectionism
17. b, Topic: Comparative Advantage
18. b, Topic: Economies of Scale and Creating Competition
19. d, Topics: Division of Knowledge *and* Economies of Scale and Creating Competition
20. a, Topic: Winners and Losers from Trade

## Answers to Short-Answer Questions

21. The economics of trade does not vary whether it is between two parties within a country or two parties in different countries. Two parties trade when each expects to be made better off by the trade.

    **Topics: Division of Knowledge *and* Economies of Scale and Creating Competition**

22. Division of knowledge is important as it allows people to specialize. The farmer need only know about farming, the attorney need only know about the law, and the chef need only know about cooking. Division of knowledge allows each individual to know more about their area than if to operate a restaurant one person grows the crops, knows enough law to set up the business enterprise, and finally knows enough about food preparation to be the chef. Economies of scale are cost per unit savings that come with the size of an enterprise. Division of knowledge allows enterprises to grow larger and take advantage of economies of scale. The farmer-attorney-chef scenario described above would not grow enough wheat to take advantage of combine threshers, but a specialist farmer that grows wheat to sell to others, can realize such economies of scale and produce at lower per unit costs. Trade allows people to specialize in production and take advantage of division of knowledge and economies of scale.

    **Topics: Division of Knowledge *and* Economies of Scale and Creating Competition**

23. One has a comparative advantage in producing those goods that one can produce for the lowest opportunity cost. This concept can be contrasted with absolute advantage, that is, when one can produce using fewer resources than other producers. Everyone will have a comparative advantage in something, even if they do not have an absolute advantage in any one good. This applies to both people individually and the people of a country. Exploiting comparative advantage can be summed up as it was in the text as "sell what you can make at low cost and buy what you can make only at high cost."

    **Topic: Comparative Advantage**

24. The table below contains the filled-in boxes.

    |        | Labor Units Required to Produce... | | Opportunity cost of... | |
    |--------|:---:|:---:|:---:|:---:|
    |        | 1 salad | 1 hamburger | 1 salad | 1 hamburger |
    | Bonnie | 1 | 5 | 0.2 hamburger | 5 salad |
    | Clyde  | 3 | 3 | 1 hamburger | 1 salad |

    Bonnie has a comparative and absolute advantage in producing salads. Clyde has a comparative and absolute advantage in producing hamburgers.

    **Topic: Comparative Advantage**

25. The deadweight loss would be $H + I$, which has have a value of $5 × 200/2 or $500.

   **Topic: The Costs of Protectionism**

26. Area $H$ is a loss of efficiency due to less efficient domestic producers replacing relatively efficient foreign producers in the market. Area $I$ is a consumption loss due to exchanges that previously took place being pushed out of the market due to the protectionist policy.

   **Topic: The Costs of Protectionism**

27. Protectionism is an economic policy of restraining trade through quotas, tariffs, or other regulations that burden foreign producers but not domestic producers. A tariff is a tax on imports. A trade quota is a quantity restriction where imports greater than the quota amount are forbidden.

   **Topic: The Costs of Protectionism**

28. Protectionism, in general, raises the price of imported goods by reducing supply in the domestic market. This will lead to an increase in price of the domestic substitutes for the foreign good too, as the supply of the good, domestic plus foreign, will be reduced.

   **Topic: The Costs of Protectionism**

29. Trade between individuals and countries can lead to gains by both sides. Trade only takes place when both sides expect to gain. Also, since wages depend on productivity, by encouraging workers to move to relatively productive industries, international trade can cause wages in both countries to rise. With international trade, jobs are lost in some industries, but jobs grow in other industries. Child labor is related to the income of the people of a country as is free trade. So free trade can increase incomes in poorer countries and thereby reduce child labor.

   **Topics: Trade and Jobs *and* Child Labor**

30. The winners with a tariff include domestic workers and firms that produce the product. They get to produce more and their surplus goes up. Another winner is the government that collects the tariff revenue. The losers include consumers who pay more and consume less. Thus, their surplus falls. The economy as a whole loses because what the winner gains is smaller than what the losers lose.

   **Topic: Trade and Globalization**

# 19 (32)

# International Finance

## Why Learn about International Finance?

Almost everyone should care about this topic because we all trade with people in our own country and people in other countries. Among those who will be particularly interested in this topic are:

> International studies majors will care about international finance because trade deficits, capital surpluses, and exchange rates are common issues at international treaties. These students will care about the economic as well as political relationships between countries

> Students who want to protest the IMF and World Bank will care because understanding what the IMF does will help students make more intelligent protests.

> Business majors will care because exchange rates and how changes in exchange rates can affect the profits of a business is very important to firms who do business internationally.

## Summary

International finance combines international trade as well as currency exchange. It looks hard but has three main points.

> Gains from trade occur when people trade across different countries with different currencies, just as gains from trade occur within a single nation with a single currency.

> The rate of savings is a key variable in understanding international trade and finance.
> Market equilibrium means that, at the margin, the gains from holding or spending one currency are equal to the gains from holding or spending some other currency. That sounds simple but we'll see that this principle will be a building block for understanding the market value of one currency relative to another.

In terms of goods, a country can have a trade deficit or a trade surplus. A **trade deficit** occurs when the value of a country's imports exceeds the value of its exports.

A **trade surplus** occurs when the value of a country's exports exceeds the value of its imports.

The **balance of payments** is a yearly summary of all the economic transactions between residents of one country and residents of the rest of the world. Keep in mind that the balance of payments is a combination of trade and financial transfers. A country runs a **capital surplus** when the inflow of foreign capital is greater than the outflow of domestic capital to other nations.

The **current account** is the sum of the balance of trade, net income on capital held abroad, and net transfer payments.

The **capital account** measures changes in foreign ownership of domestic assets, including financial assets likes stocks and bonds as well as physical assets.

In relation to currencies, an **exchange rate** is the price of one currency in another currency. An exchange rate **appreciation** is an increase in the price of one currency in terms of another currency. An exchange rate **depreciation** is a decrease in the price of a currency in terms of another currency. The **nominal exchange rate** is the rate at which you can exchange one currency for another. The **real exchange rate** is the rate at which you can exchange the goods and services of one country for the goods and services of another. A **fixed** or **pegged exchange rate** means that a government or central bank has promised to convert its currency into another currency at a fixed rate. A **floating exchange rate** is one determined primarily by market forces. A **dirty** or **managed float** is a currency whose value is not pegged, but governments will intervene extensively in the market to keep the value within a certain range. **Dollarization** occurs when a foreign country uses the U.S. dollar as its currency.

The real exchange rate relates to purchasing power parity and the law of one price. The **purchasing power parity (PPP) theorem** says that the real purchasing power of money should be the same, whether it is spent at home or converted into another currency and spent abroad. The **law of one price** says that if trade were free, then identical goods should sell for about the same price throughout the world. An ounce of gold will sell for the same price no matter where it is. But be careful. Some products don't ship well or are expensive to ship. Some products such as services can't be shipped easily.

# Key Terms

**trade deficit** occurs when the value of a country's imports exceeds the value of its exports

**trade surplus** occurs when the value of a country's exports exceeds the value of its imports

**balance of payments** is a yearly summary of all the economic transactions between residents of one country and residents of the rest of the world

**capital surplus** occurs when the inflow of a country's foreign capital is greater than the outflow of domestic capital to other nations

**current account** is the sum of the balance of trade, net income on capital held abroad, and net transfer payments

**capital account** measures changes in foreign ownership of domestic assets including financial assets likes stocks and bonds as well as physical assets

**exchange rate** is the price of one currency in another currency

**appreciation** is an increase in the price of one currency in terms of another currency

**depreciation** is a decrease in the price of a currency in terms of another currency

**nominal exchange rate** is the rate at which you can exchange one currency for another

**real exchange rate** is the rate at which you can exchange the goods and services of one country for the goods and services of another

the **purchasing power parity (PPP) theorem** says that the real purchasing power of a money should be the same, whether it is spent at home or converted into another currency and spent abroad

the **law of one price** says that if trade were free, then identical goods should sell for about the same price throughout the world

**floating exchange rate** is one determined primarily by market forces

**fixed or pegged exchange rate** means that a government or central bank has promised to convert its currency into another currency at a fixed rate

**dollarization** occurs when a foreign country uses the U.S. dollar as its currency

**dirty or managed float** is a currency whose value is not pegged but governments will intervene extensively in the market to keep the value within a certain range

## Tips, Traps, and Hints

### Understanding current and capital account.

$5 million of Orange Juice Brazil has *trade surplus* and a *current account surplus*.

$3 million of Maple Syrup and $2 million to invest. Canada has a *trade deficit* and a *current account deficit*.

But you can't invest Canadian dollars in Brazil. So Brazil gets $2 million of financial assets in Canada. If the Brazilians don't like the investment, they have to use the money to buy Canadian goods instead. Canada gets a *capital account surplus*. Brazil gets a *capital account deficit*.

When Brazilians accept having a trade surplus with Canada, that means they want to invest in Canada and have a *capital deficit*.

## Traps, Hints and Reminders

This is a vocabulary-intense chapter. Make sure that you are ready. You might try thinking of the current account as the account that is in all the news. News is supposed to be current and the news talks about the trade deficit not the capital account. The capital account is all about capital whether it is physical capital or stocks. The capital account seems very capitalistic so that may help you remember on the exam.

Don't forget that in the current account services count too. So if an Indian provides accounting for an American firm, that adds to India's current account and subtracts from the U.S. current account.

## Practice Exercises; Learning by Doing

1. What is the difference between a trade surplus and a *capital account* surplus?




2. Is it possible to have a trade surplus and a capital account deficit?

3. Why is gold more likely to sell for the same price regardless of location than are hair cuts?

4. Why wouldn't you worry about a trade deficit with one country?

★5. Practice with the balance of payments:[1]

**Current account 1 capital account 5 change in official reserves**

   a. Current account = −$10, Capital account = +$15. What is the change in reserves?
   b. Current account = −$10, Change in reserves = −$3. What is the capital account?
   c. Your college expenses = $12,000, Income from your barista job = $4,000. What is your current account? If you haven't changed your reserves (cash savings) at all, what is the capital account (i.e., borrowing from parents or bank)?

6. If the United States becomes a worse place to invest in, what will happen to the current and capital accounts?

7. If a haircut costs $20 in the United States and 27.17 Swiss Francs in Switzerland, what is the *real* exchange rate of Swiss Francs to U.S. Dollars?

---

[1]Questions marked with a ★ are also end-of-chapter questions.

## Multiple-Choice Questions

1. If China sells more goods to Germany than Germany sells to China, then China has a _____ with Germany.
   a. comparative advantage
   b. trade surplus
   c. trade deficit
   d. current account balance

2. If China is bringing in more money from other countries than it sends to other countries, then China has a
   a. capital surplus.
   b. trade surplus
   c. trade deficit.
   d. current account balance.

3. The yearly summary of all the economic transactions between residents of one country and residents of the rest of the world is
   a. capital surplus.
   b. trade surplus.
   c. trade deficit.
   c. balance of payments.

4. What are the three main parts of the *investments* part of the capital account?
   a. foreign direct investment, portfolio investment, and other investments (such as shifting bank deposits)
   b. foreign direct investment, portfolio investment, and changing coin collections
   c. foreign direct investment, portfolio investment, and movements in Treasury gold
   d. foreign direct investment, foreign aid, and bank investment

5. If your country has a trade deficit that is not being balanced by foreign direct investment, portfolio investment, and other investments (such as shifting bank deposits), that implies that the balance is being made up where?
   a. official reserves
   b. capital account
   c. current account
   d. oil futures

6. If your country has a trade deficit, then which of the following is probably in surplus?

   a. capital account

   b. current account

   c. oil futures

   d. official reserves

7. If the French think that the United States is a better place to invest than France, then the United States is likely to have _____ with France.

   a. a trade surplus

   b. a capital account surplus

   c. a capital account deficit

   d. decreasing bank reserves

*Use the following table (from July 12, 2009) for questions 8-11.*

| Currency Last Trade | US $ | Yen | Euro | Can $ | UK £ | AU $ | Swiss Franc |
|---|---|---|---|---|---|---|---|
| 1 US $ | – | 92.5850 | 0.7179 | 1.1638 | 0.6197 | 1.2858 | 1.0867 |
| 1 Yen | 0.0108 | – | 0.0078 | 0.0126 | 0.0067 | 0.0139 | 0.0117 |
| 1 Euro | 1.3930 | 128.9664 | – | 1.6211 | 0.8632 | 1.7911 | 1.5137 |
| 1 Can $ | 0.8593 | 79.5540 | 0.6169 | – | 0.5325 | 1.1048 | 0.9338 |
| 1 UK £ | 1.6137 | 149.4029 | 1.1585 | 1.8780 | – | 2.0749 | 1.7536 |
| 1 AU $ | 0.7777 | 72.0058 | 0.5583 | 0.9051 | 0.4820 | – | 0.8452 |
| 1 Swiss Franc | 0.9202 | 85.1983 | 0.6606 | 1.0709 | 0.5703 | 1.1832 | – |

8. Which is it more valuable to have one of?

   a. 1 US $

   b. 1 Yen

   c. 1 UK £

   d. 1 Euro

9. If an American wants to buy 20 Swiss Francs with U.S. dollars, how many dollars does she need?

   a. 92.02

   b. 18.40

   c. 37.34

   d. 9.20

10. How many Australian dollars are required to purchase 1 Canadian dollar? (rounded)
    a. 1
    b. 1.10
    c. .90
    d. .719

11. If a haircut costs $20 in the United States and 27.17 Swiss Francs in Switzerland, what is the *real* exchange rate between Switzerland and the United States?
    a. 1.0867
    b. .9202
    c. 1.3585
    d. .79993

12. *Ceteris paribus*, an increase in a country's exports, will
    a. increase demand for that country's currency and tend to increase the value of its currency.
    b. increase demand for that country's currency and tend to decrease the value of its currency.
    c. decrease demand for that country's currency and tend to increase the value of its currency.
    d. Exports and exchange rates are unrelated.

13. If a country becomes more desirable as a place to invest, then its currency will
    a. appreciate.
    b. depreciate.
    c. be unaffected.
    d. appreciate and then depreciate.

14. If a country's central bank increases the supply of its currency, then its currency will
    a. appreciate.
    b. depreciate.
    c. It is unclear from this example what will happen.
    d. be unaffected.

15. If a country's central bank increases the supply of its currency but at the same time the country becomes a better place for foreigners to invest, then the currency will

    a. appreciate.

    b. depreciate.

    c. It is unclear from this example what will happen.

    d. be unaffected.

16. Which of the following would you expect to most closely fulfill the law of one price?

    a. 1 gallon of oil

    b. a shave at the barber

    c. cement

    d. an apartment

17. When a country allows its currency to change value at the whims of the market, this is known as

    a. dollarization.

    b. flexible exchange rates.

    c. dirty or managed float.

    d. fixed or pegged rates.

## Short-Answer Questions

18. If an Argentine buys stock in a Spanish company in 2009 and gets dividend income in 2010, what happens to the current and capital accounts of Argentina?

19. Explain the difference between the nominal and real exchange rates.

20. Show the effect on the entire economy when there is a depreciation of the currency.

**21.** Explain how fiscal policy can affect the current account and the capital account.

**★22.** Consider two headlines; "Money is fleeing the United States faster than ever" versus "Record U.S. trade surplus." How can both be true simultaneously?[1]

**23.** Why is gold more likely to sell for the same price regardless of location than lawyer services?

**24.** Why wouldn't you worry about your trade deficit with one company?

---

[1]Questions marked with a ★ are also end-of-chapter questions.

# Answer Key

## Practice Exercises: Learning by Doing

1. The difference between a trade surplus and a capital surplus is that a trade surplus says that your country has exported more goods and services to other countries than it has imported from other countries. A capital surplus says that countries have shipped more financial assets to your country than you have sent to other countries. In reality, these are two sides of the same coin. If Germany imports more goods from the UK, then it exports to the UK (trade deficit), that means that Germany is sending money to UK that isn't getting sent back. That money is being invested in the UK.

   **Topic: The Capital Account, Sometimes Called the Financial Account**

2. Not only is it possible to have a trade surplus and a capital deficit together, it makes sense to have both. If you are shipping more goods abroad than you are importing, you are accepting foreign currency which is invested in that foreign country. This means that you are building capital away from home (capital account deficit) while having a current account surplus.

   **Topic: Two Sides, One Coin**

3. Gold is likely to sell for the same price regardless of location (law of one price) than hair cuts because you can easily ship gold. You can't easily ship haircuts. If the price of gold is cheap in one country, entrepreneurs will go to that country and buy gold to ship elsewhere.

   **Topic: The Purchasing Power Parity Theorem**

4. First, a trade deficit may occur because people want to invest money in your country instead of buying your goods. Second, a trade deficit with one country might be balanced out by a trade surplus with other countries.

   **Topic: The U.S. Trade Deficit and Your Trade Deficit**

5. Practice with the balance of payments:★

   Current account + capital account = change in official reserves

   a. Current account = $-$$10, Capital account = $+$$ 15. The change in reserves = $5.

   b. Current account = $-$$10, Change in reserves = $-$$3. The capital account is $7.

   c. Your college expenses = $12,000. Income from your barista job = $4,000. Your current account is $-$$8,000. If you haven't changed your reserves (cash savings) at all, the capital account (i.e. borrowing from parents or bank), is $-$$8,000.

   **Topic: The Balance of Payments**

6. If the United States becomes a worse place to invest in, people will prefer to take our merchandise instead of investing in the United States. Our current account will be in less of a deficit and our capital account will be in less of a surplus.

   **Topic: Two Sides, One Coin**

7. US to SF Nominal exchange rate * ($ Price / SF price) =

   20/27.17 × 1.0867 = .79993 So, in *real* terms, a haircut is more than 20% cheaper in Switzerland than in the United States.

   **Topic: Exchange Rate Determination in the Long Run**

## Answers to Multiple-Choice Questions

1. b, Topic: The U.S. Trade Deficit and Your Trade Deficit
2. a, Topic: The Balance of Payments
3. d, Topic: The Balance of Payments
4. a, Topic: The Balance of Payments
5. a, Topic: The Balance of Payments
6. a, Topic: The Balance of Payments
7. b, Topic: The Balance of Payments
8. c, Topic: What Are Exchange Rates?
9. b Topic: What Are Exchange Rates?
10. b, Topic: What Are Exchange Rates?
11. d, Topic: What Are Exchange Rates?
12. a, Topic: What Are Exchange Rates?
13. a, Topic: What Are Exchange Rates
14. b, Topic: Exchange Rate Determination in the Short Run
15. c, Topic: Exchange Rate Determination in the Short Run
16. a, Topic: Exchange Rate Determination in the Long Run
17. b, Topic: How Monetary and Fiscal Policy Affect Exchange Rates *and* How Exchange Rates Affect Aggregate Demand

## Answers to Short-Answer Questions

18. When an Argentine buys stock in a Spanish company in 2009, this increases the Spanish *capital account*. When that Argentine gets a dividend check a year later, the Argentine *current account* goes up and the Spanish capital account goes down.

    **Topic: The Balance of Payments**

19. The difference between nominal and real exchange rates is based on the idea that the price of a good in another country is based on the exchange rate and the nominal price in the other country. When you compare the nominal prices and the exchange rate, you get the real *exchange rate*. If purchasing power parity holds, then the real rate will be 1.

   **Topic: Exchange Rate Determination in the Long Run**

20.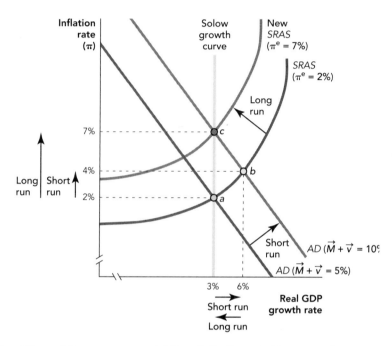

   **Topic: How Monetary and Fiscal Policy Affect Exchange Rates *and* How Exchange Rates Affect Aggregate Demand**

21. Fiscal policy must be paid for. Since this often occurs through borrowing, it raises the real interest rate. The higher interest rate attracts more foreign capital; that is, foreigners are increasingly interested in investing in the United States with its high interest rates. However, this means that foreigners are using their U.S. dollars to purchase financial assets instead of to purchase goods and services. The U.S. current account goes into deficit, but the U.S. capital account goes into surplus.

   **Topic: How Monetary and Fiscal Policy Affect Exchange Rates *and* How Exchange Rates Affect Aggregate Demand: Fiscal Policy**

*22. The two headlines; "Money is fleeing the United States faster than ever" versus "Record U.S. trade surplus" make sense because the trade surplus is the mirror image of the capital deficit. When the United States sells more goods than it brings in, that means that Americans are taking foreign currency and investing abroad instead of buying foreign goods.

   **Topic: Two Sides, One Coin**

23. Gold is more likely to sell for the same price regardless of location than are lawyer services because it is very easy to ship gold from one place to another if there is a price discrepancy. It is very hard to ship German lawyer services to Canada because the legal system is different in the two countries.

**Topic: The Purchasing Power Parity Theorem**

24. You don't need to worry about your trade deficit with one company because it is probably made up by a trade surplus with another company.

**Topic: The U.S. Trade Deficit and Your Trade Deficit**